Sharing This Walk

A BOOK IN THE SERIES LATIN AMERICA IN TRANSLATION /
EN TRADUCCIÓN / EM TRADUÇÃO

This book was sponsored by the Consortium in Latin American Studies at the University of North Carolina at Chapel Hill and Duke University

Sharing This Walk

An Ethnography of Prison Life and the PCC in Brazil

Karina Biondi

EDITED AND TRANSLATED BY

John F. Collins

The University of North Carolina Press CHAPEL HILL

With appreciation for Florence and James Peacock and their generous support of the University of North Carolina Press.

The University of North Carolina Press has been a member of the
Green Press Initiative since 2003.

Cover illustrations: Photographs by Karina Biondi.

Library of Congress Cataloging-in-Publication Data
Names: Biondi, Karina, author. | Collins, John F., 1965 April 19– editor, translator.
Title: Sharing this walk : an ethnography of prison life and the PCC in Brazil /
    Karina Biondi ; edited and translated by John F. Collins.
Other titles: Junto e misturado. English | Latin America in translation/en traducción/
    em tradução.
Description: Chapel Hill : University of North Carolina Press, [2016] | Series: Latin
    America in translation/en traducción/em tradução | Includes bibliographical
    references and index.
Identifiers: LCCN 2016018926| ISBN 9781469630304 (cloth : alk. paper) |
    ISBN 9781469623405 (pbk : alk. paper) | ISBN 9781469630311 (ebook)
Subjects: LCSH: Primeiro Comando da Capital. | Prison gangs—Brazil—
    São Paulo (State) | Organized crime—Brazil—São Paulo (State) | Prisons—
    Brazil—São Paulo (State)—Social conditions. | Prisoners—Brazil—
    São Paulo (State)—Social conditions.
Classification: LCC HV6453.B63 P7313 2016 | DDC 364.106/6098161—dc23 LC record
    available at https://lccn.loc.gov/2016018926

Originally published in Portuguese with the title *Junto e Misturado: Uma Etnographia
do PCC* (São Paulo: Editora Terceiro Nome, 2010).

Contents

Illustrations

Note from the Editor-Translator

With over 610,000 of its citizens now serving sentences or awaiting trial for criminal offenses, Brazil trails only the United States, China, and Russia in its total number of prisoners. Yet, in 1990, Brazil's incarcerated population totaled about 90,000, meaning that Latin America's most populous democracy had at that time one of the lower rates of confinement in the Americas, and even worldwide, especially when compared with similarly large, economically unequal, industrialized settler societies and nations that have suffered through authoritarian regimes.[1] Brazil thus seems to present a paradox to social scientific common sense in that during the first decades of the new millennium growing numbers of citizens found themselves imprisoned even as exports boomed, working people availed themselves of cheap credit to consume at rates that dwarfed those of previous decades, socioeconomic indicators registered small but significant declines in inequality, and wide-ranging programs ranging from food aid to families and affirmative action efforts in an expanding university system gained momentum under former labor leader and Workers Party president Luis Inácio "Lula" da Silva and his successor, Dilma Roussef. How or why, then, is it that in the decade and a half prior to the political economic upheaval surrounding president Roussef's questionable impeachment in 2016 Brazil, a nation in the midst of a deepening redemocratization, an economic expansion, and a burgeoning commitment to social justice backed by a leftist-party president increased its prison population nearly sevenfold?

Those seeking explanations for Brazil's spiraling imprisonment rates might pay attention to changes to the penal code instituted in the 1990s in response to U.S. hemispheric programs to combat drug trafficking or to a decriminalization of the possession of small quantities of marijuana in 2006 that seems to have spurred police efforts to charge newly decriminalized consumers with trafficking.[2] One might also point to shifting rates and spatial distributions of crime, improved policing techniques, and novel public safety initiatives, or argue that vigilante death squads may have declined as better-trained and better-paid police patrols now see to it that a higher number of offenders actually arrive at the station house and proceed into the court system rather than facing extermination in the streets or sitting, often uncounted and unaccounted for, in precinct holding pens. In fact, authorities and journalists have often put forth one or more such arguments to explain Brazil's shifting crime and incarceration figures. Yet those explanations may very well be wildly incorrect. For example, at least in the city of Rio de Janeiro, extrajudicial killings ascribed to police have increased during the runup to the 2016 Olympics, and the security secretary for the state of Sao Paulo recently banned police from providing first aid to victims at crime scenes since such "aid" was often used to cover up police shootings or even to plant evidence.[3] What is apparent, however, is that a massive rise in incarceration rates has accompanied the democratic initiatives and the rather impressive, at least in terms of economic indicators, consumption and natural resources-based expansion of the Brazilian economy over the last fifteen years.

Could it be, as Brazilian intellectuals have long argued in relation to the rise of a nascent, nineteenth-century modern and Atlantic liberal democratic political order, that the perspectives offered from a Brazil where "political science finds a limit in the henchman's head"[4] make visible the assumptions and ideological convictions that gird democratic theory and faith in developmentalism elsewhere?[5] Or might one observe, rather simply, that an overheating capitalist economy may give rise to serious conflicts that require some state and nonstate actors to rely increasingly on incarceration to make that restrictive economy hum?

Anthropologist Karina Biondi takes neither tack in *Sharing This Walk: An Ethnography of Prison Life and the PCC in Brazil*, her wildly insightful and remarkably personal ethnography of prison life and politics in São Paulo, Brazil's most populous and economically important state. Instead, while weaving an account that stretches across the first decade of the twenty-first century to follow the incarceration of one of the people most dear to her, Biondi describes the influence, iconoclastic motility, and constitutive tensions between equality and hierarchy—or what Biondi, following Gilles Deleuze and Félix Guattari, describes as an immanence and a transcendence—at play in the rise across the 1990s of the political force and labile collectivity known as the Primeiro Comando da Capital (PCC, or First Command of the Capital).

Biondi mostly avoids the statistics that would formally describe the PCC. And she refuses to accept the rather thin explanations offered by journalists fascinated, and state and civil society actors deeply concerned, by the PCC's ostensible coalescence as what is usually referred to in government documents and by news outlets as a "criminal organization." Instead, she looks closely, and ethnographically, at the everyday workings and remarkable fluidity and strategic materializations of the PCC. But she does not seek to reconcile competing tendencies or bald contradictions. On the contrary, she takes seriously the claims and practices of prisoners and begins to rethink how she understands "organization" and moral transformation while challenging a social science that would rest on statistics about political associations conceived of as collections of individual actors as well as the purifying, single-stranded interpretations that so often accompany those assumptions smuggled into anthropological field sites. In contrast to such attempts to clarify through simplicity, Biondi offers a "descriptive analytic" through which she follows multiple threads, or virtual connections and unexpected affinities, without reducing these phenomena to a single explanation, analytic plane, or a representation of some deeper, underlying reality that she is authorized to interpret. This more symmetrical anthropology predicated on avoiding interpretations that are external to practices verified during fieldwork raises an issue that is potentially more significant than an explanation of the curious rise of the PCC throughout the 1990s, and thus one that is less easily responded to by aiming to improve policy initiatives and statistics or mapping out cause-and-effect relationships as part of some growth in or accumulation of individual agencies: What is a democratic community, how does it arise, and how might it be encouraged to grow in relation to the real needs of its participants and those who live and work around them? Additionally, and importantly, what sort of social science is qualified to map the twists and turns, as well as internally differentiated workings, of such a collectivity?

Readers may find it troubling to encounter the translator leaning on democracy in order to preface an English-language version of an ethnography of the PCC, a group that many commentators consider a prison gang and violent criminal organization. Let me be clear: To consider the PCC and democratic struggle is not to fail to note, as anthropologist Jorge Villela emphasizes in his preface to the original Brazilian edition of *Sharing This Walk*, that large numbers of the incarcerated men with whom Biondi conducted research have been convicted of serious, often violent, vcrimes. Nor is it to celebrate or even naturalize and explain illegal actions or the members of the PCC as social bandits or "primitive rebels" whose transgressions make sense in relation to specific political economic forms, as Eric Hobsbawm did in discussing nineteenth-century outlaws in northeastern Brazil.[6] But it is to follow, closely, openly, and as ethnographers, as prisoners who suffer under stunningly brutal prison regimes develop shared forms for enunciating political will and organizing daily life—the "walk" (*caminhada*) referred to in this book's title—that Biondi argues have drastically reduced homicide rates in São Paulo, both inside and outside prison. But according to Biondi, the PCC has not simply reduced homicides. Relieved of the obligation to find an anchor in specific territories, it has morphed into a shape-shifting entity that articulates a series of democratizing impulses that Biondi's research suggests are typically covered up, or even actively repressed, by the normal activities of modern states and associated social scientific experts.

To analyze the PCC in relation to democratic impulses made real in the violent spaces of prison and prisoners' attempts to counter the state while appropriating and redirecting certain of its technologies is to attempt to understand how men who are accused of breaking the law—or even living outside the law and society as what in Brazil are commonly and tellingly dubbed marginals (*marginais*)—participate in a rhizomatic association whose disengagement from more standard modern attachments to territory and stable hierarchy permits them to agitate for legal rights and to work to inhibit abuses in a prison system made up of multiple, and very different, carceral institutions. According to Biondi, the prisoners associated with the PCC thus perform their de-individualizing labors and self-productions not as some sort of parallel power or as a copy of the state and its categories, imperatives, and prejudices but rather in relation to a radically libertarian ethos tied to what readers of this book will come to recognize as "the Crime" (*o Crime*) and a tightly packed and vibrating "Walk" (a *caminhada*). Yet, in order to be maintained and be effective, this ethos and its associated dispositions predicated on multiple manifestations of sympathetic attunement, or precisely the multiplicity of engagements that gave rise to the book's original Portuguese title— *Juntos e misturados*, meaning "Alongside and Mixed Together"—require also a rather specific recourse by participants to what may take on the appearance of a fearsome hierarchy or a fixity of social positions and the imposition of desires on the weak. This interplay of accumulated intensities, or a virtual field that takes form as the necessary conditions for the actualization of experience, is what leads Biondi, drawing especially on the work of Gilles Deleuze and Félix Guattari, to argue that everyday prison practices directed at the maintenance of equality nonetheless give rise to a type of transcendental claim that entifies the PCC as the hierarchical, fearsome, and bloodthirsty organization identified by most commentators in Brazil.[7] Yet that which appears transcendental is always composed in sympathy with an immanent critique, or the often stylized "debates" (*debates*) constrained by specific rules of evidence and propriety put forth between prisoners, that entangles PCC hierarchies in assertions of equality. These plays of immanence and transcendence that Biondi argues make the PCC real gesture at the theoretical situation, and novelty, of both the PCC and *Sharing This Walk*.

Successful ethnography typically depends on entering into, and in some sense appreciating, the practices and worldviews of those with whom the researcher interacts. Brazil today is a fulcrum of ethnographic innovation, a vital intellectual space that continues to produce not simply data for metropolitan investigators but practical and theoretical stances that challenge the assumptions and the often unexamined claims to expertise on the part of social scientists working in North America and Europe. As a creative and especially well-researched first book by a Brazilian anthropologist, *Sharing This Walk* typifies, and pushes the limits of, this contemporary ethnographic work. Biondi eschews the push-pull models of structure and agency and the tired pronouncements about some undifferentiated set of relations called "society" that still function as black boxes for too many social scientific explanations. Drawing in part on creative rereadings of the works of Deleuze and Guattari, Bruno Latour, Eduardo Viveiros de Castro, Claude Lévi-Strauss, Pierre Clastres, Jacques Monod, and Marilyn Strathern—and, above all, on the richness of her ethnographic material—she offers instead a grounded, patently and often painfully ethnographic path into democratic forms of life. And these life-forms are produced in the most unexpected places on earth, namely prisons in São Paulo. Key to this walk, and thus this lived situation shared in some way by the ethnographer and her putative "subjects," is transformation.

Transformation is fundamental to Biondi's account in a number of ways. Most basically, the introduction, four chapters, and conclusion, as well as the afterword prepared subsequently for this English-language edition, describe the rise and reverberations of a walk or an ethics that emerges in relation to everyday attempts to survive in jail. This struggle takes place within a carceral system in which, before the rise of the PCC, prisoners often required their less powerful neighbors to pay "rent" in exchange for the right to sleep in a cell, maintain their physical integrity, and even survive. Biondi details how, in the midst of such violence experienced by men who are themselves either accused or convicted of transgressions, there emerge internal critiques and dispositions. These provoke certain types of opposition and slippery, or mobile, forms of cohesion among prisoners. But such ethical positioning, as Jorge Vilella points out about the PCC's democratic impulses in this book's original preface, is not some frontal countering or some resolute negation on the part of a force that takes on its definitive form in relation to that which oppresses. Nor can it be oversimplified as an intentional attempt simply to inflect, in an ameliorative way, the forms of discipline and prejudice that oppress or are represented by prisoners as illegitimate.

The transformations activated and experienced by the members of—or, put better, the participants in—the PCC with whom Biondi conducts her ethnography are not the sorts of mutations that produce the docile prisoners or self-policing citizens described in terms of the panoptic gaze excavated in Michel Foucault's *Discipline and Punish*. More like the Irish Republican Army prisoners in British institutions described by Allen Feldman in *Formations of Violence*, the "Brothers" (prisoners baptized into the PCC) who push Biondi's account forward defy expectations about who they are and who they are meant to be. Like the figures described by Friedrich Nietzsche in *Beyond Good and Evil*, these prisoners who make up the feared PCC are much more than the evil inverse of the proper citizen. But nor are they humble sufferers: As participants in what Biondi brings to life as "the Crime," the prisoners who walk with the PCC are experts at transformation, camouflage, and contingency, qualities that Biondi analyzes through concepts and "native" categories such as "Ideas," "Rhythms," and "Reverberations." As agents of transformation, the men reveal the importance of perspective, and thus the fact that, examined in a particular light or faced with a seemingly given situation, the members of the PCC are neither resistant tricksters nor resolutely dangerous lawbreakers who stand outside society. One might instead understand the Brothers as iconoclastic expressions, and activators, of basic impulses that compose us all, albeit differentially. How those intensities are activated is in part a function of how we face difficult decisions, striking moments of blowback and fear, long periods of boredom or unexplained twists of fate, and the humming semiotic strands that make up both the PCC and everyday life in São Paulo's prisons. Perspective, then, is everything.

A concern with difference as an ontological condition is critical not only to Biondi's ethnographic text and to her conceptualization of fieldwork conducted in prisons and across networks without a firm territorial border or contextualizing fundament but also to her identity as a researcher and a person. Without going too deeply into the author's self-situation and positioning in formulating her account, here I foreshadow her introduction and alert the reader that her unplanned "insertion" into her field site required that she rethink her own ongoing, mutating crystallizations as a subject and a partner. Biondi's struggles to do so highlight the constructedness of—and I would argue the incomplete and unsatisfactory insights so often emanating from—an anthropology conducted by researchers who choose their next project by searching for a topic that "interests" them or that promises to add to or even prop up an existing political orientation. That was not a luxury entertained by Biondi, who necessarily shared a difficult walk in order to write this book. Her analysis is more a pragmatic, obligatory ethnography. Her "research" was not simply a way of figuring things out. It was also an essential component of her life that emanated from that life itself rather than from questions that seemed interesting to a relatively detached observer but did not touch directly or arise materially from the anthropologist's own situation in entangled, rather than conveniently distinct, worlds.

In *Sharing this Walk*, Karina Biondi is never some expert in charge of representing those supposedly unable to speak for themselves. She recalls instead, and travels alongside, the jailed subjects and families of prisoners with whom she learned to interact as a function of the corporeal and affective dispositions expected of—or, put better, necessarily cultivated by—a woman who visits a PCC prison. Dropped into a situation she neither desired nor expected, Biondi thus reflects the disciplinary processes and related, but often unexpected or even novel, transformations undergone by the prisoners themselves. Respected by prisoners whose everyday habits do so much to constitute the PCC, and treated at times as a criminal by guards, military police, and those on the "outside" who associate the PCC and all those touched by it with organized crime, Biondi is thus alternatingly forceful, admired, and even transcendental in her apparent crystallization as what some who appear in this book misrecognize as a leader. At other moments, she wavers or finds herself stuck. And this oscillation between transcendence and immanence is metonymic of the movements, or rhythms and ideas, experienced and made manifest by her research subjects.

The PCC described by Biondi is not structured by charismatic individuals. It is organized as a consequence of tensions between the construction of such individuals and the political offices they fill and an immanent agitation that renders untenable the sorts of hierarchical structures that social scientists typically associate with charismatic leaders. The contradictions between the two positions make up the space from which Biondi enunciates the text now before you. The contradictions that generate Biondi's scholarly production are also the genesis, and the source of the ongoing political power, of the PCC. Understood this way, the PCC, however much it arises from the violence of the prison and the activities of its participants, is neither a mirror image of Brazilian "society" nor a parallel organization that should be misrecognized as a copy dependent on some original. It is simply a different expression of the forces that are expressed more directly in the impossibly simple approaches to good, evil, and the negotiation of sociality faced by all those actors seemingly enmeshed in what anthropologists customarily dub "society."

Foreword

JORGE MATTAR VILLELA

Sharing This Walk: An Ethnography of Prison Life and the PCC in Brazil is an anthropological book. More specifically, it is an ethnography directed at understanding the First Command of the Capital (PCC). The PCC is often described as Brazil's most powerful prison gang, and there is no doubt that it is an organization with substantial reach beyond prison walls and across the nation. Yet the description of the PCC that follows goes far beyond imagining the PCC as some sort of hierarchical organization. Nonetheless, although like many of the most interesting social scientific studies, it is inflected by the author's training as an anthropologist, it may also be read fruitfully by the nonanthropologist. This is due in large part to the fact that its subject matter interests all of us, whether experts or readers with but a passing interest in the politics of prison life in São Paulo and beyond. It is also because Karina Biondi's way of writing ethnography permits us to enter the text via different paths. In short, however we engage this text, it offers much, including many surprises.

Biondi's ethnography describes the prison environment and thus the indignities faced by an enormous number of people (the prisoners) in the state of São Paulo who, over the last few decades, have put together a significant political struggle. This in turn has given rise to a collectivity, force, or group—an adequate label is difficult to find—that has played an essential role in the everyday lives of millions of people over the last two decades. *Sharing This Walk* thus strikes me as being of interest to a wide readership because one of its principal foci is a concept, and a word, that should interest all of us and about which we should reflect in detail. This word is "democracy." Yet the democracy opened up by Biondi's account is not a low-intensity, minimalist democracy based simply on the right to vote or a tepid freedom of expression. Rather, this book approaches democracy in a manner that recalls Isabelle Stengers's discussion of a democracy made up of diverse struggles developed by emergent collective formations in the present. According to Stengers, large numbers of people have long been subjected to police, juridical, and scientific knowledge. As a result, they have been configured as incapable of directing their own struggles or constructing their own forms of knowledge about that which they consider important. So, drawing on Stengers's own examples, what illegal drug abusers and HIV-positive citizens once faced is even more the case for the imprisoned. And here it is worth recalling that, among many other factors, what gave rise to the PCC was a legal demand, namely that prison authorities follow Brazil's laws governing incarceration and the prison population. Such demands are legitimate and should be taken seriously in a densely democratic society, or one worked out in practice and in opposition to "democracy" understood as but an ideal or march toward that preformed ideal. This is because, drawing again on the work of Stengers, as part of a movement toward a more complete democracy, we need to create a situation in which there no longer exist "real groups" whose knowledge and practices are neglected.

How might we take up this idea of real groups (or groupings) and their knowledge practices and politics, a concept shared by Stengers and Tobie Nathan? What the two refer to as "real groups" are not the opposite of fictitious, false, and other such apparently "unreal" groups. Rather, real groups stand in contradistinction to "natural groups," or those Stengers argues are forged by statistics and manufactured by biological knowledges and its cognates. For example, a school group is not a real group but a natural one. It is put together on the basis of age sets and even alphabetical orders. We all know that within a school classroom there arise a number of alternatives—real groups—that are the collectivities that educators, parents, and psychologists might call "the crowd" with which an adolescent hangs out. But unlike such crowds, or what in the introduction to a book about organizations other than the PCC in São Paulo's prisons we might call the "gang" of friends with whom someone hangs out, the national state is not a real group. It is instead a natural group, and within its interior there arise a number of real groups that the state does its best to squash by means of its diverse powers and legislative agendas. For example, etiological or nosological categories applied to mental health clients describe natural groups but not real groups. And even a family—a naturally occurring group—runs the risk of losing its status as a real group. This is what happens to the inhabitants of a prison or a carceral state. But the PCC, in its activity, makes up a real group, albeit only in the schematic sense defined in this paragraph. After all, as we will learn throughout Biondi's account, it is difficult to refer to the PCC as a group.

One of the most important features of Karina Biondi's work is her ongoing rejection of a certain type of reducibility, something she has developed in relation to what Isabelle Stengers has approached as an ability to force back the forms of knowledge and judgment that drive us to certainties. This involves avoiding the transformation of anything into an entity open to judgment or knowledge. A similar attempt at forestalling the hermeneutics so much a part of modernist social science permits Biondi's readers to gain a view not only of the PCC, but of many PCCs. They are thus privy to the multiple movements, tensions, and desires that compose what is supposedly a unified group called the PCC as well as Biondi's creative approach to ethnography. And as a result of this rejection of reducibility and her ability to retain a focus on multiple semiotic processes, Biondi stresses that we cannot treat the PCC as an "organization," a firm, or a diagram. Instead, as this book emphasizes, the PCC is a collectivity made up of men who committed crimes, many of those crimes extremely serious. Thus, the narrative that follows is not an attempt at mystification or redemption. Nor is it a response to some scholarly urge to test whether the PCC as a collectivity responds to political interests. In fact, as she does with Aristotle's Law of Excluded Middle, which asserts that either a proposition is true or its negation is necessarily true, Biondi sets aside the well-known social scientific injunction to test her fieldwork materials or data. Something similar occurs with the population of a prison managed by a state or country. In fact, Biondi's ethnography makes it clear that, rather than some test of assertions about sets of practices defined as "the social," the story of the PCC is a political one that refrains from announcing its endpoints in advance or predicting what will happen. On the contrary, the experiences narrated in *Sharing This Walk* are so singular that they hide in plain sight, squarely in front of the eyes of less attentive citizens. And whether this political experience is truly democratic or antidemocratic is not the task of the ethnographer to decide. Her assignment is much richer, even more important, and achieved admirably in this book: to produce a value judgment-free, analytic account of the PCC experience in contemporary São Paulo. After all, working as an anthropologist committed to resisting the urge to impose anthropological forms of knowledge on a real community that has developed vastly different, albeit complementary, forms of political practice, it would make no sense for Karina Biondi to raise questions or postulate perspectives that are not a part of the lives of the people and the actions of the institutions described in her account.

Nonetheless, it is important to raise here at least two critical points, directed especially at those who would point fingers without understanding the task and the practices described in *Sharing This Walk*. First, this social scientific research is in no way an apology for the actions or viewpoints of any of the people described. Neither Biondi nor her principal fieldwork collaborator described in the following pages is a member of the PCC. Thus, in spite of any future methodological innovations her anthropological approaches might encourage, Karina Biondi cannot be described as that special sort of ethnographer who has one foot in anthropology and the other in her object of study, a "halfie" in the words of Lila Abu-Lughod.[1] Instead, and as will become apparent to readers, the PCC came into—or, put better, came to cross—the life of Karina Biondi. And this orthogonal relationship would have remained but a small mark on that life were it not entified, and described in analytic detail, in the present study begun at Brazil's Federal University of São Carlos and the University of São Paulo.

None of the preceding discussion should be interpreted as suggesting that *Sharing This Walk* is a neutral book written from some anthropologically impossible, neutral standpoint. As I emphasize, this is a political book, in multiple ways and in the widest, most important sense. On one level, it reveals something that is otherwise hidden or denied, namely the life within and functioning of the prison, or what Michel Foucault referred to in *Discipline and Punish* as an "austere institution." But the task at hand is more complex than a simple submission of the carceral institution to an ethnographic gaze.

Karina Biondi attempts to describe analytically the working pieces of the still-unknown machinery that inflects all of our lives while nonetheless remaining obscure owing to its constant movement and the difficulty of discerning it. And this machinery is an important point of concern on the part of public, security, judicial, and academic authorities. It is also a focus of concern for millions of Brazilians who receive representations of the world constructed by the press and thus, at least in part, by such authorities. And all this takes form, and place, in spite of the fact that the very name of the ethnographic object at hand is itself a target of restrictions and prohibitions instituted by public officials of the state of São Paulo. But these are not the only reasons that the ethnography to come is a political text.

Sharing This Walk is a political text because it helps realize anthropology's historical mission, the attempt to give voice to and argue for the legitimacy of the viewpoints of those who fall under the ethnographic gaze. It attempts to do so without relegating the institutions and human beings engaged by Biondi's fieldwork to the status of objects whose worries, fears, and practices might thus become explainable as but the fruit of ignorance, brutality, irrationality, and superstition. That said, it strikes me that Biondi pushes far beyond the standard anthropological engagement of fieldwork voices in her approach and in her pluralistic treatment of the subjects she engages. Over the course of her writing, we see that her approach to her fieldwork and her interlocutors is always plural, diverse, and varied.

In the end, then, this is a political text because it seeks to describe analytically a political experience, namely the activities and outlines of the PCC in today's prisons in the Brazilian state of São Paulo, the nation's center of economic power. Despite its genesis in the shadows of prison life, this is an experience that cannot be understood as state-centered. Nor should it be approached as somehow "against," below, or beyond the state. And it is by no means a simple synthesis of the two positionings just mentioned. Neither is it a function of the existence or lack of existence of social hierarchies in the PCC and in jail.

Biondi describes complex and creative relations that emanate from fieldwork in ways that push a deeper engagement with immanence and transcendence as philosophical concepts. This is an immanence that draws frequently on a transcendence that guarantees its immanent character while also gaining existence as a transcendent form located in the breast of such immanence. In the PCC, no one is better than anyone else, and there is no one who orders and no one who obeys. Such lack of commands and obeisance is not guaranteed by the good nature of participants or by the iron hand of a tyrant. Nor is it the fruit of a pact or a legal agreement. Rather, the PCC described in this book is the unstable result of a conjuncture of variable and relatively undefined enunciations that find themselves transformed each time the pure relations of immanence appropriate to the organization's field of activities are disturbed. One example of such disturbance involves the attempt to command, give orders, and appropriate the desires and designs of another incarcerated person. Nonetheless, a key exigency of everyday life in prison involves the battle to conquer one's own existential space in the interior of the cell and as part of everyday relations with those who share it. The standard recommendation is to avoid commanding others as well as avoid being commanded by those others. It is also suggested that one avoid seeking out or producing a totalizing hierarchy in prisons. And, paradoxically, it is the side of the PCC that Biondi dubs "transcendental" that helps avoid the grave error of commanding or being commanded.

In order to elucidate the compelling and yet potentially contradictory ethnographic situation outlined earlier, Biondi argues that there exist two PCCs, and they are in a perpetual communication that means that the one always resonates in the other. These are the transcendental PCC and the immanent PCC (as defined or outlined in chapters 2 and 3, respectively). Here Biondi's paradoxical argument and prisoners' experiences in relation to these two facets of what passes as a single organization mean that readers will have to let go of or question two pillars of Western thought. These include, on the one hand, the principle of noncontradiction, or the argument that two contradictory affirmations cannot be correct at the same time. On the other lies Aristotle's aforementioned Law of Excluded Middle, or a dictum that requires that a statement be either true or false as a function of the evaluation of its contradiction. It is important to leave aside this principle of noncontradiction because, as so often occurs, the PCC may evince, at the same moment, a variety of characteristics in tandem with their opposites. In fact, the PCC is made up of apparent contradictions, and it may be both hierarchical and nonhierarchical. As a result, it will also be necessary to leave aside the Law of Excluded Middle because, in addition to being something and not being its opposite, the PCC is still other things.

In addition to avoiding so many modern conceptual addictions, *Sharing This Walk* puts forth a delicate reflection for all of us who do anthropology: How does one face problems of moral order and moral orders when one studies groups or phenomena that strike at the heart of a modern political order constantly instituted and reinstituted over the last three centuries?[2] In her response, Biondi leaves well enough alone the moral relativism so central to anthropological investigations and resultant claims. She focuses instead on a central axis in the formation and everyday activities of the PCC, namely the ethics and record of conduct referred to in São Paulo's prisons as the *proceder*. This historicized disposition and specific type of conduct related to an inmate's comportment inside and outside prison—but always within the ambit of "the Crime" (*o Crime*)—is critical to the organization of prison life today. How, then, does the PCC function in the prison environment? This is the key question addressed in *Sharing This Walk* by means of its detailed ethnographic engagement. Thus, in her attempt at a response, what exactly does Karina Biondi make visible?

As part of a journey that includes freeing herself of notional or conceptual baggage such as epistemological models that would fetishize the state, the organism, the corporation, or society and culture, Biondi works to permit a new sort of object to arise, slowly. This object's definition is rather complicated, in the sense of a complexity that any ethnography worthy of its name highlights. Rather than sweeping the world's real intricacy under the rug of grand concepts or forcing concepts to conform to the epistemological claims of the anthropologist's own community of sense, Biondi engages her experiences with a deft hand and in their proper difficulty. What she finds is not exactly a society, a group, a bundle of relations between individuals, or even an "organization." And here is where the need to discard the principle of noncontradiction and the Law of Excluded Middle arises once again: Even though the PCC is not exactly a society as defined by traditional social science, the people associated with the PCC who collaborated with Biondi in her research return tirelessly to the concept of "society." Meanwhile, although the PCC is not exactly a group, Biondi reveals that there arise incessant groupings in cells and across prisons. And, at the same time, although participants in the PCC do not establish firm relations with other individuals, they constantly establish partnerships and alliances so as to participate in collective actions.

According to Karina Biondi's fieldwork, the PCC is a species of figure without a border. It looks somewhat like the works of English painter William Turner, whose shapes fall apart continuously. The figure called PCC, then, seems to oscillate continuously between the pre- and postformal, or between a status antecedent to yet somehow beyond the taking of a definitive shape.[3] Thus, the PCC is not quite a group. It takes form as a society based on collective bonds but without coercion or the social. It does so as the product of subjects formed in the tensions and alliances between the immanent relations between those subjects and the claims to transcendence put forth in words and conduct that are misinterpreted by precisely those actors who make up the PCC.

By casting off a view of human action based on judgment-based sliding scales of rights and obligations, a move indebted to anthropologist Edmund Leach's post–World War II theorizing, Karina Biondi illustrates how the workings of the entity we call the PCC—a moniker suggestive of a concept of group identity whose suitability to the phenomena observed will be questioned severely throughout the chapters that follow—are not predicated on social codes that simply sanction lawbreakers and reward obedient subjects.[4] Biondi's text follows in this tradition of rejecting explanations based on an inside and outside whose borders are dependent on what appear as relatively fixed codes and behaviors. But the schemes of belonging that cohere as the PCC seem to function instead as more of a long, multistranded cord that pulls together recommendations and a voluntary form of conduct. Beyond the borders of this entangled path in the case of the PCC lie consequences (*consequências*) rather than legal or social sanctions. This suggests that belonging to the PCC might be understood more clearly through the metaphor of diet rather than the law: As most of us know, there is little actual direct, socially mediated punishment for the person who eats a poor diet. In fact, as far as I know, no one goes to jail for eating fat, sugars, and carbohydrates in excess. But there are consequences. A series of diseases, impediments, and aches and pains may arise, even though this is not assured in all cases by the fact that the subject has consumed an improper diet. And this is what takes place instead of punishment in environments controlled by the PCC. There is no punishment, but there are consequences. And here, lest we fall back into the immature game of contradicting that which we are shown in our ethnography, it is important to take seriously the vocabulary employed by those with whom Karina Biondi studies.

To lean on the native term "consequences" is not simply to effect a rhetorical shift or don a verbal disguise. Rather, it is, as we are privileged to learn in *Sharing This Walk*, part of the experience of exploring the different facets, meanings, and results of the actual ways prisoners communicate. Instead of seeking to contradict or correct such lexicons, Biondi struggles to engage native vocabularies on their own terms so as to confer greater intelligibility on the PCC and its actions in Brazil's prisons. In other words, *Sharing This Walk* is a real ethnography.

It is again worth remembering that to confer intelligibility is not necessarily to simplify. On the contrary, to make things understandable in the case at hand is to replace with an analytical description of the PCC the inadequate and simplistic versions of this story put forth so far by the juridical and police institutions that are unable to comprehend its real complexity. This involves replacing the simple questions, to which responses take form as little more than modest predictions—"Is it political? Is it not political? Is it good? Is it not good?"—with the rawness of ethnography, with the exhaustive work of salvaging meaning, and with the detailing of the relations and forces at play in any interaction.

Now, as I near the end of this preface, whose brevity emanates from my desire to free readers up to enter Biondi's text proper, I would like to highlight just one more aspect of the work, one that should be clear upon reading *Sharing This Walk*. This has to do with Karina Biondi's insertion into her fieldwork site. The book's powerful introduction, no doubt captivating for anyone who reads this work, pushes us without pity into Biondi's research universe, into the harshness of the conditions under which she researched, and toward the raw existence of the prison milieu. But this introduction also makes clear the sources of, and the subsequent approach to, the data on which she bases her account. This story of fieldwork is a methodological exposition of a research program as well as the emotional base for what will come next.

Finally, then, I emphasize that *Sharing This Walk* is innovative in quite a number of ways, including its research method, since the data that support the account arise from a rather special type of insertion into the anthropological "field." The contents of the book, and Karina's descriptions, are also original in that they show otherwise unknown sides of a phenomenon that is nonetheless much discussed across Brazil. Instead of choosing to reveal the ostensibly obscure forces that some might argue stand behind or motivate a collectivity like the PCC, Biondi has focused on the group's internal workings and efficacious means of coming together. Instead of denouncing untruths or actions, Biondi has described the cogs and gears that make them possible. And when Biondi imports concepts and vocabularies not found in the world of the PCC and the prison, she makes sure to follow them diligently in their uses, content, and ultimate consequences. But *Sharing This Walk* is most original owing to the fact that it takes seriously a political experience faithful to itself, produced in an environment and by an unbearable mode of existence that we are too accustomed to ignoring, judging, or even encouraging in its brutal, spiraling multiplication, which is so much a part of how the world is today.

Sharing This Walk

SKETCH OF THE SÃO BERNARDO DO CAMPO CENTER FOR TEMPORARY DETENTION (CDP)

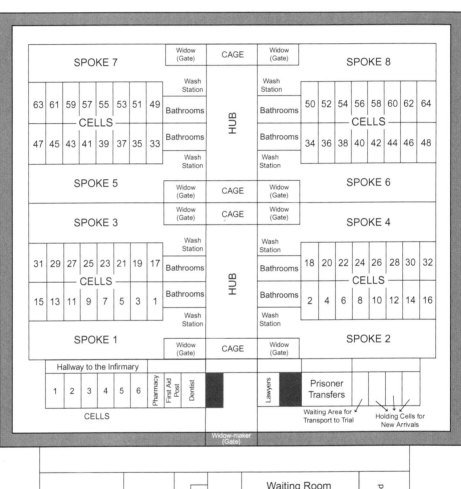

Introduction

> I am on the edge of the crowd, at the periphery; but I belong to
> it, I am attached to it by one of my extremities, a hand or foot.
> I know that the periphery is the only place I can be, that I would
> die if I let myself be drawn into the center of the spoke, but just
> as certainly if I let go of the crowd. This is not an easy position
> to stay in, it is even very difficult to hold.
>
> —GILLES DELEUZE AND FÉLIX GUATTARI,
>   *A Thousand Plateaus*

The main avenues of São Paulo are never deserted. How could they be?
According to official statistics, the world's fourth most populous metropolitan region and Brazil's "city that never sleeps" is filled with over 20
million people.[1] This urban escape hatch was once considered an oasis,
a place of opportunity capable of absorbing multiple waves of migrants
from across Brazil and around the globe. The city's riches, however, are
punctuated by its social divides. To open one's eyes in São Paulo is to
come face-to-face with gilded condominiums flanked by favelas made
up of homes with tile, or even scavenged wood, roofs. And it is precisely
this sort of contrast that I face while driving: My car is just one among
so many that move along the city's central Roberto Marinho Avenue as
Friday night blends into Saturday morning. The reasons people are out
and about at this hour are too numerous to count. But there is one cruel
reason for leaving one's home at this hour, and I have come to know it all
too well.

Today is a visiting day for the relatives of the hundreds of thousands
of citizens—mostly men—incarcerated across São Paulo State, a majority
of whom arrive in rural prisons from the streets of the state capital of the
same name. On my right, I notice two women sharing the burden of a
heavy sack, probably filled with food for an imprisoned relative. Noting
the hour and watching them struggle, I recognize the motivating power
of a spatiotemporal constellation commonly referred to as "jail."

I came to be able to make out the women's patterned, symptomatic
movements only after my husband was locked up in early 2003, or at about
the time I began the "research" described throughout this book. One

result of our experiences was nearly six years of highly unorthodox ethnography attuned to my involuntary insertion into visiting day, or what prisoners refer to as "the visit" (*a visita*). This nomenclature describes a spatiotemporal opening constructed with kin and friends, as well as the kin and friends themselves. From the perspective outlined throughout the pages that follow, then, the battle to deal with my husband's incarceration did not congeal as a neat and easily narratable collection of discrete units of time or experiences I might circumscribe as "fieldwork." In fact, and at least initially, much of what I try to communicate in the chapters that follow took place unnoticed, in ways that did not even suggest that I should take notes about what was happening or relate my experiences to that classic site of social science research, "the field." Often, I returned home after visits without making a single mark in my notebooks, thinking, "Today I didn't go to the field." But later, as my interactions with the São Paulo prison system thickened, I began to understand the importance of certain events, and formerly overlooked, or even unappreciated, information gained visibility and importance in ways that have become fundamental to my conclusions.

I conceive of my fieldwork as a process, albeit a fragmented and always partial one. My reflections in this book are the fruit of experiences, lived over the course of six years, on both the "outside" and in sections of prison units in which my husband was incarcerated. I bring together these descriptions and events in an attempt to confer a certain intelligibility on them through description. As such, and as presented in this book, they might be thought of as the end of a ball of twine whose lines cross, unite, distance themselves from one another, and, at times, become lost or indistinct. In this play of entanglement and unwinding, each lived moment carries with it traces of experiences in other times and other places. I open myself to, and thus invite, these conjunctures to compose our present. They serve as fragments of the already-gone formations I work ethnographically to couple with the here and the now in a process that gives rise to rather specific conjunctures. And these conjunctures would not exist if it were not for the specific mechanisms that make such an assemblage possible. In fact, the mechanisms that permit all of us to assemble our approaches to an often unjust or bewildering world are one of my central concerns in analyzing the experience of incarceration and the growth of what most analysts consider to be one of the world's most hierarchical and powerful criminal organizations.

There is little doubt that a nonsystematic approach to the field and anthropological fieldwork has helped me more clearly make out the lines of the nonsystematic existence of my object of study, the Primeiro Comando da Capital (First Command of the Capital, PCC). The PCC, also called the "Command," "the Party," "Fifteen," and "the Family" and often referred to in this book as a collectivity and in the press as an organization or even a "gang," arose in São Paulo's prisons in the 1990s. Today it is present in 90 percent of the state's prisons, and the greater part of its urban areas.[2] The expansion of the PCC has been accompanied by a significant decline, beginning inside the state's prisons, in homicides in São Paulo. To give some idea of the magnitude of the drop in homicides, in 1999 the São Paulo prison system, which housed 52,117 inmates, registered 117 homicides in its units. In 2007, this number fell to 11 deaths even though the prison population had climbed to 153,056. Shortly thereafter, criminologists began to note a decline in homicides in the urban areas in which the Command had made itself present. Perhaps the best known of these cases is that of the section of São Paulo known as Jardim Ângela, a neighborhood with indices of violent crime akin to those usually noted in civil war zones (97.9 homicides per 100,000 inhabitants each year), which led it to be highlighted by the United Nations in 1996 as the world's then-most violent urban space. These numbers continued to rise and reached 123.3 homicides per 100,000 inhabitants by 2001. Together with nearby regions Capão Redondo and Jardim São Luis, Jardim Ângela made up one tip of the "Triangle of Death" on São Paulo's periphery. But, since 2002, the homicide numbers have dropped precipitously, and today the murder rate in that region is approximately 16.9 homicides per 100,000 inhabitants. This drop reflects a similar tendency across the entire state: In 1999, São Paulo registered 44.1 homicides per 100,000 residents. But in 2009 this had reduced to 15.4 homicides per 100,000 residents.

Authorities present the numbers cited here as evidence of successful security policies implemented by the political party in power over the last fifteen years. But there are others who provide rather different explanations for the drop in murders. For example, prisoners as well as residents of regions that were considered extremely violent (meaning that everyday life often involved either killing or being killed) customarily attribute the decrease to the arrival of the PCC. During my fieldwork, one woman was quite clear, stating, "In the old days, it was an everyday occurrence to find a body on my doorstep. Today, thanks to the PCC, that does not happen." From this citizen's perspective, then, the drop in homicide rates is related to the main theme of this book. This is the "politics of the PCC," a concept I relate to a term used within the Command: the "discipline of the PCC" or "PCC discipline."

In an attempt to introduce readers to PCC politics and its relationship to "discipline" while making clear the particular positioning from which I began to produce the knowledge that girds this book, I invite my readers to accompany me on a visit to a men's prison. The narrative vehicle through which I seek to make sense of, and invite you into, this experience—or the text before you right now—is something I have put together on the basis of diverse fragments and memories from many visiting days. As should become clear from this compendium of often jarring and disparate experiences, and the struggles inside and outside of prison that I associate with them, my object of study took form in relation to a rather special sort of ethnographic experience.

IT IS TWO O'CLOCK in the morning as I arrive at the Centro de Detenção Provisória (Center for Provisionary Detention, CDP) da Vila Independência, a neighborhood located in an impoverished area of São Paulo's working-class eastern side (*zona leste*). A large group of people, mostly women, is gathered around the main gate. Many are asleep on mattresses, in parked cars, or in tents set up along the sidewalk and under an overpass located on the other side of the street. I approach a group of women talking among themselves, and I ask who is distributing the "numbers." They point to a small, covered space alongside a public bathroom and the prison entrance. There I ask again, and one of the women moves to notify someone sleeping nearby, who they call "Joana." Confused, and ashamed that they will have to interrupt her rest, I make clear that I am prepared to wait. But they warn me quickly, "If you don't wake her up, another person will. Stop playing around or you'll lose your space in line."

I called out two or three times, and Joana awoke. Eyes cloudy with sleep, she asked my name, the "spoke" (*raio*) or pavilion, and the cell in which my husband was housed. She wrote this information down in a notebook. Next, scanning her stacks of numbered papers, she gave me a chit: number 239. I couldn't believe it. It was only 2 A.M., and 238 people had arrived before me! I would soon learn that the first thirty chits had been distributed the previous Thursday and that those who had received these numbers had been in front of the CDP since that day. I sought to calculate the time it would take me to arrive at the CDP. Without a doubt, the wait would be long. Another woman who had just picked up a chit complained loudly to no one in particular, "Every time I come here it's fuller. They arrest, arrest, and don't want to hear about letting anyone out." We exchanged a few short words. She compared the CDP in Vila Independência to other institutions her husband had passed through, and I began to consider how I was being brought into a world of visits and transfers that are so frequent and so intense that prisoners and their families come to trace in detail the similarities and differences between São Paulo's diverse penal institutions.

Back inside my car, resting before preparing to enter the prison, I recalled that each of the jails that I had visited possessed its own dynamics. These included specific approaches to searching visitors, deciding what foods would be prohibited, and often contradictory variations in the lists of documents necessary to obtain permission to enter on visiting day. The amount of time one would be left waiting to enter also varied between sites. The Vila Independência CDP was, without a doubt, one of the slowest.

At 6 A.M., the rays of the sun began to hit my car's windows. I decided to buy a cup of coffee from a vendor who, from his improvised counter set up under an overpass, also rented tents and sold bags, tools, snacks, and cigarettes. The women who had rented the tents were already getting themselves ready for the meetings that awaited them. They helped one another put on makeup and fix their hair.

I approached the CDP gate.

At exactly 7 A.M., clutching a notebook and a pen, Joana began to organize the visitors who had received chits for the line reserved for pregnant women and those accompanied by children younger than two years of age. Almost immediately, the urgent appeal to join the other, regular line went out. Yet the visitor holding ticket 95 did not appear when called by her number and then by the name listed in the line monitor's notebook. This was enough to spur Joana to warn us, "Listen up! I don't earn anything by organizing this garbage. They asked for my help because up until last week this line looked like a brothel—the person in charge jumped ship and they asked me to take charge. You have to realize that if I'm here, it's for your own good, so that there's no double-dealing on line. Be sure to stick around while I call out your numbers and you take your place on line. I'm not going to wait on anyone!"

I recalled that the line had been much less organized before Joana appeared. Nonetheless, I knew nothing about how those who took care

Children's Day celebration at the Santo André CDP. The bicycles, purchased by the prisoners themselves, were raffled among the children present on visiting day. The cages made of metal bars (*viúva* or *gaiola*) that are visible in the photograph connect the detention facility's central "hub" (*radial*) to the cell block (*raio*), thus permitting prison personnel to isolate the cell blocks. Photograph by Karina Biondi, 2005.

of the lines were chosen. In fact, visitors do not usually perceive women like Joana as holding any institutional authority; their success in organizing the line, and thus in earning the respect of their colleagues, depends entirely on their abilities. And the relationship between abilities, institutions, and authority is central to this book and my analysis of how the PCC functions and takes form as a collectivity.

My husband, although not a member of the PCC, lived its internal routines quite intensely because he spent the length of his incarceration assigned to a prison within the Command's network. As will become apparent throughout this book, the PCC controls not simply its own members but all those who serve time within its territories. While imprisoned, my husband was therefore extremely serious about conducting himself in accordance with PCC ethics. He embraced the Command's emphasis on pedagogy and thus the expectation that he should instruct me on how to behave on visiting days. He stressed that I needed to respect my place and the other members of the line since he would be the one to suffer the consequences if it were determined that he had not tutored his visitor correctly. Nonetheless, and in spite of the extent to which all visitors necessarily became familiar with and usually adhered to this particular form of inmate-supported, systematized prison sociability, things did not necessarily fall into place in ways that suggested our etiquette on visiting day was a shared social convention respected by all.

Most women who entered with me on visiting days seemed unsurprised by attitudes that clashed with PCC recommendations. In fact, strict attention to behaviors constructed as exemplary or ideal was not expected. As a result, and alongside the recommendation that we should respect the other visitors—who we referred to as "colleagues"—we were advised to avoid trusting anyone; to refuse to hold onto anything for others; to watch carefully over our "jumbos," or packages of goods intended for our imprisoned relatives; and to refrain from saving a space in line if asked by our neighbors in line. These suggestions were justified by worries that someone might steal our belongings, take our colleagues' spaces in line, or try to smuggle illegal drugs into the prison.

Over the course of my multiple pilgrimages to São Paulo's jails, I often heard stories about unfortunate visitors such as the elderly woman who asked another person to take care of her bags while she went off to buy cigarettes. This second woman, knowing that her linemate's son was imprisoned in the same cell block as her companion, placed drugs in the bags she had promised to watch. When the guard searched the elderly woman at the entrance, they found contraband and arrested her for trafficking drugs. People warned me that it would make no difference if, facing the same situation, I were to argue that the items were not my own.

Even though the PCC orients visitors to respect those who join them on visiting day, we were advised not to trust anyone and, in return, not to expect the other visitors to respect us. In other words, although we hoped that all those present would respect our places on line, we also learned that we could not confide in an unknown person's supposedly respectful intentions. As my peers reported to me, "There is always someone who's trying to be better than those around them." Once, Joana, facing a woman who was arguing that she always entered the line as number 65 and who thus sought to claim that chit from the person to whom it had been assigned, pointed out that "no one is the owner of any number." She continued, arguing that if things had worked that way earlier, they were now different: Under Joana's guidance, the line would be put together in the order of arrival. The complainant thus threatened to call her husband, a cell block leader who is referred to by prisoners as a "Housekeeper" (*faxina*) or member of the "cleanup squad," who would see to it that Joana was punished. Joana challenged the woman to pick up the phone, saying that she had nothing to fear since she was "acting correctly" and that, in the end, it would be the woman's husband who would find himself in trouble.

According to Joana, "There are women who want to be even slicker than their jailed husbands. This ends up causing problems for those guys as they do their time. But, look, I've already spent ten years at the prison door and all I can say is that every woman mirrors the man she's coming to visit: When the woman is no good, you can bet her husband has no future either." So in response to the challenge to her authority, Joana called the prisoner she suggested was responsible for the line. She reported that he offered her support for her decisions and said that if anyone had a problem about the line's organization, they should bring it up with the prisoners they were visiting. These men would in turn pass on the information to their cell block leaders, and in this way the message would get back to the prisoner in charge of the line: "Listen, they asked me to take care of the line and here I am, out of my own good will. But things have to go at my speed. The only people who get to stand on the preferential line are pregnant women and those with kids younger than two. If someone thinks they're being treated unfairly, let that be known inside. Go explain your situation and the guys inside are going to take up your case and, if necessary, they'll let me know the name of the person who should be put on the preferential line."

Over the course of five years of visits, I had never heard of a prisoner who was in charge of the line. I found Joana's statement strange and novel since in all the jails I visited it was the visitors themselves who decided on the criteria for the preferential line. I recall that once, in a different CDP, a guard responded to an elderly woman's complaint about her right to priority entrance by saying, "If your colleagues permit it, we'll put you up front. But we don't really get involved in your organizing. If you're going to complain, complain to your friends." At that moment, I heard a colleague already on line for a Sunday visit say, "Hey, Joana! You're putting together Saturday's line along the same rhythm as ours!" In fact, it was common to hear prisoners affirm that each "prison has its own rhythm." But in this case the commentary called attention to subtle differences between the queues and thus also to differences between the cell blocks.

Finally, Joana called my number. I turned my chit over and took my place. I checked the numbers of the people in front of and behind me. Indeed, I was in the correct place. We started commenting on the growth in the number of visitors each week. We speculated about reasons for this rapid increase: A spiraling prison population, lazy guards' unhurried searches, and the holiday season were all offered up as explanations. Next, as was our habit, we began discussing the movements through the penal bureaucracy of the prisoners we intended to visit. As my colleagues told their stories about these chokepoints, I thought about the huge number of accounts I'd hear during my upcoming visits. And each account in this storm of stories, containing thousands of names, faces, and gestures, would be so singular as to make it impossible to speak accurately about "the native."

So what should I call this multitude? Any term that I might use to refer to this heterogeneous collection of actions and meeting points carries with it the risk of reducing it to a homogeneous conjuncture. Friedrich Nietzsche alerts us to the problems at hand when he points out that, "Every concept arises from the equation of unequal things. Just as it is certain that one leaf is never totally the same as another, so it is certain that the concept 'leaf' is formed by arbitrarily discarding these individual differences and by forgetting the distinguishing aspects. This awakens the idea that, in addition to the leaves, there exists in nature the 'leaf': the original model according to which all the leaves were perhaps woven, sketched, measured, colored, curled, and painted—but by incompetent hands, so that no specimen has turned out to be a correct, trustworthy, and faithful likeness of the original model."[3] Nonetheless, and following Brazilian anthropologist Otávio Velho (2007) in recognizing that the word and the concept can never be true in and to themselves, I consider myself authorized to speak of "the jailed," "prisoners," and the powerful group referred to in this account and in São Paulo's prisons as "Brothers." I use this term as part of a discursive strategy I necessarily draw on in order to refer to a variety of practices and identities that are nonetheless irreducible to stable identities, or similarities. They are marked instead by the ways and extent to which they are drawn into a symphony of sorts, by means of what prisoners refer to as "the walk" (*a caminhada*).

At the same time that my interlocutors claim that they are all part of the same walk, or a corresponding and shared destiny worked out in experience, they emphasize over and over again that each participant is responsible for creating his or her own path. "The walk," then, is a term that refers to a specific situation but nonetheless implies a sense of movement and includes a consideration of the particular ways each person will engage or get by within this unfolding situation. The reach and densities of such walks vary in relation to participants' experiences and the ways they weave their relations, construct their reputations, sketch out strategies, and demonstrate their dispositions and willingness to act. In the case of the women who work to accompany their partners through São Paulo's criminal bureaucracies, the quality of the walk is directly related to their dedication to their husband. Thus, the walk, as performed and understood by Sandra, one of the women with whom I waited to enter the prison that day, took form as I stood on line at the Vila Independência CDP: "I've walked the walk for eight years already, but my husband has been imprisoned for eleven. When I met Roberto, he was already incarcerated. At the time I used to visit my brother, who also did time. Shoot, I knew a lot about the jails already! And then I started to visit Roberto and we got married. Later, he was released. . . . We got together, but just a month later he was hit with another indictment and arrested again."

Our conversation was interrupted when the CDP door swung open to allow a bus from the Secretaria de Administração Penitenciária (Secretariat of Penitentiary Administration, SAP) to leave on its route transferring prisoners to other sites across São Paulo State. Many women approached this vehicle, known among prisoners and their families as a *bonde* (trolley), in a vain attempt to get a closer look that might reveal whether their loved ones were among those being transferred. One of my linemates claimed that there was a good chance that her husband was on the trolley, since he had requested a transfer to a space, and a status, within the penitentiary system from which he might begin the long process toward parole.[4] Such early release, or a work release–based movement toward freedom, is not possible from within a CDP. The woman admitted that, even though the transfer was in her husband's best interests, she was nervous because she found herself imagining what might befall him inside the trolley: "They suffer so much inside that thing." I answered by adding that I also knew about this, since I had heard many prisoners complaining about the conditions in which they were transported, whether between prison units or to court for hearings and judgments.

On transport day, between thirty and forty prisoners are handcuffed to one another, with their hands inverted—a prisoner's right wrist is cuffed to the left wrist of the man to his left. There is not enough room for all to sit, and guards make no provisions for the circulation of air and light. In one of their most common shared complaints, prisoners report that what does circulate across the trolley is the smell of diesel fuel. To make matters worse, passengers are not usually being sent to the same places. Thus, the trolley makes as many stops as are necessary to complete its rounds, adding to the length of time spent there. Many prisoners vomit, urinate, and defecate. Some pass out.

Some of my colleagues began to cry in light of the possibility that their relatives were aboard the trolley. Their crying was not a result of the transfer itself and the impossibility of seeing their partners that day but part of their attunement to the suffering that awaited all those who entered the prison vehicle. As the trolley passed through the CDP doors, many called out, hoping to learn whether their partners were inside. Half an hour later, a list of the transported prisoners was stuck to the wall by an official. People balled up to get a look, and those who recognized names on the list began to seek more information from CDP functionaries: Where had their relatives gone? The corrections officers requested that they call on Monday for this information and the women unable to visit their relatives walked off, taking with them the bags of food they had prepared.

Problems surrounding the trolley kept the line stalled for almost half an hour, and it was midday by the time I reached the first guardhouse. There I had to present my identity documents and receive a stamp with the number of the pavilion in which my husband was imprisoned. As usual, the employee did not respond to my "Good Morning." And I did not make a special effort to establish a dialogue, since this would be looked on poorly by my linemates and might even generate suspicion about "being on their [prison guards'] side" or, worse, informing. As a result, my verbal exchanges with the prison employees were always clipped and focused on the specific goal of gaining entrance to the facility. Yet I never adopted a confrontational posture in these interactions, even in the face of attitudes that I understood as intended to provoke a reaction in me. So when, for example, guards barred me from entering by claiming that the very clothes I had worn the previous week were no longer appropriate, I preferred to go home and change my clothes rather than contest the edicts. Although some of my linemates adopted positions like my own, another group argued that any and all *simpatia* (sympathy, niceness, or shared affect) with prison functionaries must be avoided. But irrespective of the correctness and utility of either position, the fact that I was conducting anthropological fieldwork did not mean that I gained, or wanted, any greater access to jail employees than was necessary for entering the space of the jail.

Since I was not carrying food, I could go straight to the long string of people awaiting the "intimate search" (*revista íntima*), but not before facing the judgmental eyes of linemates who had made a point of carrying pots and pots of food to their relatives. Their time of arrival for the visit and the quality and quantity of food carried into the prison is, for those women, indicative of their level of dedication to the prisoner they visit. For example, when I used to visit my husband at the CDP in the city of São Bernardo do Campo, a linemate once proposed that we both arrive at the unit twenty-four hours before visiting day so as to be able to get the very first numbers. She boasted, "That way you'll be the first to enter. No, not the first; first me! You're gonna be the second!"

But on the day I sought to enter the Vila Independência CDP from a space farther back in line, almost forty minutes passed until, after clearing the metal detector, I was called into the cabin reserved for the "intimate search," As usual, I took off all my clothes, turned the garments over to a jailor, and awaited instructions. She asked me to squat down three times and then, on the third squat, to cough while remaining in a squatting position. I followed her instructions. Next, she asked me to lean my trunk back against the wall and to continue to cough. Squinting, she said, "I'm not able to see all the way up there," and she lay down on the floor in an attempt to get a better view. This surprised me, as nothing of the sort had ever happened before. In most prisons, it is enough to take off one's clothes, bend down, open one's mouth, and shake one's hair. They used to ask us to cough also in the Vila Independência CDP, but I had never experienced a search that reached the point that a functionary would lie on the floor to "get a better look up there."

"Go to it! Cough!"

"Uff, Uff, C-uhhf."

"Strange . . . I can't see anything. . . . Open it up!"

"What!"

"Open it up with your hands, so I can get a look inside."

I felt incredibly embarrassed by what was going on, but there was nothing I could do to avoid the request. I remembered one young woman who felt so ashamed on her first visit to prison that she turned around and fled the institution. The employee who was supposed to conduct the search followed her all the way out, screaming, "You think I'm a weak fool? I know you have drugs inside of you! Who do you think you are? You think you can just stop? Ah . . . it's because you know that the drugs're gonna fall out, right? Get back here and face our search. I'll get you and you'll never get out of jail!"

The woman who was searching me decided to call her colleagues over to look at, and into, me. Five moved in a group to the front of the cabin and asked me to cough again. Still bent over, I did as they told me. After they talked among themselves for a while, the woman who had examined me first, visibly upset, shook her head negatively and bellowed, "Go, get dressed!"

I couldn't hold back the tears. I had come to understand what the prisoners called "humiliation" (*humilhação*), or a sense of impotence mixed with revolt that may lead to hate. I crossed the patio to the doors that separated me from the pavilion where I would conduct my visit. The last door through which I had to pass was located within a wide corridor, called the hub (*radial*) because it gives access to four additional doors on each of its two sides. These entrances were blocked by large iron grates secured with a huge padlock. Each of these gates in turn opened to one of the eight pavilions, or "spokes" (*raios*). Today was visiting day for the even-numbered spokes on my right, and Sunday would be visiting day for the odd-numbered ones on the left.

Seeing me crying, the jailor in charge of opening the door to the spoke where I would visit my husband asked, "What happened? Did someone treat you badly?" I shook my head negatively. "If you have any problems, tell us and we'll see what can be done," he said. I entered into the cage (*gaiola*), or the space just before the main patio. When they hear the door to the spoke open, the prisoners watch the cage intently in search of a known face about to enter their patio. But if they fail to recognize anyone, prisoners return quickly to their activities—domino games, cards, walking, conversations, singing groups—since to look at another prisoner's visitors is to commit a grave offense within a PCC-controlled prison. Sometimes women on their first visit would ask us how they would manage to find their loved one inside. Our response was always the same: "You don't need to worry. It's them who're going to find you. When the door opens, stay still and they'll come to you. It's not right for a visitor to go walking around the spoke alone. But stay calm because it's impressive how fast they find us. It's also impressive how, with so many people inside, we are able to meet up with the guy we visit."

Entering, I located my husband visually, in an instant. He had already seen me and was walking toward the cage. His smile of happiness shifted quickly to an expression of worry. We embraced, and he asked me what was going on; why was I crying? It was not the first time that I had felt the need to cry after experiencing the guards' searches. But, like the other women, I always choked back my sobs so as not to worry my husband. But this time I couldn't help it, and the tears rolled down my face. I told him the patdown had been difficult. At this moment, two prisoners approached us, touched my husband's shoulder, and, their backs turned to me, whispered something in his ear. It is rare for one prisoner to speak with another prisoner's visitor. In addition to the injunction against looking at or speaking to another's visitor, there are a number of specific bodily postures and injunctions whose proper exercise is essential to such interactions. This is why the two other prisoners turned their backs on me. Their demeanor, which in other contexts might indicate a lack of respect, was here a demonstration of esteem since a prisoner should avoid turning his genital region toward the *senhora* (a formal term for wife) of one of his peers. In fact, even when it is impossible for prisoners to approach another's wife with their backs turned, they do so in a sideways manner. Additionally, verbal interactions are initiated with other prisoners' wives only in relation to very specific issues, and they are typically mediated by the prisoner who receives the visitor. Thus, I could not circulate freely around the prison yard as an anthropologist, asking questions of other prisoners. I needed to conform to the behavior expected of the visitor, and the wife, of one of their own.

I do not exaggerate when I report that my research would have been impossible without the cooperation and support of my husband. In each of the conversations I was able to engage in, in all the penal units in which I worked, it was my husband who opened up the possibility of dialogue. Without his mediation, I would never have been able to conduct this research. When I was interested in a particular point, I would ask my husband, and he would open up the questioning by approaching those around him or those best positioned to converse about the topic. Only when the dialogue had thickened would he call me into the conversation. But even with his support, we always exercised great care in interactions with other prisoners, especially with regard to corporeal and communicative conventions.

In spite of the need to rely on my husband's mediation, it would be a mistake to take our stylized engagements as somehow derivative or "artificial." The interactions between prisoners and visitors were real enough to produce quite concrete effects that in turn revealed the extent to which our relations were in many ways the results of a series of quite different policies implemented in São Paulo's prisons across the 1990s with the rise of the PCC. This is something I will address in greater detail in the next chapter. But here I emphasize simply that the effects of the interactions between visitors and prisoners emanate rather directly not from what one does, but from what one fails to do to make them real. So, for example, by policing his body and way of speaking in the presence of another's wife, the prisoner avoids the potential for being dubbed a *talarico*, or someone who pays too much attention to prisoners' wives and thus faces the threat of assassination.[5]

On the day I underwent the highly intrusive search, I did not need to ask my husband to initiate any dialogue: He whispered something into the ear of another prisoner, and that man asked me directly, "Did the functionaries oppress you, ma'am?" I answered, "They were a little rough around the edges during the search." It didn't make sense to add any details. The other prisoner spat out, "Those vermin!" Then he continued, "We're gathering complaints so as to join in putting together a common solution to this problem."

"You got it, man," responded my husband, as we left the two other prisoners. As we continued on toward his cell, he let me know that I was not the only one, that other women had arrived crying and complaining of poor treatment suffered as they tried to enter the prison on visiting day. He explained that men linked to the two prisoners who had met us and inquired about my treatment—a group of inmates associated with the PCC and thus referred to as "Brothers" (*irmãos*)—had vowed to find a solution to the problem, something they identified as an abuse on the part of the guards and prison employees. Here it is worth recalling the reaction of the Brothers in the CDP located in São Bernardo do Campo when faced with the same issue. As soon as they became aware of the first case of humiliation, they asked for a general meeting with the institution's director:

Senhor, we are here due to some unfortunate things that are taking place on visiting day. Here's what's up: we are bandits and we are paying the price. But our families have nothing to do with what we did and don't need to be punished. Would you like it if it were your mother who had to crouch down on all fours, opening her legs so that others could look in? No? Then don't play around with our families. Respect has to be mutual, sir. We're here taking the lead so as to resolve daily problems in the jails. Within the Command we have our discipline. Now sir, if you are not showing respect for our families and the families of our compatriots and someday when one of your employees is inside locking us down and some *malandro* [slick or tough guy] with nothing to lose decides to wring your guy's neck, I'm just not going to be able to do anything, sir. . . . It's really very lamentable. You see, you gotta respect in order to be respected. And we demand the same respect that we show to you, sir. So the searches are gonna go down like this: " 'Take off the clothes, bend down three times,' and that's it." There is no need for anything beyond that; understood?

As I walked to the cell, I noticed that many of the prisoners I had seen on my last visit were no longer on the patio. Instead, I saw new faces. Each spoke has about four hundred prisoners who sleep in the cells that abut the pavilion, and there is a lot of turnover in that population. Each week, I came across different people, since prisoners enter and leave the prison unit almost every day. This was one factor that made it difficult for me to update everyone about my ongoing research. Additionally, any research position—no matter what that position may involve—will necessarily fail in capturing the intensity of the unruly affectivity of visiting day. This is a moment when all attention is focused on the interactions between prisoners, their families, and the concerns that permeate the encounter. To interrupt such meetings would be seen as a sign of disrespect. Instead, I used to try to observe, feel, hear, and experience each moment of this intense space called visiting day and then put together specific questions on those rare occasions when I engaged in conversations with prisoners other than my husband.

I could always count on my husband's unflinching support. He would alert me to new developments in the prison, and he worked actively to put me in contact with people who might talk to me about these and other experiences. In short, this research would have been impossible were it not for my husband's dual commitment to my research and to acting correctly in the environment in which he found himself.

We talked about many things on the day the prison employees decided to put me through the difficult inspection. One issue that especially troubled my husband involved a young man who lived in his cell. He had accumulated a number of debts and, unable to pay, had asked for protection in the special lockup. Claiming that his life was at risk, the man had thus made the symbolically resonant move of turning to the prison administration for protection from his peers. As was normal, then, the guards reacted by putting him in the special area reserved for inmates who faced threats if left in the general population. The main problem in this case was that the prisoner was supposed to receive a television set that would arrive filled with contraband, including three cell phones intended for other prisoners.

The prisoners who were supposed to receive the cell phones began to worry about being turned in when the inmate moved to the special unit. This augmented my husband's biggest fear: He had been the one to introduce the inmate to the intended recipients of the cell phones. And since they knew one another on the outside, it had been my husband who had made the critical move of offering the young man a space in his cell. In the wake of such an invitation, it is assumed that the inmate is "giving his word" (*dando a palavra*), or endorsing the new arrival's behavior, character, and, most of all, history of proper orientation in the world, or prison universe (*proceder*).[6] So my husband was the one responsible for offering the new arrival instructions on how to live in their particular prison unit. And these instructions should have included pointed warnings about running up debts in addition to descriptions of the sanctions meted out to informants. Given his responsibilities and his acquaintance's subsequent behavior, my husband therefore had already run through his head all the arguments he would bring to bear in defending himself if it became necessary to resolve the situation with the discursive tool, discussed at length throughout this book, that prisoners call a "debate" (*debate*).

When we heard the whir of the siren announcing the end of visiting day, we said our goodbyes. I wished my husband well in the debate that would come. I learned days later that he had been able to control the situation and demonstrate that he had acted correctly in spite of the other man's mistakes. But I would learn the details only during our next visit, two weeks later.

When the Anthropologist Is a Visitor

As I have begun to spell out, a visit to the "field" is not a self-contained event conducted by an individual self. It is instead a compendium of experiences that emanate from multiple additional times, spaces, and experiences on which one necessarily leans in an attempt to make that moment intelligible. In other words, in order to comprehend one's lived experience, it is often necessary to draw on past experiences. Thus, the research trajectory described in this book is not about a neatly delimited space and time but rather about the effort to establish connections that go beyond the limits of a space and a time called "the field."

So far, we have seen how the impossibility of gaining access to all the inhabitants of any single spoke, or pavilion, together with prisoners' continual transfer between institutions, made it difficult for me to announce my research to them publicly and in detail. For the prisoners, I was a visitor like any other, and they permitted me to see only what all the other visitors saw. The difference between my linemates and me did not arise at my research site or at the moment of my visit to my husband, but subsequently as I wrote down what my interlocutors had offered and converted it into something definable as social scientific knowledge. In spite of such translations or transfers of knowledge, I did not in the end fear the possibility of retaliation for writing about issues that some might see as unsuitable for presentation to a larger public.

One of my principal preoccupations when I first began anthropological research as an undergraduate at the University of São Paulo involved the dangers associated with divulging information about prison life. I worried intensely about being considered a stool pigeon (*cagueta*) and thus being faced with threats on my life. But I soon arrived at a partial solution: I attempted to move through the prison in ways that would enable me to draw on "native" logics that would in turn permit me to represent the experience without incurring sanctions for revealing my ethnographic data. This "solution" arose as part of my examination of the prison-based classificatory system where a "Brother" (*irmão*) is a baptized member of the PCC; a "Cousin" (*primo*) is an inmate who lives in prisons controlled by the PCC while remaining unbaptized; and a "thing" (*coisa*) is an enemy. Prison employees and members of rival criminal factions are thus "things." In the logics of the PCC, and thus prison, anyone who is not involved with and thus "of Crime" (*do Crime*) cannot be such a Brother, Cousin, or thing. All noninvolved subjects are referred to instead, and pejoratively, as "Zé Povinho," or "Joe Public."[7]

As configured by the logics employed by the PCC, my status as Zé Povinho left me untouched by the group's imperatives and permitted me to publish my research. But rather than an absolute identity, such self-positioning relied on different actors' potential for argumentation and discussion of my status, something that could be deployed as necessary. Nonetheless, throughout my first fieldwork period, I never had to explicitly deploy a Zé Povinho status because no one questioned me about my research, in part because it was developed anonymously. No one, neither the jailors nor the prisoners, knew about that stage of research.

After I began to publish the results of my initial fieldwork,[8] my use of native categories in establishing or justifying my research position began to seem a bit fragile. Most basically, I began to understand that the categories adopted by inmates were not as rigid as I had made them out to be. In fact, the vast majority were evaluated contextually and manipulated frequently. I noticed also that, precisely because of his position outside PCC norms, "Joe Public" tended to be mistrusted as a potential snitch since citizens (who are not "of Crime") tend to rely for security on precisely the systems of control that gird prisoners' detention and conviction. Secondly, on the heels of my initial fieldwork, I decided that I would no longer perform an ethnography of prison as an institution but rather an ethnography of the existence of the PCC. So I thought it prudent to gain some form of assent from the "natives" at the center of my study. This would lead me to begin negotiations with the Brothers, the full-fledged members of the PCC.

One problem with my new research methodology was that negotiations with participants in the PCC could put me in a delicate position in relation to the legal authorities, for whom the PCC is a criminal organization. Thus, it might be argued that those who enter into dialogue with it are involved with crime. Additionally, citizens who give voice to criminals in the type of descriptive move so common among anthropologists might be interpreted as committing an "apology for crime." This is a crime, or an offense codified within Brazil's National Penal Code. Nonetheless, as Brazilian anthropologists Ana Marques and Jorge Villela have pointed out in a different fieldwork setting, "dedication to understanding everything that takes place in such processes should not be confused with an apology for them."[9] Furthermore, to "go against the moral consensus is not to apologize (for crime), but to feed controversy

as part of a search for alternatives that arise from the pluralities immanent in multiple ways of being."[10] In light of such insights from my
peers, I gained the confidence to approach certain prisoners to discuss
the possibility of continuing and extending my initial fieldwork. And
my tense negotiations of the possibility of studying the PCC turned into
a full-fledged research project when I passed on a copy of one of my
articles. To my surprise, and in a reaction that eased my fears, my account was received quite well: "You know more about the prisons than
many of the guys in here!" a number of people told me. And my readers
seemed to be confident that I had no intention of following up on crimes
or informing on anyone. That is how I was granted a "license" (aval)
from one group of Brothers to continue with my research.

Nonetheless, the Brothers' authorization of my research did not release me from the category of "visitor" (visita), and there were a variety
of forms of obedience and codes of conduct I still needed to follow. This
position required that I adopt the posture considered appropriate to a
woman visiting her imprisoned relative. Through such interactions, I
learned that the condition of "visitor," although not the same as being a
prisoner, does not exempt that guest from the same basic codes that orient the lives of those who are imprisoned. After all, as I mentioned, if
all prisoners are expected to instruct their visitors in proper etiquette,
then those prisoners may be held accountable for any mistakes made by
those visitors.

I was both an insider and an outsider. Drawing on this ambiguous
position, I sought to learn native practices without giving up a perspective that would permit me to put together my own standpoint in relation to one key facet of the experience, namely the visit. Since a variety
of observances and taboos are activated on visiting day, my particular
mode of inserting myself into fieldwork meant that I had to remain subject to certain specific conditions. In the first place, I was expected to
know certain rules of etiquette and behave in the manner expected of a
visitor. Secondly, the prisoners treated me as a visitor invited by one of
their own. And this created for me, paradoxically, a concomitant invisibility that arose from this insider status.

Respect for visitors is one of the basic rules of prisons controlled by
the PCC, especially as it relates to women. For example, when a female
visitor passes through a corridor occupied by prisoners other than her
companion, these men are expected to turn toward the wall so as not to
look at her directly. Additionally, I was strongly discouraged from giving

anything to anyone but my husband. And conversations without a specific objective were also frowned on. Here, in the specific forms of non-interaction characteristic of visiting day, gender rises rather forcefully to the fore since among the prisoners women are treated as something that belongs to a particular prisoner. Perhaps paradoxically, such an apparent constriction of possibility granted me a strange sort of access to the self-representations, or forms of self-fashioning, put together by the people at the core of my study. Or, seen slightly differently, my specific fieldwork situation permitted me to begin to sense what was latent or hidden in that field site, and thus to gain a certain access to that which remained unexpressed or filled with contradiction.[11] Additionally, my five-year period of research generated a rather extensive collection of materials. It also permitted me to gain the trust of people and develop a level of familiarity that enabled me to understand the relationship between what must be enunciated and what must be left unsaid, in order to trace the relations that constitute the PCC.[12]

My insertion into the field as a visitor or as an ethnographer who knows the prison "from within" (*de dentro*) granted me a privileged position for getting close to the collectivity known as the PCC both inside and outside prison. This is because I now possess the affective, often embodied, grammars and moral and ethical values that only "those on the inside" can really know. Out there, on the "Outside" (*Mundão*), I can engage those who share my "walk" (*caminhada*) just as I can approach ex-prisoners as well as people who live in areas under the influence of the PCC.[13] And I am able to engage these people, intensely and without fear of discrimination and incrimination, in ways that permit me to hone in on the relations that surround and constitute them.[14]

This becomes even clearer when I reveal my position as the wife of a prisoner, whether it involves ex-prisoners, prisoners' families, or even just residents of the periphery of any of Brazil's cities. At such moments, I am usually treated with greater intimacy and significantly less suspicion than the typical researcher. Thus, an approach to the field as a visitor imposes certain obligations on me. But it also opens up a series of critical perspectives that speak to how anthropology is established as a system of knowledge. My experiences suggest the possibility of a form of experimentation, or something Loïc Wacquant describes as "the need to understand and fully master a transformative experience that I had neither desired nor anticipated, and that long remained confusing and obscure to me, that drove me to thematize the necessity of a sociology not only *of* the body, in the sense of object, but also from the body, that is, deploying the body as tool of inquiry and vector of knowledge."[15]

In the sense highlighted by Wacquant, the very process of gaining authorization to conduct my research was revelatory because it challenges the idea that the PCC is a hierarchical organization. Since each participant speaks for the "Command" (*Comando*), it was not necessary to negotiate different levels of authority or even have my project discussed by large groups. As a result, when I encountered someone who did not know about my ethnography, all I had to do was explain that such and such a Brother had granted me license.[16] This meant that although my authorization was granted by a specific Brother, he, just like all the other members of the PCC, held the power and the authority to speak in the name of the group.[17]

The interactions that shaped my approach to the PCC enabled me to see and hear things that are rarely revealed to outsiders. They also sucked me, emotionally, into the midst of practices and relations that I hoped and prayed I could engage as but a simple observer. This whirlwind forced me to transform such "'participation' into a tool for producing knowledge" that might permit me to make sense of things that are not usually revealed to an ethnographer.[18] I needed to transform my emotional involvement into a calibrated instrument of knowledge production, and thus of specific, posterior claims.

Problems

It became apparent, even as I conducted my initial ethnography in the CDP in São Paulo, that it was difficult to determine whether what I was being told was representative of anything beyond people's experience of that particular institution. And yet what I observed was a series of actions within the jail that, either directly or indirectly, pointed insistently at the PCC. I was confused by the fact that an institution that no one—neither the press, the state, nor even the prisoners—considered any sort of PCC command center seemed to me to be a powerful site for the group's self-production. So while it would be wrong to insist that the CDP was "the" site of PCC activities, neither could I argue that the group was absent or lacked influence there. Yet I could not even claim with any certainty that all those who helped reproduce the PCC were in fact members of the group! This issue became even thornier when I asked a well-placed interlocutor from São Paulo's prison system for juvenile offenders, known at the time as the State Foundation for Juvenile Well-Being (Fundação Estadual para o Bem Estar do Menor [FEBEM]), about the existence of the PCC in his units:

"What? Junior-PCC? No! That doesn't exist," he exclaimed.

"So you're saying that within the FEBEM the prisoners don't follow any of the PCC orientations?" I pressed him. My source replied,

"Look here: They answer to the PCC, but juveniles are not baptized members," the official concluded

This short dialogue reveals that the PCC may be present even where it is absent, or, put better, in sites where we do not encounter any of its members. Such a perspective challenges not simply media portrayals of the group across Brazil but also the models of social structure offered up as analytical tools by a standard, modernist anthropology. And this experience has led me, in presenting the account here, to engage recent anthropological work that questions neat concepts of "society," "culture," "group," and "individual."[19]

Although it makes a certain sense, the attempt to classify prisoners as either members or nonmembers of the PCC would end up reifying the group as an isolated or discrete entity, something that would fail to get at its highly specific composition, history, and effects. To isolate the PCC in such a way would be to do violence to a complex system of relations put together by a quite diverse array of actors who influence its shape. This is part of a larger issue related to a traditional Anglophone and modern social scientific perspective for which the social comes to be seen as a thing to be explained, constituted, and "invented" instead of being approached as a series of relations in flux.[20] So instead of seeking to delimit, and thus limit, my object of study, I have sought to move beyond an approach to society as a concatenation of individuals or some sort of transcendental force that provides its members with a frame within which to act and to know themselves.

Marilyn Strathern and Christina Toren have defended the argument that "society," or an idea related to notions of localization and unity, is not really about individuals, nor is it "superior" to them. In effect, Strathern (1996) and Toren (1996) deny the existence of a higher entity— society—that would provide a necessary framework for those who are born into it or supposedly move and live within it as a milieu. Their analysis also suggests some of the problems that accompany a reliance on society as a transcendental or preconceived structure whose existence researchers presuppose when they examine particular relations imagined as existing "within" or composing that society. Strathern and Toren encourage us instead to think through everyday relations as forces and flows.

In spite of the usefulness of such insights, one might critique this position by noting the ways that "society" serves as a word used in a variety of communities.[21] Indeed, in São Paulo, prisoners speak of "society" when referring to life outside the jails. And this is not a simple physical space but the space beyond crime itself.[22] According to the prisoners, "society" is "Joe Nobody" or "the system"—it is the person who judges, incarcerates, and serves as a target of crimes. Nonetheless, and independently of the different uses made of "society," the central question put forth by Strathern and Toren involves the social scientific use of concepts that presuppose the existence of transcendental entities—whether "society," "culture," "language," or "group"—that are treated as a prioris that exist over and above individuals. For these two thinkers, "society" is nothing more than the conceptual forms that emerge from strong transcendental tendencies in Western thought. And it is precisely this tradition that may obscure the productive relations that they argue actually constitute human existence.

From the sort of perspective advocated by Strathern and Toren, to think the PCC as a "society" (or even a group) presupposes that it is a locatable, delimitable entity formed by a united cluster of members who are molded by forces understood as coercive and external to them. Instead, I think this relation through the lens of "sociality," a concept proposed by Strathern (1996) that leads me to discard anything that comes before, and thus delimits or constrains, the phenomenon at hand. From the ethnographic perspective taken here, then, analytical positions associated with a reliance on the social carry a marked risk of homogenizing or conferring a unity onto the real diversity of the PCC. My entwined ethnographic and analytical positioning thus helps mitigate against deterministic explanations, as well as interpretations that are external to practices verified during fieldwork. And this book is, quite centrally, an attempt to put together a description that avoids eclipsing or interrupting what I witnessed during fieldwork. Hence, a deactivation of the concept of "society" in favor of "sociality" is not some academic play on words but a methodological choice that supports novel fieldwork approaches and, consequently, different sorts of analytical work and outputs.

Bruno Latour (2005) suggests that ethnographers should follow their interlocutors and not tolerate the interruptions in analyses presented by ready-made concepts. This perspective offers powerful insights for an ethnography of the inconsistencies and instabilities, and thus the associations and disassociations, that constitute what we call the PCC. But even though I accept the power of such suggestions, if I were to lock the Command into Latour's actor network theory, I might find myself ignoring the claims to transcendence or transcendental unities put forth by members of the PCC who may at times attribute to the group something overarching, something akin at times to social scientists' "society."

Prisoners in São Paulo fail to see themselves as residing inside what they consider "society." They employ the term quite specifically to refer to those outside the prison walls. Yet they are not free of what I refer to throughout this book as a type of transcendental thought. This reappears in other guises, as concepts that include "PCC," "Crime," and the "Command." As should become clear, then, the people with whom I conducted my research consider the PCC an enduring force capable of exercising control over its participants. The particular ways in which I "followed the natives" have thus led me to consider whether there exists some "Super-PCC" that determines local societal relations.

In the chapters that follow, I put together an ethnography that permits us to consider the possibility that, however much an eschewal of the social and an insistence on actual practices reveals in relation to the rejection of a prioris, to follow the PCC without accepting the importance and possibility of certain strands of mystical, overarching thinking would be to miss how certain transcendental claims do indeed operate and hold great value among the Brothers. And their recourse to overarching, enduring concepts is not simply some instrumental appropriation of "the social" among those who participate in the Command.[23] Instead, the Brothers of the PCC are themselves part of a Western tradition of thought in which certain ideas come to the fore, and make sense, in ways that configure those ideas formally as structuring principles that precede or carry value above and beyond the experiences of those who create such structures. This gives rise to a situation in which the recommendations for a postsocial sociology of the type proposed by Latour— who rejects models in which superior forces such as culture, society, or group mold the human—fail to account for native theories and tend to trip up analyses of what is really going on. The basic problem here is that concepts and theories, whatever they are, are "collective assemblages of enunciation."[24] As such, they supercode other concepts and assemblages in ways that impose an alien form on the object of analysis.[25] They work to impose on the object of analysis a shape that is strange to that object. Or, put slightly differently, anthropology's standard toolbox is capable of all too neatly cutting off the rough edges that outline a still-indeterminate path. In the process, ruptures and declensions are covered up by arbitrary selections and surgical maneuvers that emanate from the observer's instruments of analysis.

How, then, might ethnographers put together an anthropological praxis without a blinding reliance on those seductive toolboxes, whether they be the now-consecrated classics of modern social science or newer ideas such as Latour's actor network theory? One path into a more complex and faithful engagement with objects of analysis involves resisting the urge to trace out theories—whether timeworn or novel—and instead create maps based on the very challenges thrown up by our objects of study.[26] This is why I direct so much attention to understanding how transcendental figures and claims are constructed and become efficacious. This involves the difficult, and perhaps contradictory, task of considering the transcendental without imagining that it preexists. In other words, I seek to think of transcendentalism by valorizing its immanent qualities, or the potentials within it, as both products and producers of what appears, or takes form, as a transcendent PCC. Central to this project is to observe an entity's local instantiations and quotidian appearances in the most subtle and casual of relations as established between interlocutors. This involves looking also at how a particular figure is produced and in what ways this force of production acts as something exterior to the situation or context.

What I propose is an immanent anthropology directed at the native construction of transcendence and transcendental ideas or institutions: If I affirm that the PCC holds a certain influence within the prison system, it is not because I consider the PCC to be an established, pregiven force that maintains power over prisoners in order to dictate what they should and should not do. Rather, it is the name placed on a much wider formation being constructed and operated locally. At play is the local production of a transcendental form that, in this case, also holds the capacity to act agentively and produce the relations developed between prisoners.

Again, even though a tendency toward the transcendental thinking so much a part of Western thought and modern social science flows through the Brothers who work to establish or cognize a stable, cohesive PCC, or a totality, as an exterior force that exercises coercion on individuals, I opt for the concept of "sociality."[27] This permits me to move closer to the heterogeneity of my object of study and offers the potential for more powerful analysis. Additionally, and so as not to fall into the temptation of offering theoretical interpretations that would delegitimize the real perspectives of my interlocutors by treating them as simple beliefs, I propose the idea of a PCC group, a PCC structure, and a PCC "totality" as objects that the Brothers seek to realize or construct.[28] Since the Brothers can do little alone, their objective is to link themselves up in search of stability-by-association, even if this means conjuring up a transcendental unity, the PCC.

For the observer, analyzing stability implies investigating why a certain conjuncture has gained a measure of "success." But it is also to analyze instability and to think through the circumstances that have provoked change alongside the ideal, but still real, potentials that accompany as well as threaten such fragile stability. And to take up such a focus is not necessarily about following, or disagreeing with, the PCC. Nor is it even about undermining their desire for stability in the interest of the creation of a group.

To opt for or choose between "society" and "sociality" or stability and instability can be fruitless. Thus, my project is not simply about opposing the figure of the rhizome celebrated by Gilles Deleuze and Félix Guattari against the more ossified figure of the root, or immanence against the transcendence I have suggested has much to do with modern social science's overdetermination of its objects of analysis. After all, as Deleuze and Guattari point out, there are more hardened treelike formations in the creative forms of association they dub "rhizomes," and there are "rhizomatic" formations in putatively stable and stabilizing roots. Thus, my object is to work rhizomatically in order to begin to make out how a particular form of sociality made real by way of the PCC is constructed. It is thus fitting that the rhizome is a concept put together by Deleuze and Guattari to engage multiplicities, or nonhierarchical forms in which "any point ... can be connected to anything other, and must be."[29] In fact, the best-known example of a rhizome might be the underground stems that bind together sod and which, no matter where they are cut, grow back and recompose themselves from their middles since they depend on no central organ for their development. Adjacent roots, on the other hand, are metaphors par excellence for hierarchical forms and centralized systems in relation to a "law of the One that becomes two, then of the two that become four.... Binary logic is the spiritual reality of the root-tree."[30] Nonetheless, Deleuze and Guattari emphasize that neither the root nor the rhizome is ever found in its pure form since "there are knots of arborescence in rhizomes, and rhizomatic offshoots in roots."[31]

The challenge when mapping flows and forces inside and outside São Paulo's prison system involves identifying a particular reality today without forgetting that what I understand as arboreal, or relatively transcendent, social forms persist within the state's prison units. In this context, a questioning of dualities does not necessarily mean hiding or negating them. Thus, as long as the opposing sides are undone by a powerful back-and-forth movement that eventually escapes those bounds to leak into all extremities, my attempt to hold onto a certain duality as a jumping-off point does not mean that the analysis that follows is dualist.[32] In fact, one can successfully avoid splitting or abruptly interrupting one's analysis by permitting an oscillation between the two to invade the both so that novel lines of analysis split off in all directions, leaving the two opposing points empty.

Again, in dissolving dichotomies, I rely, above all else, on my object of study. The rhizomatic prison universe generates a particular type of movement in relation to attempts to analyze its more fixed formations, in the process tirelessly inventing multiple series of different repressive—or, in the language of Deleuze and Guattari, "arboreal"—mechanisms that it insists on replacing within itself. This may at times arise from attempts to stifle competing forces that reproduce, on a small scale and with all its corresponding shorthands, the power of the state. And yet this is not simply an example of the production of the transcendental by that which is immanent to it. Rather, it is about the tense standoff between two nonentities, or two assemblages that do not exist except as agentive forces in a conflictual relationship.

It would appear that in examining the PCC we find ourselves before a collectivity that, excluded from life within society and thus occupying a space nearly consonant with the very objective of incarceration, produces incessant attempts to negate the state that isolates the collectivity. But in doing so the PCC is unable to avoid a certain idea or debt to a transcendence that seems to offer the potential to materialize powers typically seen as belonging to that state. So, if the object of the struggle of the Brothers of the PCC is the consolidation of their Command, then success involves forms of totalization from which they nonetheless seek to escape. And yet they are ultimately unable to form either a root or a bulb that would connect to it: When the objective seems near, it disappears into the haze.[33] Such oscillation between—or, put better, such interpenetration across—immanence and transcendence is one of the most basic dynamics I set out to explore in this book.

Order of the Chapters

Elaborating the account before you forced me to face a number of problems that, although not quite resolved, did make me choose certain theories, methods, and ways of putting together this text. One such choice forced on me by the still-incomplete attempt to overcome multiple challenges involves the order of the text. When I would develop the narrative in one way, I would begin to note that all the lines I chose as starting points failed to account for certain of their precedents, even as they ended up converging with other lines. I found myself unable to recover a perfect opening that would prepare the ground, and my readers, for what comes next. All my choices were the results of, or emanated from, other choices that ended up converging at certain points and diverging at others. So there are excellent reasons that a "native" term for conceptualizing this relationship—the phrase "Mixed Up and Together" (standing together, as one)—served as this book's original title in Portuguese (*Junto e misturado*). Not only do the natives examined here argue that they work toward the logically or rhetorically inconsistent goal of keeping themselves alongside one another as a single unit, but the border between immanence and transcendence in this collective is markedly indistinct.

Even though my difficulties in encountering a neat starting point may very well be the positive effect of an ethnographer's attempt to escape the a priori, I have tried in chapter 1 to overcome this confusion and produce a short and fairly standard history of the PCC and the individuals and spaces that will follow in successive chapters. Chapter 1, then, will move from discussions of the skills and baptismal rituals essential to the construction of a Brother to the production of PCC territories. This production of territory, especially regarding relations of command and leadership, is the main focus of chapter 2, "Politics and Pedagogy: Inside the University." There I describe the political positions that put into operation sets of practices shaped by native theories that strive to produce a coherence between those politics and concerns with equality. They do so in ways that hold forth the possibility of stamping out the exercise of power by individuals or groups over other individuals and groups. Improvisation and careful strategizing come together in this project, and this politics, which resist top-down commands.

Here it is worth introducing the conceptualization of politics that inspires and orients this book. Over the course of significant periods of the discipline's development, anthropologists focused on understanding how, in the absence of a state, primitive societies were able to organize themselves successfully. Thus, among anthropologists working in Africa, for example, kinship and lineage systems were thought of as forms of corporate identification that took the place of modern state institutions.[34] Meanwhile, in the 1970s, the French ethnographer of Amerindian societies Pierre Clastres began to put together an analysis that would disengage the nearly reflexive association of modern political organization with the state. For Clastres (2003), the absence of state institutions was not a problem to be solved through functionalist analysis or overcome in relation to so-called modernization. On the contrary, he began to argue that in certain societies—even in the twentieth century—there existed a number of mechanisms that actively inhibited the presence or growth of state institutions or statelike formations.

According to Clastres, the Amerindian groups with whom he conducted research put together a politics that was not simply dissociated from the state but also actively resisted the construction of top-down power structures that might support the installation of state and statelike institutions in their societies. These communities are, in Clastres's words, "societies against the state." The ethnographer thus offers possibilities for thinking through the ongoing exercise of micropolitics disassociated from the state and its institutions. I argue that it is this type of politics—a politics that has nothing to do with disputes between parties, for example—that prisoners in São Paulo's jails participate in today. For example, in chapter 3, "The Politics of Immanence," I examine moments when prisoners lose control as part of an attempt to understand the labile workings of the rationality associated with such strategizing. Here, what I refer to as "dispositions" function as motors that permit the coexistence and interaction of what I approach as projects, manipulative efforts, chance, strategies, unexpected as well as carefully manipulated twists, and improvisations.

The fragile consistency generated by the diverse processes described in chapter 3 gains stability when it takes on a more transcendental form that is both the product and the producer of the immanence that permeates it.

Hence, the ways that what I refer to as "deindividualizing" processes operate in the materialization of a power that gains autonomy from and superiority over its producers—or, put another way, the ways such a transcendent force makes de-individualization possible—are the subject of chapter 4, "The Politics of Transcendence." This chapter makes clear the efficacy and strength of a force field called the PCC by offering an analysis of territorializing processes that take place alongside the phenomenon of deindividualization. Or, put a bit too simply, chapter 4 focuses on a form of power that supports the existence of a collectivity without an enduring, stable tie to territory. Most importantly, in that chapter 4, I also seek to describe the construction of a localized form of transcendence, or the establishment of an imaginative figure whose perplexing concreteness avoids ultimate transcendence by working as a machine that seeks liberty and resists all subjectification in its avoidance of the constitution of power as put forth by the state.

CHAPTER ONE

The PCC

São Paulo's Carandiru House of Detention was inaugurated in the 1920s as a model prison designed to house 1,200 inmates. Over time, Carandiru came to hold approximately 8,000 men, a number that granted it the dubious distinction of being Latin America's largest prison. In 1992, something took place in Carandiru that would have critical consequences for São Paulo's prison system: A police "intervention" intended to quell a rebellion in Pavilion 9 resulted in the deaths of 111 inmates. This event would come to be known as the "massacre of Carandiru," or what I refer to simply as "the Massacre."[1]

The Massacre garnered significant attention from a variety of actors, both Brazilian and international, and ended up making Brazil the target of legal action in the Organization of American States' (OEA) International Court. A number of commentators have also suggested that the killings made clear a series of fissures in Brazil's ongoing redemocratization by highlighting the continued place of torture and violent practices that appear to have been inherited from the military dictatorship that ruled from 1964 to 1985. Although the military legacy is open to debate, the slaughter gave rise to change by sparking the creation of the Secretaria de Administração Penitenciária (Secretariat of Penitentiary Administration, SAP), a new institution charged with paving the way for the deactivation of violent, decrepit, and overcrowded Carandiru.[2] And, indeed, during the period between the Massacre and Carandiru's deactivation in 2002, São Paulo's prison system underwent significant transformations. These were the result of a series of simultaneous yet distinct processes that constantly crossed into and influenced one another.

The first transformation involved the vertiginous growth of the incarcerated population. In 1992, São Paulo State's prisons confined 52,000 prisoners in forty-three different prison units. But by the end of 2002, there were nearly 110,000 prisoners in eighty units.[3] Such rapid growth failed to generate significant notice across the state, in part because social movement actors had begun to turn their gaze away from prisoners and prison conditions following the release of political prisoners detained during the dictatorship. But the principal reason for the public's lack of attention involved a basic transformation in the prison system in the wake of the Massacre.

Among the initiatives pushed forward by SAP was the deactivation of urban public jail units, or those run by specific police battalions and neighborhood precincts. This meant the end of the small jails that once pockmarked São Paulo's urban fabric. Instead, the SAP worked to construct large prisons in suburbs and rural areas. This created a situation in which an increase in cells meant not simply that the state could incarcerate more people, but also that those prisoners formerly concentrated in a disparate array of jails from which they often escaped and thus garnering neighbors' attention, would be spread across suburban and rural São Paulo. This distribution of the incarcerated across São Paulo State—a political unit approximately the same size as the entire United Kingdom—meant that the new politics of mass imprisonment put in place by successive administrations could be camouflaged by the dispersion of prisoners and the facilities that housed them. Yet the construction of new, state of the art units failed to keep up with the rapid growth in the number of people incarcerated. As a result, the deactivation of the Carandiru House of Detention was postponed on multiple occasions. It was only after Carandiru came to be considered a source and command center of the "megarebellion" of September 2001, in which approximately 28,000 prisoners detained in twenty-nine penitentiaries rebelled simultaneously, that it was closed for good.

The 2001 megarebellion was the first large action put forth by the PCC, whose birth and early growth occurred silently and without being perceived by the great majority of São Paulo's populace. The rise of the PCC constitutes the third of the processes responsible for the changes in the prison universe in the wake of the Massacre. And Carandiru's deactivation constitutes something of a nodal point that brings together this megarebellion, the spike in prison population, and the shifts in the nature of carceral institutions in São Paulo State. From this point on, commuters on subways and buses would no longer catch glimpses of prisoners in their cells, residents whose houses abutted police stations stopped living in fear of (relatively common) escape attempts, and prison facilities came to be hidden, no longer a part of the everyday experience of living in São Paulo. However much their numbers grew, these prisoners were no longer so visible to most *paulistanos*. The transfer of prisons from city centers to peripheries, and then on to distant, rural areas, meant that the PCC also became a distant, or less visible, phenomenon. And this scattering of adherents and their associates, like the PCC's tendency to act most forcibly at the margins of the city, meant that the Command took shape in what for many Brazilians were distant or forgotten areas.

I AM UNABLE TO SPECIFY precisely the date and exact circumstances of the PCC's birth. Over the course of my research, I collected different versions of the Command's origin stories. According to some, the PCC arose in 1989, in Carandiru. Other versions of the Party's foundational myth claimed it came into being in 1991 in the prison near the city of Araraquara, located a little over 250 kilometers northwest of the state capital. Some of my sources argued that the PCC emanated from earlier prison groups, including the "Black Serpent" (Serpente Negra) or "Warriors of David" (Guerreiros de David). Some even claimed that the group originated in a soccer game. It is also widely claimed—but extremely rarely on the part of Brothers—that the PCC arose as part of the engagements between political prisoners imprisoned by the military regime and the "common" criminals who served time alongside them.

Whatever the real beginning of the PCC, one version of its birth came to be accepted over others in the prison universe after the publication in 2004 of *Cobras e Lagartos* (Snakes and Lizards) by São Paulo–based crime reporter Josmar Jozino. Within months of the book's publication, prisoners came to accept Jozino's version of events. So although I cannot trace exactly how this account came to be accepted to the detriment of others, I remain surprised by how quickly it took form and gained credence. The rise of the origin story based on *Cobras e Lagartos* took place in an environment in which it seemed that alternative accounts had never existed. And this stands as one of many cases of "collective amnesia," or the term I employ to describe situations in which debates that burbled and boiled would cool down and disappear rather rapidly. For reasons as diverse as the impulses that first generated them, it would appear as if these debates had never existed.

One such impulse involved the polemic generated around information potentially revealed about prisoners and their actions—soon after the publication of *Cobras e Lagartos*, one of the prisoners cited in the account argued astutely that he had not yet been tried for one of the crimes described in the text and that it would therefore be incorrect to associate him with the action. This prisoner saw Jozino as a stool pigeon. Three years later, I came into contact with other prisoners who said they had known Jozino and contributed to his book. They affirmed that Jozino was not at risk as an informer because he had not "fingered" anyone, since everything he published had been authorized by the protagonists. Whatever the truth of these varied claims, the work's repercussions inside São Paulo's prisons were significant, and this density of discourse helped authenticate the origin myth published by Jozino.

According to *Cobras e Lagartos*, the PCC took definitive form on August 31, 1993, during a soccer match held in an annex of the Casa de Custódia e Tratamento de Taubaté, a jail generally considered one of the most rigorous in Brazil. The fight that erupted during the game between the Comando Caipira (Redneck Command, or loose affiliation of prisoners) and the First Command of the Capital led to the deaths of two members of the Comando Caipira. To protect themselves from retribution and prison abuse by authorities—most commonly beatings—all members of the First Command of the Capital team signed an agreement promising that any punishment of any member of the team would give rise to a serious response by all members of the team.[4] Soon the soccer players were able to count on the support of numerous other prisoners. Next, an inmate named Mizael, recognized subsequently as one of the PCC's founders, put together a constitution that enunciated two broad lines of action. First, it theorized a jailhouse organizing project aimed at ending the mistreatment he claimed was so basic to life in carceral institutions. Second, it brought together language that sought to regulate the relations between prisoners so that their actions would not be a part of the mistreatment described in the statute. This intervention into prisoners' relations turned on the claim that since all prisoners faced the same brutal conditions, they needed to unite in order to demand dignified treatment within the prison system. According to Jozino, the wives of a number of the inmates involved in the demand got together immediately afterward in São Paulo's City Council to discuss prison conditions.

Many prisoners today see the creation of the PCC as having extinguished the climate of constant war, of "all against all," in which the basis for life in jail was "everyone for himself" and "survival of the strongest." Up until that point, physical punishment from guards and violence between inmates was common in an environment in which the most minor of slights or disagreements might lead to a "decision by the knife," or a contest in which only one participant would emerge alive. Additionally, before the rise of the PCC, sexual violence was quite common.

Often, the only way to resist such attacks involved killing the aggressor, adding another charge to a prisoner's record. And in a phenomenon that added to sexual and interpersonal violence, inmates would seek to control any available resources, from a roll of toilet paper to the cell itself, in order to sell them to other prisoners who could not obtain them through force. But this changed with the rise of the PCC. As a Protestant minister known as Pastor Adair put it, "I'm not looking to support or excuse any crimes, but before the PCC came into existence those imprisoned here really suffered. They suffered because they were organized into rival gangs. And there was a lot of extortion, rape, and deaths over nothing. But when in 1988, I came to know the Party as a pastor I began to observe their way of working and to note how jail was changing. The cell that you once had to buy, today you don't buy any more. Rape no longer exists in jail. And those banal deaths no longer take place. So it would seem that there has been a change . . . for me it's been a change for the better."[5]

When I asked one prisoner, who had spent more than thirty years of his life in prison, whether there had been any change following the emergence of the PCC, he cracked a wide smile and told me, with his eyes gleaming, "Ah, . . . the Party! With the Party our situation has gotten so much better. There's no comparison." The PCC's proposal, which involved a change in ethics within the prisons, was seductive. For this reason, it gained adherents inside and outside the prisons. But in spite of such growth inside prison walls, the PCC remained largely invisible on the "outside." This had much to do with the position taken by authorities in relation to the PCC.

The state's first reaction was to cover up the group, to hide its existence. But at the end of 1995, television reporter Fátima Souza broadcast an interview with the leader of a prison rebellion in Hortolândia, a city located in the interior of São Paulo, near Campinas, a university center. The prisoner declared himself a member "of a fraternity, a command that has spread across the jails" in order to "fight against injustices, against the prison system . . . against the judicial system . . . and for our rights."[6] Authorities quickly denied the prisoner's claims and transferred him to a "more secure" jail. But the name of the prisoner's "fraternity" had not been revealed. Not until 1997 would the acronym PCC be made public, as part of the efforts of the same reporter. But, again, the government denied the facts of the report. In fact, Secretary of Penitentiary Administration João Benedito de Azevedo Marques declared it a "fiction, idiocy. It's complete garbage. I am completely convinced of this. I've been Secretary for almost two years and I've never seen any sign of this group."[7]

And yet, finally, in September 1997, during a rebellion in a prison in the interior of São Paulo State, the secretary came face-to-face with public evidence of the PCC's existence when a group of prisoners unfurled a banner reading "PCC" while Azevedo Marques was conducting a group interview. Nonetheless, it was not until 1999, following the PCC's "rescue" of a group of prisoners from a police station's holding pens, that the government of the state of São Paulo asked police to investigate the group. This inquiry, concluded in 2000, turned up significant evidence about the Command's strength. But the state government continued to treat the PCC as but a small group of convicts, without much influence inside or outside prison walls. Nonetheless, authorities decided to transfer PCC leaders to prisons in other regions of Brazil. But if the plan was to weaken the group, the result was the opposite: The transfers permitted the PCC's expansion into other states and the building of alliances with other criminal groups, including the Comando Vermelho (Red Command) of Rio de Janeiro.

But the real coalescence of the PCC in São Paulo's prisons, as well as official and definitive government recognition of its existence, came with Brazil's megarebellion of February 2001. The well-coordinated actions that came to be referred to as the "megarebellion" did much to push the PCC's expansion: After 2001, the PCC came to act not simply in the overwhelming majority of São Paulo's penal institutions but across most of its urban spaces. Only in the wake of overwhelming evidence of the group's presence inside and outside prison walls did the government begin to publicly recognize the group's existence.[8] In June 2011, the Public Advocate's Office (Ministerio Público) denounced the PCC as a "criminal organization." Nonetheless, one secretary of the Penitentiary Administration, Nagashi Furukawa, announced that "criminal organizations are a minority within our jails."[9] But, by this point, leaders of the PCC had ceased trying to remain anonymous, and they struggled to make their acronym visible whenever possible. As a result, and in an attempt to calm the public, any mention of PCC, the number 15.3.3, or even the name Primeiro Comando da Capital was prohibited by the editors of certain news organizations. According to Josmar Jozino, who at the time worked as a reporter for the *Diario de São Paulo*, a newspaper owned by Brazil's powerful Globo News Network (Rede Globo), the editorial board "prohibited the use of the acronym PCC, the number

15.3.3, and even the name 'Primeiro Comando da Capital.' More specifically, the acronym was barred, for an undetermined time period, from use in texts, titles, captions, headlines and first page news. Reporters were instructed to refer to the PCC only as the 'criminal faction that dominates São Paulo's prisons' or else a 'criminal group' or 'criminal faction.' This decision was then applied to the other newspapers, magazines, and television networks of this [Rede Globo] group headquartered in Rio de Janeiro. The acronym 'CV' and title 'Comando Vermelho' [Red Command] were also outlawed."[10] As a result, the Party's activities remained unmentioned for years in the pages of Brazil's major dailies or by the reporters of Rede Globo, one of the world's most-watched noncable television networks.

In November 2002, Saulo de Castro Abreu Filho, then secretary of public safety, made public a collective interview and organizational chart of the PCC. This diagram included "bosses," "sub-bosses," and "pilots" and was based on the testimony of Geleião, one of the founders of the command, who had nonetheless been forced out subsequently. That same year, authorities had completed the Presidio Presidente Bernardes, a maximum-security institution designed to isolate the leadership of the PCC. And eleven of the prisoners cited in the organizational chart offered up by the secretary of public safety were transferred to Presidente Bernardes. Godofredo Bittencourt, the director of the Departamento de Investigações sobre o Crime Organizado (Department for the Investigation of Organized Crime, DEIC), characterized this transfer of prisoners as a victory, arguing that "the PCC is a failed organization. I can't say it's dead, because it's a powerful symbol, kind of like a cancer, always popping up. But now it's a cancer in remission that, with patience, we are going to kill off."[11]

Yet the activities of the PCC continued to gain notice. In November 2003, the Command sponsored seventy actions against public authorities, principally the police, in an attempt to pressure the government to transfer its leaders out of the Presidente Bernardes maximum-security facility. And in 2004, 8,000 people massed in front of the headquarters of the Secretariat of Penitentiary Administration to demand new rules for visiting prisons. The year 2006 would usher in the most powerful actions related to the rise of the PCC. In May, Brazil's second megarebellion took shape in eighty-four penitentiaries, including ten outside São Paulo State. And this megarebellion had a significant effect beyond prison walls, as eighty-two municipal buses were burned, seventeen banks were bombed, and 299 state institutions were attacked. This focused violence resulted in the deaths of forty-two public safety agents and police officers and the wounding of thirty-eight other agents and officers.

As a collectivity that many imagined existed only on urban peripheries and inside jails gained visibility by means of violence in the centers of Brazil's most important cities, the scope of the second megarebellion quashed most Brazilians' doubts about the presence of the PCC outside São Paulo's penitentiaries. In the wake of the 2006 attacks, intellectuals were called on to explain what was happening. This gave rise to the publication of a special journal issue, *Dossiê Crime Organizado* (Organized Crime Dossier), by one of Latin America's most important institutions of social analysis, the highly regarded Instituto de Estudos Avançados at the University of São Paulo.[12]

In the Dossier's very first article, well-known social scientists Fernando Salla and Sérgio Adorno claim that the powerful impact of the second megarebellion was the fruit of the PCC's organizational structure, one "maintained by its hierarchical universe of 'functionaries,' or disciplined and obedient members ready to carry out orders without question," in an environment in which Brazil's laws and social policies had not kept up with changes in society.[13] The authors go on to suggest that the PCC was able to come into being only as a result of a weakness, a lack of rigor, on the part of public institutions that failed to inhibit its organizational efforts. Additionally, and as part of an analysis that contradicted that moment's commonsensical assumptions, they argue that "there is strong evidence that mass incarceration related to attempts to constrain the leaderships of organized crime groups has produced unexpected effects" like the 2006 attacks, events the two social scientists classified as both "moments of social effervescence"[14] and "moments of war."[15] In this way, and even as they see prisons as "environments in which social relations are arranged precariously, lacking in reciprocity," they interpret the PCC actions in 2006 as junctures at which "the solidarity between 'brothers' is reinforced, as is also the case in relation to the bonds between those who are imprisoned and those on the outside."[16] In fact, Adorno and Salla affirm that, for the PCC, "What is at play are interests related to business ... [the PCC] has no political project for the construction of a democratic society. Its conception of society is weak, based on loyalty between 'brothers' and a social conception of extensive family, or a constellation of moral and material interests."[17]

In the same special issue, and in accordance with UN classificatory norms, Getúlio Bezerra Santos portrays the PCC as a "structured group" composed of "jailed criminals who in the name of a false solidarity assumed command of the jails, due to a lack of effective state presence. That is why I call it the 'social security system' of the prisons—since inmates are lazy and the majority are condemned for crimes, living in an almost pathological condition, they organize themselves into associations that permit them to continue to commit crimes by operating under the guise of providing some (false) protection to the families of inmates on the part of gangs like the Primeiro Comando da Capital. The PCC has become something of a fashion or fad."[18]

In the arguments described, the authors present the PCC as something of a poorly produced copy of the state, or a hierarchical structure blessed with a chain of command that is more efficient than the state's structures because it does not depend on the bureaucratic entanglements too often thought to be so constitutive of the Brazilian state. This image of the PCC as a vertically or pyramidally structured business with purely economic interests is common among intellectuals as well as among legal professionals and journalists. But my fieldwork contradicts such representations rather forcefully.

In producing their arguments, Adorno and Salla do not really engage the philosophical bases of the state, instead limiting their analysis to a critique of the government's methods in managing prison populations and attempting to control crime. Too often, then, the activities and workings of the state become analogies that may filter into and even guide what might otherwise be analyses of a fundamentally different type of politics waged by the PCC. As a result, in working to understand how my fieldwork data contradict such a representation, throughout this book I draw on the philosophical reflections of Gilles Deleuze and Félix Guattari. These thinkers have helped alert me to the shortcomings of a philosophy and social science guided by statelike assumptions that continually and erroneously slip the state and its epistemological models into the analysis. In the hands of Salla and Adorno, the result of this confusion is a characterization of the PCC as a parallel state. But this interpretation is diametrically opposed to research by French ethnologist Pierre Clastres that inspired Deleuze and Guattari. For Clastres (2003), the absence of state institutions among the indigenous populations he researched is not a deficiency that must be filled by alternative structures that perform the same function. On the contrary, Clastres's interlocutors actively rejected the rise of social hierarchies and leaders who relied on the power of command and would therefore lead them to a statelike form of political organization.

Throughout this book, I present data that suggest that the PCC is not primarily an economically focused hierarchical institution—or parallel power to the Brazilian state—thus arguing that the concept of "organized crime" is not an adequate lens for understanding what has taken place inside and outside Brazil's prisons over the last three decades. My point of departure for developing such an understanding of the PCC and its politics involves a number of issues, including territoriality. For this reason, the next section of this chapter presents a survey of the ways that prisoners engage and make use of the spaces presented by institutions directed at "rehabilitation."

Territorialities

According to research performed by Brazil's National Department of Penitentiaries, in December 2007, 153,056 of the 422,590 prisoners who made up the nation's total incarcerated population were housed in the state of São Paulo. To give some sense of the magnitude of this number, the state of Rio de Janeiro, which tends to garner the most attention in national as well as international journalists' accounts of violence in Brazil, had only 26,523 prisoners in custody.

In 1993, São Paulo became the first city to create a secretariat directed exclusively at prison administration. Today, the Secretaria de Administração Penitenciária (SAP) oversees thirty-four Centros de Detencão Provisoria (Centers for Temporary Detention, CDPs), seventy-four Penitenciárias (Penitentiaries) for inmates who have been judged guilty, twenty-two Centros de Ressocializacão (Centers for Resocialization, CRs), seven Centros de Progressão Penitenciária (Centers for Furlough and Return to Civilian Life), two Institutos Penais Agricolas (Penal Agricultural Colonies), five hospitals, and three maximum-security units.[19] Ideally, prisoners are distributed between these units in relation to where they stand in the completion of their sentences. According to Decree 44,708 of February 10, 2000, the state-level measure that defined the different prison units, CDPs are "directed at the custodianship of provisionary prisoners" who await legal judgment. Once sentenced, prisoners are supposed to be sent to penitentiaries in order to begin serving their sentences. Meanwhile, the CRs and the Centros de

Progressão Penitenciária (or what prisoners refer to as the *colonias*, or prison colonies) are reserved for inmates who are nearing the completion of their sentences. Many of the members of this latter group are completing the final segments of their sentences in what in Brazil is called a "semi-open regime" (*regime semi-aberta*), in which they leave prison grounds during the day and return to sleep at night. Finally, the maximum-security units (*Unidades de Segurança Máxima*) are reserved for prisoners considered extremely dangerous or who have committed disciplinary infractions considered serious by the SAP. However, the ostensibly rational taxonomy of apparently discrete types of prisons does not prevent an often promiscuous transfer of inmates across and between the different units.

Centros de Detencão Provisoria, or those supposedly "provisional" spaces of detention in which I conducted the majority of my fieldwork, occupy a special place in the transfer and categorization of prisoners. This is especially true in the city of São Paulo, where the number of penitentiaries is significantly lower than the number of CDPs. So even though these facilities were created to house inmates for short periods of time, in practice many of the imprisoned end up completing their entire sentences in the CDPs. Additionally, upon finally reaching trial, prisoners commonly find that they have spent a period in the CDPs that is as long or nearly as long as their sentences. In other words, they end up serving their sentences before being judged guilty. In other cases, prisoners request a transfer to be closer to family members, and they end up being transferred to a CDP owing to the relatively small number of penitentiary spaces in urban centers in the wake of the still recent reorganization of São Paulo's jails. Finally, it is also common for prisoners who are already serving time in a distant penitentiary to find themselves transferred back to a CDP in the city of São Paulo to facilitate their transportation to hearings.

Although I have not been able to come close to quantifying in any satisfying way the numbers of prisoners involved in each of the three challenges to ostensible distinctions between CDPs and penitentiaries, my ethnographic experiences suggest just how commonplace it is for CDPs to house prisoners who find themselves at rather different junctures in their passage through the penal system. Thus, CDPs take form as heterogeneous spaces capable of housing prisoners who find themselves facing the very beginning of their loss of freedom alongside prisoners who have spent decades incarcerated, prisoners who have already passed through dozens of institutions and prisoners who are experiencing their first contact with incarceration, physically disabled and mentally ill prisoners, foreigners, those arrested for minor offenses but who boast long rap sheets, and people accused of major offenses but who are nonetheless innocent.

Most of São Paulo's CDPs are modeled on a single architectural style, and thus they are composed of an infirmary and eight sequentially numbered pavilions or spokes (*raios*) that give access to long lines of cells. Each spoke has an official capacity of 768 inmates. As mentioned in this book's introduction, these spokes are accessed from doors located on another long, and somewhat wider, corridor. The prisoners refer to this central passageway as a *radial* (hub) since it leads off into the spoke, or pavilion, which in turn opens onto cells (see the Sketch of the São Bernardo Do Campo Center for Temporary Detention at the beginning of this book). This hub or passageway is a closed space, surrounded by bars. A prisoner enters, and guards then open doors that lead inside only after an opposing set of doors that connect to the corridor that leads to the main prison yard have been closed and locked. Thus the eight spokes, each of which typically boasts a prison yard punctuated by a pair of goals and/or the lines of a soccer field, are central to prison life because they grant access to the cells that house inmates.

The CDPs, designed for short- and medium-term confinement, have no spaces for classes or for prison work programs. But ludic, pedagogical, work-based, and cultural activities are almost never offered to inmates. Meanwhile, guards and prison personnel have great latitude in setting the standards for the units since Decree 44,708, which legally established the administrative outlines of the CDPs, permits guards to determine:

1. the rights, obligations, and freedoms conferred on prisoners
2. means and criteria for the application of disciplinary measures
3. appropriate ways of acting in each unit
4. the obligations of penitentiary employees in relation to the treatment of inmates
5. all other pertinent issues

As a result, the CDPs do not function in a prescribed or even homogeneous manner but rather in relation to their directors' decisions. I felt such differences in the skin during my fieldwork, whether in relation to visitation rules, the days on which visits were scheduled, or by means of the issuance of the *carteirinha*, the visitor pass that permitted my access to the spokes. In fact, looking simply at the rules for visitors' dress, the degree to which "correct" procedures varied from one CDP to another became apparent. In the CDP located in the city of São Caetano, female visitors could not wear long dresses. In Santo André, those who sought entry were permitted to wear sneakers. Meanwhile, in São Bernardo do Campo, visitors were not allowed to enter wearing any blue-colored clothing. And in the Vila Independência CDP, visitors were not allowed to enter wearing blue jeans.

Rules could change from week to week. This might come about in relation to sanctions imposed by administrators—as in the case of one CDP when, following a prisoner's use of a chocolate bar to induce an episode of vomiting intended to facilitate escape, the administration imposed a prohibition on chocolate in that unit—or from negotiations between prisoners and the guards. As a result, each CDP appeared to take on its own particular quotidian and bureaucratic rhythms. And each of these rhythms might shift, often without prior notice.

In all of the institutions that I came to know, the relationship between prisoners and jailors is tense. There are harsh boundaries between the two, which are continually remade in a process that makes clear the ever-present possibility of strife. When the São Bernardo do Campo CDP was inaugurated, a large number of its new guards spoke in the cadences of rural São Paulo that suggested they were new to the career and without certain of the habits of more seasoned personnel. As a result, and even though the new guards treated inmates and visitors without hostility, the prisoners immediately sought to construct a necessary frontier between employees and prisoners. In CDPs, guards enter the spokes only to perform their daily count of inmates, for sporadic searches, in cases of death, or, when requested by the prisoners, who are locked into their cells after sundown, to extract someone during the night. And guards' direct observation of the occupants of the cell blocks is typically limited to the view from the doors of the *raio* and the facility's internal camera system. This situation helps explain what once happened in São Bernardo do Campo when an agent entered a cell unexpectedly and its occupant blurted out, "Hey, what's going on, sir?"

The guard responded, "I came to check up on the cells," which led the inmate to observe, "Take a look at the cells? Hold up, boss (*chefão*), you're new here, right?"[20]

"I am."

"Here's how it works, boss: You come to the door, ask how many of us are in here, and we answer. Cops don't enter the bad guys' cell. Imagine if we were killing someone inside here? Or if we were digging a tunnel (*tatu*)?[21] If you were to see that you wouldn't be allowed out alive. And we'd be forced to kill you too. So why don't you go and do your job and then go home, peacefully, without any problems? This is how it works: You go and cause trouble for us thieves, preventing people from bringing in glue for stamps, a t-shirt; and then you go pissing off our visitors. . . . I understand, you're following orders. But, sir, at the moment a rebellion breaks out that guy who gave you your orders will be far away, on the other side of the wall. The guy who's gonna be here is you, with a chord around your neck. So, boss, finish out your twelve hour shift and go home, to your wife. Don't go causing trouble, you hear me?"

And in yet another CDP, an inmate reproached a jailor for having used the prisoner's nickname:

"What sort of liberty are you taking with me, boss?"

"What do you mean?"

"You called me ["nickname"]. But I don't call you by any nicknames! Respect is mutual."

"But, you see, I hear the others calling you by your nickname," responded the guard.

"No sir! Here inside, for the thieves, it's one thing. For functionaries it's quite another thing! Guards are guards and thieves are thieves. I never granted you the liberty to call me by my nickname! Who knows? Someday the guys might misinterpret that and then I'd get labeled as a rat!"

To this the guard responded, "I don't think that's gonna happen," provoking the prisoner to observe simply that, "It's not gonna happen to you, sir, but shit is crazy in jail. Respect is what counts, and I admire respect. But if you don't hold up your side of the bargain then we're going to have to see where that leads us."

In such cases, experienced inmates teach new guards how "it should be" in the CDP since, even though there is no homogeneity to the particular ways each unit is run, all facilities follow a certain basic pattern of behavior and interaction as oriented by the "discipline" associated with and directed by the PCC. But it is not simply guards who learn correct comportment in the CDPs. Even though the CDPs house many experienced prisoners—those who "are serving sentences as long as Nelson Mandela"—the "provisionary" jails are the first stop for new prisoners transferred out of police precinct holding pens. Dubbed "college" by the prisoners, the CDP is a chronotopic envelope par excellence for absorbing theories of prison life. In this liminal and yet, for some, long-term spatial and temporal configuration, inmates absorb everyday practices and come to understand the importance of the Command.

Many of the imprisoned, over the course of their stays in CDPs and penitentiaries, undergo "baptism" and become members of the PCC. They do not stop being Brothers (*irmãos*) upon release, because upon induction they entered into an "agreement with the Command."[22] On the other hand, many other prisoners join the group before incarceration. Hence, a variety of urban spaces come to be vessels for the activities of the Command and are thus brought into its disciplinary regimes.

Police investigations made public by the press indicate that the PCC divides São Paulo into regions and appoints one member to manage each sector. Significantly, in relation to my argument about the PCC as something much more than a mirror image of or parallel to the state, this political map of São Paulo does not show colored areas in which the Command operates. Rather, it divides up the city neatly and completely. In this way, questions of discipline and control come to the forefront: Does the Command's "discipline," as is suggested by the police, spread out across each of these urban spaces to percolate hierarchically and neatly through them? Although my ethnography does not allow me to answer this question definitively for São Paulo as a whole, one experience sheds light on the issue of the PCC, hierarchy, and the occupation of territory.

At one point, residents of the upper middle-class neighborhood in São Paulo proper in which I lived began to experience a large number of break-ins and even violent assaults on homes' occupants. The home invasions were typically quite ferocious, and included threats on the lives of the victims and the claim that no homes in the region would be safe from the wave of violence. So as soon as I heard about this threat, I worked to put out word that the neighborhood's population included relatives of prisoners since, as an extension of the sacred aura of the "visit" and as a function of the aforementioned "discipline of the Command," no relatives of prisoners should face harassment or attack from thieves.

Given the situation, I therefore hoped to invoke my special status to put a halt to the threats to my family and neighbors. I began the laborious task of finding the member of the Command, the Pilot (*piloto*), responsible for my part of the city. But the occupant of such a position is not usually widely or publicly named. As a result, passing on a message requires activating a series of contacts within extensive networks that lead, eventually, to the person charged with the "airplane's" navigation. The twists and turns of this network suggest that what is most important is not the person who occupies that position but rather the role played by the Pilot.

A few days later, I learned that the Brother responsible for the region in which I lived already knew about the issues facing residents. In fact, he was looking for the robbers, since he suspected they were members of a rival faction trying to attract police attention and thus dislodge the PCC from a nearby center of illegal drug sales (*boca*). Such actions in a section of the city claimed by another command were considered a direct affront to the PCC. In such a situation, the local Pilot could not necessarily guarantee the safety of those, like me, related to a prisoner in a facility overseen by the Family. For this reason, I received a telephone call one day from the Brother responsible for the region, and he informed me that he had obtained a 9 millimeter pistol that I could use to defend myself. I refused the offer.

Months later, three young men were arrested and accused of the assaults. They lived in the same neighborhood as I did, as did the man who had offered me the pistol. For a time, I suspected that the wrong people had been picked up, but the victims ended up identifying the three. This led me to question the information passed on to me that the assaults were part of a larger rivalry between commands. Word came back that originally the Pilot had indeed suspected a rival group but that the men who committed the assaults were simply local crack addicts (*noias*).[23] In reaction to this information, the messengers argued that proper comportment on the part of those involved in a life of crime rests on respecting the illegal business actions (*correria*) of other groups, even much-maligned crack abusers. I then asked whether it was more important to respect other group's "*correria*"—a term that may also be used to refer to the collectivity made up of actors involved in revenue-producing illegal activities—or to respect the home of someone imprisoned in a PCC-controlled facility. They responded that no one is obliged to know the owners of the house one prepares to rob. On the contrary, it is up to the victim to be skillful, to talk to the perpetrators (*desenrolar as ideias*), and thus to stop or mitigate the assault. I argued in turn that, as far as I had been told, to beat one's victims after getting what one seeks in a robbery is looked down on since that is the type of behavior in which the police engage. The Brothers agreed, but responded, "Yeah, you see, but that neighborhood is a place for rich kids. There are some people who run with the Command, but how is one supposed to know exactly who that is?"

The wave of assaults, and the reaction by the Brothers, taught me how one goes about activating networks in order to get to the person in charge of a neighborhood or prison. But it also taught me something more profound: In spite of the extent to which the Command's "discipline" was so frequently evoked by a broad spectrum of actors as being almost a compass, as something that set the tone for or directed everything around it, this discipline was really something more contextual or circumstantially constructed. It was not a rigorous code or prescription. PCC discipline was not a given or an objectively existing code of conduct but rather the result of its modes of actualizing potentials brought to bear by those actors who oriented themselves within the network and thus, in some way, made up the PCC.[24] In other words, the Command, by means of its very motility, brings in and multiplies its membership by treating it as transitory and thus always requiring that belonging or not be evaluated in relation to particular sets of circumstances.

Composing Selves, Making Up Positions

CDPs are privileged locations for prisoners to make their reputations as they move from the status of first-timer (*primário*) to resident (*residente*). These two terms, although they are also drawn on by representatives of the state to differentiate new and older inmates, have special meaning, of a distinctly relational character, for prisoners. In principle, a prisoner is a first-timer upon being arrested for the first time, and he becomes a resident after serving one year or when arrested a second time. But that same resident, even with more than a year of prison under his belt, may take on the status of first-timer in relation to someone who has served more time. And even without completing a year of prison, he may be perceived as a resident in relation to someone just brought in by police. Thus, an inmate may be a first-timer and a resident at the same time.

When a prisoner is considered a first-timer in a particular situation, his errors tend to be tolerated a bit more since he is understood to be undergoing an apprenticeship. As an apprentice, his mistakes may be explained situationally as errors on the part of the residents who orient him. But since the statuses at play here are relational categories, they can be manipulated—as on those occasions when a prisoner claims first-timer status so as to escape sanction for an error—or disputed, as in arguments over who might sleep in a bunk or on a cell floor. And since the number of occupants of a cell is much larger than the number of beds available, a majority of prisoners in the CDPs sleep on the floor, or what they call the "beach" (*praia*).

When establishing who gets to sleep where, the Brothers rely on a variety of criteria designed to stop the sale of personal spaces and the violent appropriation of what belongs to another prisoner, or standard ways of doing business and surviving in prisons that existed before the rise of the PCC. Principal among the techniques employed to impose new rhythms on a facility is the determination that a resident has priority over a first-timer in the search for a bed. And resident status is nearly always defined in relation to uninterrupted time in prison. Thus, someone whose sentence is broken up or who spends even one day on the outside returns to the CDP as a first-timer. This innovation reverses the situation common before the mid-1990s, when the pecking order for claiming space was based on total time served. Under such a regime, an inmate whose accumulated life experiences meant he had spent a long time in jail, even if it was decades ago, would have a right to the space occupied by someone with more time in that particular prison unit. But this means of allocating space shifted under the PCC. After all, as one prisoner put it, "The Brother got out, had fun, took advantage of the Big World out there [*Mundão*]. It isn't right for him to take away the bed from another Brother who's been suffering here inside. So, 'Get off the bed, onto the beach!' doesn't quite work the same way as it used to. No one wants to be here, inside. After all, it's the toilet that's been here the longest!" Suffering, then, is an important criterion in establishing who is a resident.

Although an inmate's accumulated uninterrupted time served defines the resident in relation to the first-timer when it comes to dividing cells, at other moments the same prisoner classified as a first-timer in contests over sleeping arrangements may be accepted as a resident. Salient examples include debates that lead to decisions about positions to be taken on the everyday politics of the prison unit or decisions about the guidance offered to those first-timers entering the jail system for the first time. In these cases, the resident is defined not so much in relation to suffering within prison but in relation to that individual's experiences in prison and his reputation as a prisoner.

Despite the permeable borders of first-timer status, an inmate makes his reputation during his first few months in prison. As first-timers, prisoners will be exposed to the PCC's "college" (*faculdade*) and learn how to play the politics of reputation in the prison environment. Each prisoner will do his best to be positively evaluated by the other inmates and in this way come to be considered a "properly male subject" (*sujeito homem*) and an "upright guy" (*cara de proceder*).[25]

All prisoners, whether residents or first-timers, who are able to live safely in the general population (*convivio*) of a penal facility controlled by the PCC are considered "Cousins" (*primos*). But those who are unable to enter this milieu successfully are known as "things" (*coisas*). These include snitches (*caguetas*), hired killers associated with the police (*justiceiros*), or people who belong to other factions or who committed crimes—rape, parricide, or infanticide, for example—considered unacceptable by the Command. These prisoners must do their time in protective custody (the *seguro*), a special, segregated space outside of the general population, and insulated from the microinteractions and reworkings of relationships so important to establishing who one is and what the Command is.

I nonetheless learned of a former police officer who was able to live outside, in the general population, when serving his sentence. Prisoners informed me that this was because of his ability to demonstrate that he "ran alongside" (*corria lado ao lado*) the criminal milieu, or "the Crime" (*o crime*), and that, because he was of a certain age, he "deserved this opportunity." However, prisoners also told me that he would be their first suspect if someone began to act as an informant for the jailors. Yet even the status of "informant" is fluid: In an email exchange, the daughter of another prisoner recounted to me the story of one man's acceptance in the general population in spite of the fact that he had been labeled an informant upon his arrival in prison.

The prisoner was able to reenter the general population, and thus the social space known as "the Crime," by arguing that his revelation of details to the police had been impossible to prevent because it involved torture and his family. Although I am not interested in the ultimate veracity of this story, the prisoner's account provides an important view into how people are evaluated in prison:

> There's a guy I know, who I'll call "Tiago," who's from a really
> humble family. They're really poor.... He works illicitly because
> he was never able to study.... On Thursday the police invaded
> Tiago's home without a warrant, at 2 A.M., and they smashed to
> pieces the little he had. Finding him sleeping with his family, they

destroyed his bed, his refrigerator; they broke all his furnishings while looking for drugs. The police eventually encountered a few bricks of marijuana. . . . Tiago admitted ownership immediately, alleging that he'd bought them in a different state for his personal use. But the police refused to accept that explanation and they began to beat him in front of his family. One of his children, disabled, started to go into convulsions, turning purple. Tiago's wife went crazy because she was handcuffed and couldn't get to her suffering child. Only her mother could do anything, since she was the only one in the family who wasn't handcuffed.

The police wanted to know, at any price, who Tiago's boss was and where he had gotten the drugs. Their prisoner insisted that the drugs were his own, and for his own personal use. The police responded by torturing Tiago for over an hour, subjecting him to kicks, punches, and suffocation sessions. . . . But Tiago kept on insisting that the drugs were his own, and his alone . . . then one police office decided to pick up one of the children—Tiago's youngest daughter—and putting the two-year-old on his lap, inserted a .38 caliber revolver into her mouth while asking Tiago "for the last time" whether he was going to take the police to his compatriots or not. Faced with this scene, a desperate Tiago, following his heart as a father, found himself in an untenable situation: While the policeman may have been bluffing, Tiago watched with fear as his screaming toddler twisted and turned as a stranger held a pistol in her mouth. He could not continue his bluff. Probably scared that the gun would go off, and witnessing the effect of this violence on his wife and other two children, Tiago turned his boss in to the police.

Tiago could have tricked the police by alleging that his boss lived in another city, or even another state, but Tiago had at this point been effectively kidnapped. And the police continued beating his handcuffed wife as they hustled him out to their car. Separated from his suffering family, he took the police to his boss. Arriving there with Tiago in the trunk, the police found large quantities of drugs and arms, and Tiago gained infamy as the stool pigeon who had made the raid possible.

The police radioed their compatriots back at Tiago's house and they released his wife, as if nothing had ever happened. But Tiago and his boss were taken to the police station, and now this respected man who had always walked firmly and properly alongside the Crime found himself in a difficult situation . . . overnight he had gained the label "stool pigeon." . . . As a result, he was put in a secure lockup upon arriving in jail since ratting on someone is considered an unpardonable offense and prisoners in "favorable units"—or those controlled by the PCC—do not accept snitches in their midst.

Tiago's friends followed his tribulations and tried to clean up the mess. They called a community meeting in their neighborhood in order to discuss what had happened. These men were convincing in their arguments, and they came close to arranging a safe conduct so that Tiago could rejoin his compatriots in the world of Crime and enter the general population. The only barrier was Tiago's boss, who would have to give his okay since he was well-respected in the world of Crime. Additionally, besides Tiago, he was the one who had suffered most severely because of the raid.

Whether my interlocutor was telling me the truth, or even the whole story, is not critical: The account of Tiago's trials is significant because it indicates that even if other Brothers decide that someone has acted correctly, the final word on his fate is left to the person his information impacted most severely. The boss is the one who needed to decide whether Tiago would have to pay for his revelations.

Although I was not privy to the debates surrounding the resolution of Tiago's case, I do know that he eventually returned to the general population. Nonetheless, a case such as Tiago's is an exception. In order to guarantee that no one who violates the PCC's notion of prison life comes to reside in its prisons, Brothers conduct a type of triage on recently arrived prisoners. This does not follow a predefined script but varies in relation to those involved and the issues brought to bear by the new inmate.[26] Sometimes the Brothers are guided by the semiotic information that the new arrivals carry with them or on their bodies. At other moments, the very nature and details of the crime committed or for which the prisoner is accused seem most important. And comments on that person's action and representation by inmates who may have known him on the outside are also critical to such evaluations.

Before new inmates can anchor themselves in "the (prison) life" (*se atracar no convívio*), they must respond to questions put forth by jailors as to whether "they have any problems with any prisoner inside." Meanwhile, the questioning directed at new arrivals by more established prisoners looks instead at the dispositions, or personal history or way of being and "conduct" or "comportment" (*proceder*), of the new convict.[27] Thus, prisoners who arrive in the pavilion go almost immediately to the cell of the unit's leader (again, the *faxina*), where they are asked why they are imprisoned, their home neighborhood (*quebrada*), and whether they know anyone incarcerated in their new prison unit. This greeting offered to new arrivals by members of the PCC suggests that the experience of prison in facilities controlled by the Command is rather dissimilar from the sorts of social phenomena Erving Goffman (1999) referred to as "total institutions," or those characterized by formalized and rather rigid, intrusive vigilance over all aspects of prisoners' lives.

In prison units controlled by the PCC, power is not exercised in a hierarchical manner. Nor is it localized in a single person or even a single sector of the prison. In other words, the most important relationships that come to characterize an individual's passage through São Paulo's penal system are those developed with other prisoners. Here the *proceder*, or everyday comportment, and the reputation and sense of self developed out of it become paramount. More specifically, the term is used to describe relationships developed by prisoners with one another, with prison employees, and with visitors. This indexes behavior and ethical stances adopted at each moment of interaction, and it extends into even more intimate areas, including issues of personal hygiene. But the concept of a historicized, sedimented *proceder* is most critical because it does not simply describe or sum up the prison experience but instead permeates that experience and the prison population. According to Adalton Marques (2006, 2009), the *proceder* stands as the key means of organizing divisions between the sociality of the general population and the anomie of the "protective" custody that those prisoners unable to uphold notions of correct comportment must seek. Disputes over who demonstrates correct comportment and who does not are evaluated in relation to multiple factors so as to constitute what some have called an alternative, or "other," legal system.[28]

The testing and establishment of a *proceder* takes form within strategic disputes whose "winner" can never be known in advance. Thus, comportment is not something rigid or stable; far from being seen as a tangible quality held by a person, it looks something like the theorization of possession put forth by nineteenth-century sociologist Gabriel Tarde. For Tarde (2007), possession is fragile and provisory, the result of plays of desire that give rise to a fragile state of being that in order to be maintained must be constantly renewed and renegotiated. Any mistake, any slip-up on the part of a prisoner, may be enough to spur the loss of a *proceder* and thus a descent out of the general population and into protective, isolated custody. Nonetheless, disputes over comportment that might lead directly to one participant being sent to protective custody are relatively rare. A man's *proceder*, or reputation for and ability to continue to engage in proper comportment, is understood to disappear only in light of a major error that impacts or threatens a wider network of prisoners. In order to avoid such a situation, which necessarily results in the movement of the guilty prisoner to protective custody, inmates make a major effort to ensure that cellmates act properly to avoid disruptions to their shared space (the *convivio*).

Censure and, more commonly, correction await anyone who pressures cellmates; who causes problems as they serve their time, or walk their walk (again, *a caminhada*); or provokes a conflict (*debate*) that might lead someone else to solitary confinement. Since the Command encourages all prisoners to take part in prison life, the responsibility for maintaining correct comportment and providing instruction falls primarily on the shoulders of residents, or the veterans who instruct newcomers on proper comportment. As part of this attempt to keep cellmates out of trouble, residents offer newcomers an information session known as a "lecture" (*palestra*). One of my interlocutors lived for over one year in a single cell, and he reported to me that he observed dozens of such lectures, or performances that may last up to two or three hours and that revolve around the techniques and attitudes deemed necessary for serving time properly and avoiding trouble.

Just as each jail has its own rhythm, so does each cell. Not all of the residents' lectures are three hours long, and not all first-timers receive the sort of detailed instruction that I was told was so basic to my interlocutor's cell. Perhaps this is why the long-term residents of that cell reported to me that later, following transfer or even release, a number of men who had been first-timers in that particular cell had become full-fledged members of the PCC. And these Brothers attributed their baptism to the quality of their initial reception in prison by the Command.

Yet the principal objective of the lecture is not to increase membership in the PCC. A majority of those who face instruction will never become Brothers. And some who experience the lesson will not even be able to avoid resorting to or falling into protective custody. The goal of those who offer the lectures is thus to ensure correct conduct among prisoners. However, knowledge of correct procedures and comportments constitutes one of the areas of prison life that those already a part of the Command evaluate before transforming a Cousin into a Brother. This suggests that those with more extensive prison experience have a much greater chance of becoming Brothers. Perhaps this is why there are relatively small numbers of Brothers in the CDPs, or the spaces in the penal system ostensibly reserved for those awaiting trial.

Although I do not have firm data about the exact numbers of baptized Brothers held in São Paulo's CDPs, on the basis of my fieldwork I would estimate that roughly one out of every hundred prisoners is a full-fledged member. But if the number of PCC adherents in the CDPs is small, once one moves on to the penitentiary, the proportion of inmates who belong to the group grows sharply. This spike is partly the result of the experience of moving through the CDP and becoming acquainted with the activities that become so important to the forms of belonging fomented by the Command. Additionally, and significantly—since becoming a Brother is understood as entering into a pact with that phenomenal entity dubbed "the Crime"—many prisoners opt to become full-fledged Brothers only after they are sentenced to long periods in the penitentiaries. This is a decision without return since, once baptized, the prisoner cannot abandon the life (*a caminhada*). He cannot stop being a Brother, since he is expected to honor the agreement that he accepted in joining the PCC.

If a Brother behaves in an inappropriate manner (*ramelar*), he may be suspended from his position, or "take a hook" (*tomar um gancho*), for a period of thirty or sixty days. And if he continues with or repeats misdeeds after these suspensions, he may "lose his role" (*perder o papel*) and be excluded from the Family, thus forfeiting his status as Brother. Just as I learned of Brothers who were excluded after they purposely violated codes of conduct so they could leave the PCC, so too did I witness Brothers seeking redemption in order to return to the fold.[29] But the Family does as much as possible to avoid excluding members.

Candidates for baptism tend to be men who demonstrate a capacity for oratory and negotiation, and who behave properly in prisons controlled by the Command. If the prisoner has already done something to represent the nebulous yet powerful phenomenon called "the Crime," or the ethic and the communal formation that girds the PCC, then that individual also moves closer to induction. When such a Cousin stands out from his peers, whether in relation to his general comportment or how he conducts himself in a special situation, or even because one of the Brothers knows him from somewhere else, his behavior is watched closely. Entrance into the PCC then begins once two Brothers recommend the candidate. It is significant that, for this to occur, only the initiative and the actions of the two Brothers are required.

An invitation to PCC baptism usually comes to fruition after two Brothers decide that, based on his attitude, the prisoner in question is ready to become a Brother. The invitation may also arise in the wake of a significant event that reveals that the individual is ready to "run alongside the Command" (*correr lado-a-lado com o Comando*). Activities that might indicate such readiness include participation in escape attempts or the stringing together of a powerful argument that reveals that the individual understands key aspects of how the PCC functions.

When a prisoner accepts an invitation, the two Brothers who propose his application for entrance into the Family become the new member's godparents (*padrinhos*). These fictive kin are not held responsible for what the baptized Brother might do during his time in the PCC. However, a poor choice, such as the admittance of an inmate whose past includes membership in a competing faction, resonates poorly for the sponsors.[30] For this reason, the Brothers are rather careful about their choices. One preferred technique for evaluating a potential new member is to invite that inmate to live in the *faxina*, or the "housekeeping" cell occupied by respected inmates and Brothers in leadership positions, who are then able to observe the candidate closely in a variety of situations.

The apprenticeship process through which a Cousin passes is also a technology for constructing Brothers. As I have emphasized, the position of Brother is not something conferred automatically or a specific form of rank. Rather, it is the result of a building process that rests on prison comportment—the *proceder*—that takes form as what Michel Foucault referred to as a "technology of the self."[31] After all, an invitation to baptism depends on the prisoner's ability to develop a mode of comportment deemed proper by the PCC. And whether that person remains a Cousin or becomes a Brother depends in turn on whether the individual accepts the call of the Command. Quite a number of Cousins who choose not to heed the call remain Cousins but gain the symbolic status of Brothers in specific circumstances, including meetings with jail officials. In such situations, participants assume that the inmate in question already manifests all the talents considered basic to standing as a Brother, and baptism is considered a mere, and thus potentially overlooked, formality.

Whatever the case, the prisoner in question gains recognition (*reconhecimento*), a powerful relational quality.

To gain recognition in relation to the PCC is not to assume a hierarchical position above and beyond fellow inmates. Above all, a Brother is supposed to be humble. This means engaging all prisoners as one's equals. This concept of equality (*igualdade*) lies at the core of the next chapter and is considered the most basic of the attitudes manifested by any Brother. Yet humility can never be confused with weakness—even if an inmate cannot be better than his peers, he is nonetheless never less than them. In fact, the disposition that prisoners refer to as "hairiness" (*cabulosidade*) is constantly in play in the development of a subject position in which an emphasis on the active maintenance of an ethics of equality is seen as fundamental to resisting domination.[32] Thus, equality takes on a special role in prison and in the construction of the PCC.

Even as equality and humility are basic to being Brothers, there also arise important differences between members of the Family and their Cousins who fill São Paulo's jails. Baptism marks the end of a process of self-construction that becomes manifest through its recognition by a prisoner who is himself more than "common." This is because the invitation to become a Brother must come from a person who is already somewhat special in a setting nonetheless marked by an emphasis on equality.

If the concept of equality propagated by the PCC is supposed to erase differences between prisoners, making them all Cousins, then to become a Brother is possible only through some measure of differentiation that provokes an invitation and subsequent baptism. This involves certain differences of capacity and political ability that are typically acquired over the course of a long prison stay. But the emphasis on equality offers, and turns on, an attempt to recover an egalitarian ethos in spite of the Brothers' attempts to recognize different inmates' differential capacities. Thus, the work of harmonizing the collectively held but special status of Brother with the identities and desires of those in the general prison population is in effect an attempt to erase a type difference that Brothers are not supposed to affirm but which nonetheless permits them to take on a new subject position and develop a specific politics. In fact, and as a result of his humility, a Brother is well situated to develop egalitarian relations with other members of the Family as well as with Cousins. He thus takes on the burden of guaranteeing equality among groups of Cousins as well as Brothers, and between Brothers and Cousins. But this obligation is also in itself a mark of difference.

Even though it may appear paradoxical or impossible, there exist a myriad of strong claims to equality between Cousins and Brothers in jails controlled by the PCC. For example, I once observed a Brother, upon noticing that his cellmate was reserving the bulk of desserts for members of his cell block's clean-up squad, or Housekeepers (*faxinha*), chastize another, "What's that? Why are you divvying up the sweets? Are you gonna smuggle them to your friends on the outside? Where's the equality (*igualdade*)? You've got to divide everything up equally. We're not gonna have that shit in here. It's all about equality!" On another occasion, a Cousin who lived in the cell nonetheless reserved for the Housekeepers told another Cousin to give up his bunk for a recently arrived Brother. The Cousin, who had occupied that space for some time, responded, "I don't understand anything! Where's the equality now? Here's what I'm gonna do: I'm gonna get my things and move over to Cell 8 and let the Brothers have this here special cell." A Brother who had already served time with that Cousin in another penitentiary took him aside and discussed the situation:

"Hey, man. Don't go. Stay here alongside me. You're the only one here I really know," to which the Cousin replied, "No, I'm stepping out for real. You're here with your Brothers."

"They are my Brothers," the full member of the Family responded, "but I've never served time with them before. I know you. And in prison you can't trust anyone."

"OK, it's all good. I'll stay," decided the Cousin.

His interlocutor then turned immediately to all of their cellmates. Asking them to pardon the Cousin who had ordered his fellow inmate to turn over the bunk, he requested that his companion, with whom he had shared the experience of doing hard time, remain there.

The process of building up Brothers through an emphasis on equality, which is by definition also a part of a process predicated on particular forms of differentiation that take place on another level, reveals a permanent tension between identity and difference. In spite of all the effort put into making things egalitarian in São Paulo's prisons, dissimilarities and even inequalities proliferate at every turn. In the next chapter, as I focus in on that tension, I will seek to make clear how the tension between different prison categories or roles (first-timer, resident, Cousin, Brother) and the attributes associated with them confer a distinct form of sociability on the prisons that belong to the Command.

CHAPTER TWO

Politics and Pedagogy

Inside the University

> If sailors abused the helmsman, or the sick the doctor, would
> they listen to anybody else? For how could the helmsman
> secure the safety of those in the ship, or the doctor the health
> of those whom he attends?
>
> —MARCUS AURELIUS

The PCC has undergone major transformations over the course of its existence. Initially, leadership revolved around its founders, who stood at the top of a pyramid-like structural hierarchy that included "generals" and a series of differentiated, ranked positions.[1] Jozino (2004) describes this as a period of internal disputes for power that preceded a subsequent moment when the PCC took new form only as early leaders either died or were excluded. But the real change in the organization took place when the man known as "Marcola," well known across Brazil for his starring role in testifying to the national Congress during its 2005–6 investigation of arms trafficking, rejected the label "leader" and distributed the leadership he had gained by edging out his predecessors Geleião and Cesinha. In fact, testimony offered to Congress by Geleião, or the man Marcola had removed as a leader of the PCC, confirms my fieldwork that suggests that the PCC has no real individual leader.

Geleião testified that Marcola

> is not really the type of person who wants to be the boss. I could
> give you a different story, but I've sworn to tell the truth. So, in
> spite of the fact that he is my enemy, I can tell you that I really
> don't believe that Marcola's heading things up. . . . In fact, today
> the PCC lacks leadership. Everyone is the boss. . . . Where there
> once existed a command—after all, our word was the last word and
> even though everyone had a say, our word was final—Marcola has
> now decreed that anyone who wants to rebel should rebel, that
> each and every Brother would be responsible for his own actions.
> That's not about leadership. So there's no leadership. This model
> rejects leadership, since if each and every member is going to do

what he wants, there's no reason to consult a leader. No. In our time there was no such circulating system of authority. We were the founders. We had the last word and everyone else was our Pilot. And they were truly Pilots—they obeyed and did exactly what we ordered. There was nothing about consulting two, three, four, or twenty opinions. The final word was ours."[2]

The emphasis on equality put forth after Geleião's loss of leadership is amplified by the inclusion from that point on of the word "Equality" (*Igualdade*) in the PCC motto "Peace, Justice, and Liberty" (*Paz, Justiça e Liberdade*).[3] This shift, like other alterations in the Command's organization, was not felt immediately in the same way across all prison units. In fact, there exist great differences in the politics and rhythms of different prisons since, whether large or small, the changes that occur in one jail do not necessarily migrate to other locations. One example of the heterogeneity of the techniques that compose the PCC involves rules on seniority and rights to bunks, as discussed in the previous chapter. In one prison in which I conducted research, the rights afforded by Brothers to Cousins in claiming sleeping quarters were still completely unknown. But then a prisoner I knew was transferred out of a jail in which Brothers emphasized the core concept of equality in assessing who had rights to a bed and into a new facility in which Brothers took precedence over the unbaptized. Upon arriving in the new jail with its unexpected hierarchies, the prisoner contacted the Brothers in his previous unit and asked them to pass the word along and indicate that they had developed a new, more egalitarian means of interacting with nonmembers. Yet another example of the irregular, albeit constant, forms of communication that lead to shifts in PCC practices involves a communiqué put out at the end of 2006 in relation to the theme of "Peace":

> Today, due to the peace that has taken root (in relation to those involved in criminality and imprisoned) knives have been beaten into hooks for facilitating escape, crack cocaine has been expressly prohibited in jail, "bad eggs" who committed assault, extortion, and rape while causing conflicts have been taken out of the general population and they're no longer a part of a Crime that now walks a straight line, doing the right thing (or they will be killed).
>
> This change is one of the most important changes in the Crime, and one wrought in the name of all of us. And this is what gives peace importance and meaning within the penitentiary system.

And yet, according to the same communiqué, "Peace, Justice and Liberty" are "three words that are the pillars of a motto, for which many have been sacrificed, that pushes us forward." It would thus seem that the emphasis on an ethos of equality did not arise overnight and evenly in all of the prisons and all of the announcements put forth by the PCC. Nor was it dictated from above. And yet, even after "Equality" was added to the slogan, I still came across Brothers who made reference to "soldiers" and "generals" in talking about the Command's organization. But "Equality" soon became a definitive part of the PCC motto, its symbolic repertoire, and the quotidian dispositions its members are expected to enact. And here, in what seems another example of the "collective amnesia" mentioned in the previous chapter, an emphasis on equality very quickly became a part of the Command's official positioning. This took place in a manner that effectively erased mention of the previous hierarchies. Even the hybrid, transitional period during which Brothers in different prisons emphasized or failed to emphasize equality as part of a heterogeneous set of positions seemed to disappear. Instead, "Equality" was on everyone's lips, so much so that even a number of foreign prisoners with whom I interacted and who barely spoke Portuguese incorporated into their vocabularies the Portuguese phrase "é de igual," or "it's all about equals." This phrase was typically used by the Brothers to refer to their novel, iconoclastic emphasis on equality.

The full incorporation of the ideal of equality into the PCC's ideological registers did not mean, however, that the concept or the process of incorporation was immune from tensions. In fact, the addition of "Equality" to the PCC slogan and to its ideational registers provoked a series of articulations that made the group's politics all the more complex. This is because a principle of equality clashed with the practices so much a part of forms of a quotidian environment permeated by some inmates' exercise of power over others. In this sense, to maintain equality as an ideal in the context of the Command's activities nourishes a tension that infiltrates and spreads out across the capillaries that hold the Family together. This tension turns on the spaces opened up by practices that simultaneously build up and tear down loci of power alongside related forces that similarly build up and then deconstruct social hierarchies. In other words, the addition of an emphasis on equality produces formative tensions that make certain connections and agreements necessary. In this way, a dialectic between equality on the one hand and compulsion and hierarchy on the other makes real the ligaments that tie together the PCC as an organization. At the center of this process lie efforts to formulate a Command composed of supposed equals, or a fundamental contradiction that becomes clearer upon analysis of the political dimensions of the PCC.

Political Positions

The dynamic that materializes the PCC as an organization revolves around a number of relatively specific political positions that in turn rest on Brothers' abilities and dispositions. These positions include those of "Pilot" (*piloto*), "Cleanup" or "Housekeeping" (*faxina*), and "Tower" (*torre*). Rather than lifelong statuses like that gained by the baptized Brother, to take on the position of Pilot, Housekeeper, or Tower is to occupy a transitory perch that confers on the participant a certain instability and malleability. In fact, ethnographic examination of the PCC suggests a certain disconnect between these positions and those who fill them, or what might be described as a permanence of the categories alongside constant alterations in those who shuttle through those loci. My choice of the term "position" thus reflects the persistence of political functions in light of people's fluid migrations across them.

In his testimony before Congress, Marcola sought to convince his audience that he was not the leader of the PCC precisely because he did not have a claim to such power: "There is no reason to kill me to say you killed me since real power is in the hands of other people, and it's been a long time since it flowed through my hands." Although his statement may be interpreted in a variety of ways and indeed illustrates a "complex difficulty of communication" between Congress and the witness,[4] Marcola's assertions reinforce what I observed during fieldwork: Political positions and authority within the PCC are transitory.

The most called-upon position in the PCC, and thus the one most visible in light of everyday relations, is that of the Housekeepers (again, the *faxina*). As introduced earlier, this term refers to the cell itself as well as the group of prisoners inhabiting the space out of which they oversee the internal administration of the cell block (food delivery and serving, opening and closing of cells, sanitation, and dispute resolution). Again, participants are primarily Brothers, but a number of trusted Cousins being considered for or undergoing evaluation before baptism are also often included on the housekeeping squad.

The Housekeepers operate also as spokespeople for prisoners in interactions with prison authorities, and they are the only people in the pavilions expected to speak with jailors. This means that when a prisoner has a problem for which resolution requires engagement with the prison staff, he will go to the Housekeepers and request their aid. For example, one member of the housekeeping squad is usually responsible for medicines and prescriptions. Each prisoner who requires a medicine will then send a "kite" (*pipa*), or a note, to that Housekeeper requesting the medication. The prison administration in turn sends the medicine to the designated Housekeeper, who makes sure each article is picked up by the inmate to whom it is directed.

The issues overseen or mediated by the Housekeepers that impact a large swathe of the general population are reported to "Pavilion Pilots" (*pilotos de raio*), or the Brothers who take overall responsibility for the functioning of the entire pavilion. Their tasks include responsibility for the actions of the inmates in their sectors. These Pavilion Pilots also pass on prisoners' issues and aspirations (*passam a caminhada*) to "Facility Pilots" (*pilotos de predio*), who get together with the men who occupy similar positions across the entire prison complex in order to present petitions, work out quotidian routines, and come to some sort of understanding with administrators and guards. For example, in one institution I came to know fairly well, the administration responded to all requests for medicine by sending doses of aspirin to the Housekeepers who transmitted the prisoners' needs. As a prisoner put it, "If you have a fever, they send aspirin. If you have a stomach ache, they send aspirin. In here aspirin is even used to treat AIDS!" In cases such as this, the Brothers called on the Pilots, who, engaging authorities at another level, demanded proper medications.

Yet another relationship that may often lead Pilots to intervene with prison authorities involves visiting day, especially in response to complaints by inmates' family members about the strip searches so much a part of the entrance ritual. Housekeepers and Pilots who negotiate with prison authorities thus balance a double mandate. On the one hand, they attempt to secure what they describe as the "dignified serving of one's time," a concept that extends to the prisoner's relationship to family members and others on the "outside." On the other hand, Brothers also work assiduously to guarantee order within the jail. A paradigmatic example of such balancing of order and inmate dignity involves the incident, narrated in chapter 1, involving a cell leader who called out a jailor who intruded into that personal space in violation of the pact between prisoners and authorities. As part of that exchange, the Brother informed the guard that if he did not respect the prisoners they might rebel, and the Pilots would not be able to do anything to guarantee hostages' security, since "respect has to be mutual." In other words, the Command's responsibility for institutional order is guaranteed by a "respect" that emerges as a tangible effect of negotiations between prisoners and guards.

Pilots rarely reside in the Housekeepers' cell. This is a tactical maneuver, since prison authorities typically transfer all residents of that cell to new jails in the wake of rebellions or strikes. Here it is important to note that the negotiating abilities seen as so essential to success as a Pilot serve as an ideal for all Brothers, who are expected to partake and excel at the multiscalar negotiations so much a part of survival in prison, as well as the ethical imperatives that bind members of the PCC and its relationship to the general population. In fact, all Brothers are understood to be potential Pilots. This is an important component of the PCC's organizing strategy because of the frequent transfers of prisoners, which create a void into which new participants must step. It is also essential to the process through which Pilots are chosen.

The Brother elected as a Pilot holds that position until he leaves the particular prison unit in which he was elected, an event that motivates the Command to organize another election. Thus, the inmate who serves as a Pilot in one prison is not necessarily a Pilot in another prison. And when a Pilot is transferred, the Brothers call for an election to choose a new representative. Only Brothers may participate in the voting and nomination process, which takes place during a quick meeting in which a single prisoner is typically nominated by another Brother and the group then evaluates that candidate verbally while comparing the inmate to other potential choices offered up by other Brothers. Inmates explained to me that in the wake of one Pilot's transfer, one of the remaining Pilots would call together all Brothers in that unit and, standing before them, would announce something like, "Hail, Brothers. As you all know, our brother Diógenes, who was serving as Pilot, got transferred. Now you're gonna have to tell me, out of your own free will, who is going to represent us, who is going to stand up for us.[5] Look here, I think we have César here. The Brother has already done ten years in the Command, right? He's done some time, right? He sees what's in front of him.[6]

The Brother is open to things, owes nothing, puts together ideas, and converses well. He has a vision of things. I propose him. What's your vision of things, Brother?"

This question prompted another inmate to chime in, "For a guy to step up and plan things with the director (*cabeça branca*) he's gotta be smart. If there's a need to kick around ideas, the guy needs to know how to debate. I'm not saying that we need slick tough guys (*malandros*) around here—everyone here's bad—but we need to put some real democratic thinkers out front, to represent us. The guy's gotta know how to negotiate, you hear me? Some of us are kinda hotheaded. They'll get up there and they won't know how to bargain. I nominate our Brother César. And you, Brother, who do you think we need?"

To this, another Brother responded, "I propose Brother Aurélio. The Brother is new, he just got baptized, but he deserves a chance to show what he can do." This proposal brought a swift response from another Brother, who pointed out, "Look, Brother. Look closely. Right now we're in the midst of some progress in this jail; you know that, right?[7] To put a new boy at the head at this time isn't a real good idea. That's not to denigrate the Brother in any way, you understand? It's just that this is a real hot job, a thousand degree job (*mil graus*). If we put a new guy at the front and this shit explodes, and he goes to the hole [solitary], we might face some serious repercussions.[8] I choose Cícero, okay, Brother? He's been in the life for a time. He's got a vision of things. . . . He's got some ideas. . . . He knows how to debate, something not everyone can do. Cícero's a real smooth talker."

Each Brother then stood up to express his opinion, and the person who garnered the most votes was chosen as the new Pilot. They told me that, to hold elections, the group would have to choose at least three candidates, who, typically, had not volunteered to run but were instead chosen by the group based on their reputations and skills. In response, I questioned the Brothers about the possibility of a candidate deciding to decline the nomination. I was told in response, "If they put the guy up, he's not gonna be looking to run away. He's gonna run from responsibility? The answer's easy!" And with respect to the impasse around the candidacy of the Brother who had been inducted only recently, the prisoner explained to me that, "There's 'progress'—as in an escape attempt—going on. If that escape comes down, and something goes wrong to blow up our plan, they're gonna come to us and ask, 'Didn't you see that the kid is young? We're 'making progress' and you go and put a kid in charge!

He didn't know how to get things straight and now he's in the hole. Okay, so who's gonna make it happen now? Who had the great idea of putting him in charge?' And if that happens, that guy could very well get excluded from the Command."

As noted earlier, the Brother chosen as a Pilot holds onto that position until he leaves the prison facility in which he was elected, an event that causes the Command to organize another election. In this way, a Pilot in one prison is not necessarily a Pilot in another prison. In fact, there are even moments when Cousins take on the role of Pilots—in the absence of baptized Brothers, trusted associates may play the roles of Housekeeper and Pilot. Theirs is typically a short-term role, since Cousins are often leery about taking on such responsibility. But it is a necessary one, and one usually accepted in the name of "security" and stability, especially, for example, when a new CDP is opened. If the first buses arriving at the facility don't carry any Brothers, the Cousins will quickly begin to organize a housekeeping cell. In one case recounted to me, on the first night that prisoners arrived in the penitentiary, a group of experienced prisoners met to define who would take part in the housekeeping crew.

The gathering included a Cousin who had served an especially long time in jail, a former Brother who had been excluded from the PCC (and would thus under normal circumstances be excluded from housekeeping), and another Cousin, who had once organized prison labor brigades in another facility. The three found that prisoners had little desire to serve in housekeeping, and the number of volunteers was smaller than the number of positions that needed to be filled. The three initiators were able, nonetheless, to put together a group of nine inmates who moved together to the single cell, where they began to exercise the standard functions of the Housekeepers: supervising cleaning services, overseeing the distribution of food, and requesting medicines for all on the cell block. They continued to perform these roles for two months, at which point the transfer of prisoners brought full-fledged Brothers into the prison unit. When they described this moment to me, they explained that, "It was a relief, a feeling of 'mission accomplished.'"

The fact that for a short time Cousins may take on an important role usually reserved for Brothers is significant to understanding the dynamics of prison life at a juncture when the PCC has come to play a key role in managing São Paulo's penitentiaries. These Cousins did not assume "command" through brute force. They did not need to struggle to be recognized as Housekeepers. And there was no violence involved in the assumption of the posts so important to maintaining order for all the inmates. This is because members of the general population and Brothers do not conceptualize their relationship as one of domination or subjugation, as is so commonly claimed in the specialized literature.[9] Instead, as the prisoners themselves describe it, they "run alongside" (*correm lado ao lado*) the Command.

Instead, and especially at moments when the Command negotiates with prison authorities, the Pilots and the Housekeepers support their fellow inmates by imposing certain limits on guards. But in doing so they also step up and assume a measure of responsibility for the actions of all prisoners. I was able to witness this process in the context of a 2006 rebellion in the Sao Bernardo de Campo CDP. As I arrived for a visit and went through the strip search, a heavily armed police unit surrounded the building in which I was being processed. Their goal was to stop the flight of a group of prisoners who had taken a number of guards hostage. Amid this activity, the prisoners made an effort to calm visitors and guarantee their safety. My field notes from that day read, in part:

> A young man dressed as a guard opened the door to the booth in which we were being processed and asked if there were any prison employees with us. In light of our negative response and our obvious nervousness, he tried to calm us down, demonstrating that he was in control of the situation. He explained that some prisoners had fled and another group had been caught but that everything was fine, things were under control. I didn't remember ever having seen that agent on any of my previous visits. I began to suspect that he was in fact a prisoner, but his way of speaking was ambivalent, hybrid, and he could have been either a prisoner or a guard. My suspicions were confirmed when I recognized another inmate dressed as a guard, walking alongside yet another prisoner and taking control of a particular corner of the scene unfolding before us. So we closed the booth's door again and, gazing out a small window located high up, near the roof, noticed that something seemed strange. Someone shouted out to us, "Are there any prison employees in there?" And another prisoner responded, "No, only visitors!" Then the men dressed as prison guards opened the door and told us that they were indeed prisoners and that we should not close the door again so as not to be confused with prison employees.

We began to understand better what was going on. . . . The prisoners told us to get together in a group outside the booth and huddle down in a corner, where we would be safer in case bullets started to fly.[10]

As the prison administration and the prisoners who had been unable to escape began to negotiate, we realized that the negotiations were, in a sense, pointless since both guards and inmates simply wanted the remaining inmates to return to their cells. But the prisoners needed to make sure that the guards and police atop the prison walls would hold their fire as the rebels crossed the patio that separated them from the "hub" (*radial*) that gave access to their pavilion. Meanwhile, the prison director needed to protect the employees who had been taken hostage and to make sure that no arms had been lost to prisoners.

The subsequent negotiations were tense, principally because the prison guards, who held one part of the penitentiary, and the military police, who occupied the opposite end, could not agree on a single plan to end the standoff. So while some prisoners talked with the guards, another group talked with the police. As the prisoners exchanged news, it became clear that the police and the guards were not on the same page. It even took quite a long time for the authorities to understand the prisoners' most important objective: that they return safely to their cells. In fact, this demand only began to be understood when one prisoner shouted out in frustration, "Sir, I don't know what's going on. All we want to do is to go back to the pavilion, sir!"

At that moment, the negotiations began to revolve around questions of dignity and authority. This involved the issue of whether prisoners would return to their cells clothed or, as is more typical in Brazil in such situations, naked. Prisoners, including one who exclaimed, "Naked, sir? Are you crazy, sir? We can't be naked!" refused to return to their cells unclothed because this would leave them visible to the visitors trapped in prison at the moment of the rebellion. The police also wanted all guards, including female prison employees, to strip off their shirts. The prisoners also rejected this plan, exclaiming, "They're guards, but they're women too. It's not right to walk around without clothes. You have to show respect." Police then proposed that prisoners remain in their underclothes, a proposal that was also rejected since "There are visitors in here!" This was uttered in a way that suggested that prisoners were sure that guards would understand their logic and sense of morality.

Finally, an agreement was reached that prisoners would remove their shoes and pants but that undergarments and shirts would remain, and female guards would not remove their clothing. At that point, the prisoners asked that the armed guards atop the wall be advised that they would be crossing the prison yard and that the guards should not make the mistake of shooting at them. In order to guarantee that they would not be executed as they marched across the open space, they used their hostages as shields and promised to release them as soon as they approached the entrance to their pavilion. But the guards demanded that all prisoners be released.

In the face of the difficulties encountered in beating out an agreement, a state of affairs that stemmed from a deep mutual suspicion, one of the prisoners sought to gain the guards' confidence by drawing on the sense of responsibility that accrued to his status as a leader among the Brothers. "He who speaks now is the prison's Pilot. I'm responsible and responsive to whatever arises!" he called out. With these words, he sought to indicate that he was guaranteeing that an accord would be followed by all prisoners. As I indicate in the introduction to this book, I did not have access to the guards in order to begin to work out how the message was received by authorities. Nonetheless, the prisoner who served as the Pilot seemed to hold little doubt that the guards would recognize the authority that accrues to his position, since prison authorities are well aware of the importance attributed to the Pilot's word. Yet, at that moment, the guards seemed to pay little attention to the Pilot's affirmations. And one prisoner commented, "That Pilot speech stuff isn't doing anything. They're not hearing you. They don't care about it."

But after a bit more negotiation, the prisoners began to return to their cells, taking their hostages with them to the hubs that opened into their pavilions and then liberating them as they arrived safely. The hubs, prisoners explained to me later, had been under their control, so they had been able to open the gates that led to each of the patios as well as the doors that linked up different patios, or the spokes. Here it is significant that one of the members of the housekeeping squad, upon returning to his pavilion, came on a series of broken pipes and water meters. Questioning a nearby group of inmates, he learned that they believed they effectively ended the guards' ability to ration their water supplies. But the man, in a move that surprised me initially, began to upbraid the prisoners. When I asked him later why he had taken offense at the destruction of the prison infrastructure, he responded, "Because they damaged property." Surprised, I replied, "So what?" This spurred him to exclaim, "You can't damage property—that's a crime!" The statement surprised me. I confessed to the Housekeeper that I failed to follow his logic, and he explained that the PCC had put out a communiqué (*salve*) that demanded that inmates refrain from damaging prison installations since such actions could lead to the transfer of Brothers to institutions with even harsher disciplinary regimes. This claim spurred me to recall the images of destroyed prisons that are so much a part of the Brazilian public's and my own understanding of rebellions, and I questioned the Housekeeper about this disparity. He responded that the prohibition was relatively new and that things had changed. And yet, in the wake of our conversation, I continued to come across images of prisons damaged in rebellions. My observations illustrate the extent to which decrees issued through the PCC's communiqués are not laws but rather guidelines whose valences and very form shift in relation to their effects and their incorporation into particular localized communal rhythms.

Pilots, like Housekeepers, orient and shape prisoners' actions. They also answer to authorities on behalf of prisoners while presenting those inmates' needs and desires to prison officials. These actions are often impossible to separate out neatly since what might at first glance appear to be a discrete move may in fact call up a whole series of relations whose alteration shifts the very context in which the Brothers act. An example of such relationships involves the fact that, over the course of the rebellion just described, a group of Housekeepers had come across prisoners placing a noose on the neck of one of the captured guards. As related to me, the Brothers immediately demanded, "Hey, Thief, what the fuck are you doing? You're tying the guy up by his neck? Are you crazy? Leave that chicken meat alone. Shit, things are not that bad yet!" The Housekeeper who had expressed his disagreement with the attack on the hostage then looked at the guard and asked, "Are you okay, sir? Stay strong." Then, turning immediately to another Brother, the Housekeeper exclaimed, "What the hell is this, Brother? Those Thieves pulling this sort of shit? Grabbing the rooster (*frango*) by the neck?" Next, turning to the common prisoners involved in the attempt, he explained, "Listen, we represent, we take the lead (*estamos de frente*) in this fucking prison! What you do affects (*repercute*) all of us! What labor brigade are you a part of?" When the prisoner responded that he wasn't involved in the groups organized by the Housekeepers, the Brother bellowed to another member of the PCC, "Look, the guy's not even part of a work brigade! And he's in here, showing off, fucking things up." The Brothers then ordered, "Anyone who's not on the work brigades, go back to your cell blocks! Only Brothers and workers can stay; we have visitors out here, goddammit! Respect the Command and its discipline!"

The guard who had been threatened by the inmates was the same one the Brothers had upbraided before the rebellion when he entered their cell without warning, alone. And as the Brothers had informed him on that occasion, the members of the Command who had ordered the noose removed from his neck were committed to treating guards in a manner that reflected the jailor's treatment of prisoners. Indeed, over the course of the same rebellion, the Brothers had ordered the immediate release of a veteran guard, known for his efforts at humane treatment, who had been taken hostage.

By inhibiting violence against hostages through the exercise of their power to command other prisoners, the Brothers protected themselves against direct reprisals for leading the rebellion. They also shielded the prison population as a whole from suffering under a ramping up of disciplinary measures in the wake of violence against guards. In doing so, they demonstrated to prison authorities that they maintained control over inmate populations and that they were able to answer for the actions of the men they oversaw. This led the administration to place a certain trust in the Brothers. And such trust—the fruit of their leadership rather than authorities' benevolence—would be essential to their bargaining power in future interactions. Additionally and finally, by avoiding violence against guards and reprisals from authorities, they also avoided having to answer to the PCC's Towers (*torres*), the group of high-ranking Brothers who would demand answers if someone were assassinated without authorization.

"The Towers" is the term used to describe the political positions out of which PCC directives emanate. All directives, recommendations, and communiqués to different units start with the Towers. These Towers, then, are not simply positions but also political territories. Although usually located in penitentiaries filled with veteran prisoners serving long terms, I did learn of at least one Tower located in a CDP that housed inmates awaiting trial. To complicate things, the wife of a prisoner housed in a recognized Tower informed me, after we got to know one another on visiting day, that an important pronouncement that was well known across the prison system had not arrived in her husband's

Tower. Thus, it would appear that not all of the PCC's pronouncements come from recognized Towers. Yet, given the limitations of my fieldwork, I did not come into direct contact with Towers, and I have been unable to investigate closely how these nuclei so important to structuring the Command actually function. Nonetheless, it is possible to delineate the phenomena that permit the Towers to take shape as key loci for the maintenance of prison discipline.

The general orientations transmitted to each prison are understood to emanate from Towers, never from individual actors. Whenever I asked who had given an order, the response was the same: "The Towers." In fact, there is a PCC prohibition—or, put better, an injunction that is commonly understood to arise from the Towers themselves—against naming anyone involved with these positions of authority and command. Although it may be correct to assume that such prohibitions function to protect those who participate in the PCC's upper echelons, the most basic effect of the insistence that decrees emanate from the Towers is to veil the mechanisms that produce the basic orientations and forms of discipline that structure prison life in São Paulo today. It is as if an unidentifiable and impossible-to-locate force is responsible for the specific task of ordering the circulation of power through the prison. From such a perspective, it does not really matter what prisoner occupies what position. After all, an inmate might find himself in such a position at a particular time only to face state sanctions or be transferred to another institution without warning. What counts is that the PCC's pronouncements emanate from the mysterious and powerful Towers rather than from individuals.

The prisoners who play important roles in relation to the Towers are typically described as veterans, as "Brothers who have suffered for a long time, Brothers who have long endured a venomous environment" but who have managed to uphold what the PCC defines as a proper mode of comportment (*proceder*) that earns the Brothers recognition (*reconhecimento*), respect (*respeito*), and solidarity (*solidariedade*). These inmates whose individual identities become subservient to the action of the Towers are more than veterans of long periods of incarceration. They are political theorists who have become expert in the everyday life of carceral institutions. Here, however, it is important to note that the politics in which they engage flow not from the personal authority of individuals but from actions performed by inmates who temporarily occupy a series of specific social positions.

Political Action

The positions that make up the PCC are not reserved exclusively for Brothers. And yet, with rare exceptions such as those outlined, they are normally filled by the fully baptized. This circulation of sometimes ambiguously defined PCC "members" through the structures that bring the Command to life in São Paulo's prisons is an important aspect of the collectivity's structure. Each and every Brother may be called to occupy a place in the mutating organization. Thus, each member must be ready to occupy any position without "screwing things up" (*ramelar*) in a way that would cause harm to the group. This emphasis on the interchangeability of actors and the permanence of positions and institutions, or a series of complex relationships I describe as "political actions" and that are related to the active forgetting that is so much a part of the construction of the PCC, is one reason for the careful vetting of Cousins before baptism.

Every Brother carries with him the attributes expected of a Housekeeper, a Pilot, and a Tower. In this way, the Brothers' political activities, and thus their cycling through various positions, makes up one of the fundamental aspects of the PCC's effectiveness and politics. How such actions function to make the group cohesive and operative becomes clear in the demands for, and the attribution of, responsibility in and over inmates' lives and for the prison as an institution. As I discussed in chapter 2, the negotiations entered into by the Brothers turn on an emphasis on the "dignified serving of one's sentence" (*cumprimento digno da pena*). Such dignity serves as something akin to the sorts of structuring containments of crisis in a political field described by Marc Swartz, Victor Turner, and Arthur Tuden in their classic book *Political Anthropology* (1966). In this light, prison constitutes a political arena in which disputes over objectives that are widely known and publicly discussed help constitute the PCC around a single issue: What do the Brothers put in play when they intervene in deliberations between actors with diverse interests, such as prisoners and guards, so as to push for an agreement that might resolve ongoing conflict?

Anthropologists have worked to understand social conflict by approaching their units of analysis not as stable, closed groups and institutions but as entities in flux around which attempts to resolve conflict produce the political. Here we might understand different actors as either "arbiters," "mediators," or "intermediators" in moments of crisis.[11] In the

CDPs in which I conducted most of my fieldwork, the Brothers put the prison population and the prison administration into play, structuring the relationship between the two collective actors. It is tempting to describe this as a mediatory relationship akin to what the Brazilian media typically ascribes to the PCC, namely a position of "leadership" within the nation's jails. Indeed, the very idea of a criminal gang or "faction," the term generally employed by the media to refer to the PCC, suggests the importance of leadership.

According to Ralph Nicholas (1977), factions are political groups (that may nonetheless serve private interests) characterized by the instability of their memberships, the uncertain duration of their existence, a lack of formal organization, and, above all, the presence of a charismatic individual leader. For Nicholas, these factions typically arise in unstable, conflictual situations in which a struggle for dominance is directed by a strong leader. He imagines that in the absence of this leader, the faction will fall apart. Meanwhile, for Moacir Palmeira, factions are "conflictual unities whose members are brought into line by a leader who draws on a wide array of principles."[12] For Palmeira, then, to join a faction is to situate oneself socially. Perhaps in the past, at moments when its dispute with other organizations for dominance in São Paulo's prisons was especially fierce and was structured around defined hierarchies, the PCC may have functioned like the type of faction identified by Palmeira or Nicholas. However, and for a variety of reasons, these formulations do not really describe the PCC today, a group that has added "Equality" to its motto.

Among the reasons for the PCC's adoption of a form that is quite distinct from that which characterizes a "faction" is the fact that active disputes over São Paulo's prisons are relatively rare today, with the PCC recognized as a powerful force that intervenes in nearly every aspect of prison life. Additionally, Cousins and Brothers serve time alongside one another and add to one another's efforts. The two do not constitute opposing groups or find themselves divided by a barrier between members and nonmembers. On the contrary, they oppose prison guards as a united front. And, finally, the existence of the Command does not rely on the existence of a single charismatic leader.

The terms "leader" and "leadership" are notably absent from prisoners' everyday vocabularies. This absence of reference to a leader is not simply a trick to shield the real leaders of the PCC. On the contrary, there are quite a number of reasons for the eschewal of "leadership" in prison talk and everyday relations. Principal among them is the extent to which hierarchical visions carry the stigma of obedience and subordination, negative values in the prison context. And it is thus significant that the exercise of politics on the part of the Command is not sustained through actors' occupation of hierarchical positions but rather is legitimated by a sense of respect earned through the Brother's success in negotiating between prisoners and with authorities.

Throughout my fieldwork, I heard prisoners discussing the relative skills of different Brothers who negotiated with prison administrators. For example, prisons are often patrolled by a special "Shock" (*Choque*) military police battalion, a unit feared throughout Brazil for its brutality.[13] Systematic incursions in search of cell phones, drugs, and weapons, known in Brazil as "blitzes," are common features of prison life. At one point, in the CDP in the city of Diadema, guards began to copy the Shock Battalion's tactics. They would don helmets, body armor, and masks and employ tear gas while wielding heavy nightsticks to invade cells and discourage any sort of resistance from prisoners, whom they forced to disrobe and line up in single file. Even when prisoners complied, the members of the special unit would beat them as the inmates scurried to follow orders and form lines while running a gauntlet of guards swinging nightsticks and shields. Men subject to this state violence ended up blaming members of the PCC for the situation, arguing that the Brothers were not skilled enough negotiators to put an end to the guards' abuse.

The legitimacy granted to the Brothers by their fellow prisoners, like the PCC's role in negotiating with officials, thus oscillates wildly and is built up only locally and circumstantially. Although the Brothers act as intermediaries between state officials and prisoners at moments of crisis in ways that impact how the relationship between guards and inmates takes form and shifts across time, there is no expectation of an exchange of favors or any sort of alliance between inmates and the representatives of the state who oversee their imprisonment. Any such exchange would go against the Command's basic opposition to what prisoners call the "System" (*Sistema*) and might even lead to the ouster of a Brother from the PCC.[14] In this way, the Brothers work in opposition to the systems of favor and secret dealings that were so much a part of relations between guards and inmate leaders before the rise of the PCC.[15] But the PCC put an end to such intimacy by channeling, and thus to a certain extent controlling, the relations between guards and prisoners. According to my interlocutors, by avoiding exchanges of personal favors that might end up negatively impacting other prisoners, the Brothers put an end to a relationship that often gave rise to violent interactions between inmates.

Instead of exchanging favors, interests, or expectations of mutual aid, what exists today in São Paulo's prisons is something of a dispute over resources on the part of two participants in an ongoing series of negotiations. Or, put better, what goes on in institutions controlled by the PCC is a constant effort to harness or redirect a power associated with another group or that appears to emanate from a site outside the interface between the two groups.[16] Out of this confrontation, there arise fragile agreements that threaten to dissolve at any moment. These alliances that emerge from ongoing negotiations should not be confused with exchanges of favors, in no small part because they are conceptualized as moves or strategies on a battlefield. They are thus conceptualized as treaties that do not involve future obligations but instead manifest as constantly reiterated and thus contextually reproduced attunements that might be broken in light of a novel crisis or a shift in the prison landscape.

The provisional nature of agreements mediated or activated by the PCC suggests the shortcomings of the many interpretations of prison politics that focus on competition for resources. This results partly from the extent to which such interpretive models "rely on a social topography in which power is crystallized around a monopoly over or effective control of resources by a particular class or group (what we might call the 'oligarchical thesis'); an attempt to reduce a multitude of factors that link patrons and clients into a single, braided explanation (the 'binary thesis'); and to distill all such relations into social institutions that circulate goods and services as part of an attempt to translate into a language of reciprocity the diverse motivations that link up patrons and clients."[17] A close reading of the ethnography conducted in rural northeastern Brazil by Jorge Villela suggests that the relations forged in recent decades in São Paulo's prisons are quite particular and cannot be reduced to more standard understandings of patrons and clients locked together as static, if intimate, dyads built on exchange and reciprocity. After all, the Brothers form a powerful group involved in conflicts over resources. But their positions in this struggle are legitimated by their skill at negotiation. As a result, and even as the Brothers' positioning is supported by an authority gleaned in relation to the prisons' general population, the Command's political efforts are marked by a powerful tension between equality and political action rather than an ability to curry favor in relation to unequal access to resources.

Equality and Political Action

As we have seen, when prisoners begin to express serious discontent or agitate for change, it is the job of the Brothers to transmit those demands to the administration. It is also the PCC's responsibility to guarantee that prisoners respect the "white flag" (*bandeira branca*), the agreed-on prohibition against any riots, uprisings, or rebellions.[18] However, more than anything else, the Brothers seek to accomplish their goals in harmony with their emphasis on equality. This means that, if at all possible, they act in the name of order and what they define as the correct means of serving prison terms, without claiming authority or exercising direct power over any other prisoner. And yet the Brothers' responsibility for maintaining order in prison goes beyond negotiations with administrators. It also includes the regulation of relations *between* prisoners as the Party works to avoid the extortion, rape, and fighting so characteristic of earlier periods in the history of São Paulo's prison system. And, in this context, violence between inmates has become a strategy of last resort.

Originally, the PCC inhibited only violence between Cousins, and it did so by reserving the use of force for Brothers invested in the maintenance of order. But in the wake of the new emphasis on equality, the Brothers have rejected their monopoly over violence. Aggression against Cousins, as well as Brothers, is now prohibited. Violence is sanctioned only in very specific instances, when attempts at diplomacy have failed miserably. Such outbreaks of violence are understood as resulting from one of the involved parties' inability to sustain the forms of proper comportment (again, *proceder*) expected by the Command. And once one party breaks with ideals of proper comportment, the only solution is for that party to retreat to solitary confinement and withdraw from the relationships that govern "proper" prison life.

Prisoners refer to the communicative and "diplomatic" situation that precedes cases of violence or trips to solitary as "stretching the bubble gum" (*esticar o chiclete*). This expression might be translated roughly as "taking it to the max" as well as "chewing the fact," but examined carefully and in light of its use in different situations, it means much more: To stretch the bubble gum is, most basically, to continue a discussion and to carry forward negotiations that have not yet given rise to any consensual agreement. So when one prisoner tells another that he's ready to "stretch the bubble gum," he is pointing out simply that he is willing to follow their mutually constituted path as far as it goes, whatever the consequences.

This was the case with Sérgio, an inmate who, before being transferred to a facility controlled by the PCC, spent a long time in solitary confinement in a prison controlled by a competing faction, the Comando Revolucionário Brasileiro da Criminalidade (Brazilian Revolutionary Criminality Command, CRBC). Upon Sérgio's arrival in the new prison, the Brothers speculated that he had become a "thing" since he had spent so much time with their enemies. Offended, Sérgio decided to stretch the bubble gum and make the Pilot of his new prison aware of what was going on. The Pilot happened to know Sérgio, and he reprimanded the Brothers, asking, "Are you crazy? This guy's my partner [in crime]."[19] Here the dispute could have been put to rest, but Sérgio insisted on carrying it forward: "Brother, everything looks fine right now because you're the Pilot here. But what if you weren't? I could have been tagged as the one at fault." Although I was unable to follow the ensuing negotiations to their endpoint, I learned later that the Pilot had continued to stretch the bubble gum with Sérgio and that, in the end, they made the dispute disappear.

In yet another case, and in an echo of practices common before the rise of the PCC, an inmate I will call "Silas" called his relatives on the outside and told them that a large amount of money needed to be paid to the PCC or he would be assassinated. One of his cellmates who overheard the conversation realized that the money was not for the PCC but to pay off a drug debt incurred in prison by Silas. So the cellmate stretched the bubble gum again by tipping off a Housekeeper, who called Silas onto the carpet. The inmate who had informed on Silas also participated in the encounter, as did all the Brothers on the cell block. The meeting congealed around a field of oral argument. And yet the stretched bubble gum could, at any moment, snap. And here the particularity of the expression comes clearly into view: The gum is thought to snap toward and besmirch the side of the debate taken by the party who fails to sustain his argument, finds himself without a response within the debate, or becomes entangled in contradictions.

Following the debate about Silas's request for money, all present at the meeting decided that Silas should call his mother on an open cell phone line and ask her whether she had deposited the requested money in his account. She replied, "Not yet, son. Things are really tough right now. Have they hit you yet?" To stretch the gum always supposes that those involved might reach a breaking point. And this point represents the fracturing of a relationship not simply between the particular prisoners involved but between one of the parties and the inmate community. Nonetheless, and before such a rupture, the bubble gum becomes much finer, almost stringy. This permits those present to make out relations and claims that were once internal to the spongy mass. And this indicates, in turn, that with greater visibility comes a greater danger of rupture. After all, bubble gum never breaks unless it is stretched. And therefore, in the face of the words of Silas's mother, one of the Brothers seized the telephone and said, "Good afternoon, ma'am. Your son incurred that debt with drugs and it is against the Command's policies to extort a fellow prisoner. No one here is threatening your son. That's the old way of doing things. We're not even going to make him pay what he owes. But your son is now suspended: No one may sell to or use drugs with him. And that's because it's not right to take money from the mouths of our family members in order to use drugs." In debates such as this one, Brothers seek to establish that most tenuous of states: an intense form of transparency coupled with a tautly stretched social bond that continues to link participants. In other words, they seek to push the debate in a way that makes clear what is at stake but fails to rupture the bonds that structure everyday life in the prison. And should such a rupture come about, there are necessary consequences, often in the form of sanctions: Silas, in addition to being banned from the forms of sociability that come from purchasing or using drugs, was also publicly humiliated. At the very center of the cell block, one of the Brothers shouted out: "Listen up, prison population! You see this guy here, this little brat? This guy has no class. There are always a few rotten apples among us! And here's one. He's got no future. He's not trustworthy. He's one of these idiots who runs with us but always sets us back. His word is worthless. He ran up drug debts and then he went and blabbed that the Command was extorting him—He was taxing his family, taking money from the mouths of children so that he could use drugs. He was extorting his family. Right now he's getting a serious break (*pegando o maior axé*) from the Command, because if this were an earlier time we'd rip his head off."[20]

Silas's errors created a situation that threatened an emphasis on equality, since the decision to sanction a prisoner creates an imbalance between those who determine the consequences of actions and those subject to that injunction. How, then, does one call prisoners onto the carpet without undermining the Command's emphasis on equality?

To begin with, Brothers do not use the term "punishment," because the word necessarily posits a gap between those with power and those without it. Additionally, the term presupposes that some participants are authorized to judge others, who thus take on the status of the accused. Such a situation is quite different from stretching the bubble gum, or the ligatures that link participants. Thus, the Brothers who intervene in disputes use a language of "consequences" (*consequência*) and "dunning," or "making demands" (*cobrança*). This is not simply a rhetorical strategy, since the language employed turns sanctions into the expected, or naturalized, results of one's own actions. In fact, one often hears from Brothers that "nothing is prohibited, but everything has consequences." And these consequences arrive in the form of claims through which Brothers seek to remind their interlocutors of the importance of loyalty to the PCC.

When it becomes necessary to make demands on someone, Brothers typically perform another maneuver designed to relieve them of responsibility for meting out the Command's disciplinary measures. Here the Towers play an important role: When an important decision is made, such as the violation of a ceasefire or agreement with guards, the Towers are almost always invoked as sources of the decision. And should a Brother make such a decision without consulting the elusive Towers, he may face suspension from the Command.

Even though the activities of the Brothers are limited to a local context, and the consequences prescribed in relation to specific violations are dictated by the Towers, participants deny that the relationship is hierarchical. They see the dynamic instead as one of consensus and of a Command that prevents them from making decisions in isolation or without consultation. Yet this does not mean that those involved with the Command have unproblematically left behind the ghost of hierarchy. As one woman reported to me when we discussed how messages get passed to and from the Towers, "It's really much easier to talk directly with XXXX, who is a constant visitor to Prison A. Because if you pass your message on to YYYY, whose husband is in Prison B, he's only going to have to pass it on to the Towers in Prison A, later on." When I sought clarification and asked, "So do you have to go directly to Prison A to get a message to the Towers?" the woman responded, "Well, you see, it's kind

This toilet in a cell at the Santo André prison was shared by more than forty prisoners. Photograph by Karina Biondi, 2005.

of like ... the guys in Prison A are more ... more ... [long silence]. Look, every communiqué is going to have to pass through Prison A."

My interlocutor avoided stating that the prisoners in any one unit have authority over, or more authority than, prisoners in another unit. Yet she affirmed that all information needed to pass through Prison A.[21] But if all involved make such an effort to deny hierarchies, how can we explain the edicts put forth by Towers in penitentiaries and then passed on to the CDPs filled with less experienced prisoners or inmates who have not yet been convicted?

Prisoners, whether Cousins or Brothers, do not consider the edicts that emerge from the Towers to be orders. In fact, the word translated here as "edict" is but one meaning of the term "*salve*" as employed in prison. As used by those touched by the PCC, a *salve* may be a notice, as in "If anything happens, send me a *salve*." It may also be a greeting, such as "Tell him I sent him a '*salve*,'" or a way of hailing someone or finding out if anyone is present, as in a prisoner who approaches a toilet stall and calls out "*Salve*, toilet!" The word may also refer to a message, as in the common expression "Hey, would you pass this *salve* on to him?" In each of these usages, the term carries no connotation of hierarchical ordering or authority over another. And even when prisoners in a CDP accept a *salve* from the Towers, its contents are seen as fundamentally different from concepts like "law," "order," "decree," or "rule."

There are many factors that may lead analysts to misconstrue the structures and practices around which the PCC takes form. In a discussion of Marcola's testimony before Congress that provides a basis for comprehending why so many commentators misidentify the PCC as an essentially hierarchical social formation, Adalton Marques (2010) argues that the witness formulated a remarkably specific "conceptualization of leadership" that "responds to the issue of context" but gave rise to multiple misunderstandings between Marcola and his inquisitors. In his testimony, Marcola seemed to augment the term "those in leadership" employed by the lawmakers in order to "introduce an entire deck of cards composed of anonymous prisoners" as the PCC cupula. In doing so, Marcola affirmed the importance to the inmates of seeking consensus:

> A consensus . . . someone offers up an idea, for example. Someone thinks, rationalizes, and speaks up, 'Hey, guys, what do you think about abolishing crack here in prison?' This idea is then sent out to all penitentiaries across the state. Then the prisoners in each of the penitentiaries will give their opinion of the idea. If a majority is in favor of outlawing crack, crack will be abolished. Or, for example, a majority of prisoners were against homosexuality. Guys raping other guys. This was standard practice in São Paulo's jails and the state was never ever able to wipe out the practice. And then we came across as an organization, and understood that rape is a violation of human dignity.[22]

The PCC ethos means eliminating any individual identity, or difference, from the Towers, the Pilots, the Housekeepers, and even the Brothers. What is at play here is not the desires or the initiatives of any one person. The Towers stand instead as a political position, or mode of positioning, rather than an identity. As such, they become detached from the prisoners who operate or manage the position. And thus the decisions that emanate from a Tower move from the realm of individual choices to determinations that reflect the desires of the collectivity.

In order to avoid any association of the Command with any individual, no decision may be made by a single Brother. Or, as the prisoners describe it, "decisions cannot be isolated." As a result, prisons that belong to the PCC must have at least two Unit Pilots. This helps ward off "isolated decisions" (*atitudes isoladas*), or actions that would indicate that someone was trying to go above and beyond the Command. Thus, prisoners do not approach the Brothers as inmates charged with overseeing the prison but rather with making the PCC's ideals clear and then ensuring that they are followed.

In a dynamic akin to that identified in a rather different context by Swartz, Turner, and Tuden (1966), common prisoners may charge the Brothers with the task of negotiating prison conditions, because they believe that such a situation will be beneficial to all. But such benefits typically emanate more from the directives coming from the Towers than from the actions of a Brother. Thus, the Brother is seen as simply a representative of the PCC, an organization that seems to take action independently of the individual accomplishments of its members. It is therefore up to each Brother to ignore individual desires and draw on his individual talents only in order to be able to bring to fruition the recommendations of the Command. If the Brother takes undue advantage of his authority or abuses or gives orders to other prisoners, he is accused of failing to obey the "values of the Command" and can no longer be recognized as someone through whom the PCC works. Marcola made this clear to Congress:

CONGRESSMAN PAULO PIMENTA: It was you who distributed power to the different members of the PCC. Those guys respect you.

MARCOLA: [Laughter].

CONGRESSMAN PAULO PIMENTA: Isn't that so?

MARCOLA: Please respect me; respect me.

CONGRESSMAN PAULO PIMENTA: He who delegates power can take it back when he wants to.

MARCOLA: Respect me until that moment when I [unintelligible]. As soon as I begin to cite names and people the respect is finished. And so am I.

In a similar sense, I overheard a prisoner who, upbraided for failing to follow through on an agreement to sell a radio, responded, "I'm not obligated to do anything, isn't that right, Brother?" He spat out the question as a type of threat but not of violence. What was at risk was the legitimacy of the Brother, since in the context of that interaction he stood as representative of the PCC ideal, or a guarantee of equality based on the elimination of any form of submission by one prisoner to another. And obligations or forced actions point to the existence of inequality.

When, earlier in this book, I claimed that Housekeepers are the only prisoners who may speak with guards, what I was describing was not a prohibition or an obligation. In reality, any prisoner may speak with the guards. But all actions have consequences. Or, in the words of one prisoner, "No one in here is forced to do anything and nothing is prohibited. But everything you do is gonna have consequences."

Christina Toren (2000), in her study of chiefly politics in Fiji, describes a related figure who must balance equality and hierarchy. In Toren's view, elections are structural necessities, or expressions of a politics within which hierarchies and a competing sense of equality are mutually constitutive. The two should be approached as aspects of one another, with each implicating the other. The efficacy and the continuity of the chiefly system are assured only by setting hierarchy and equality in tension, as opposites, while understanding them as emanating from social relations. According to Toren, this tension is an effect of a series of pairings of opposites that make up a totality and that are present in Fijian ideas of the person, of kinship, and of state institutions. A supreme chief is chosen by subjects on the basis of their evaluation of his efficacy in carrying out obligations, and elections force the chief to continue with his balancing act lest he be deposed. Thus, the elections offer the conditions for the maintenance of a dualism based on the fulfillment of mutual obligations.

Although it may be that mutual obligations form the basis of the tension between equality and hierarchy that support Fiji's chiefly politics, what girds the tension between equality and the Command's political practices in São Paulo's prisons is an absence of obligations. And this grants a certain flexibility to interpersonal relations, offering spaces for dynamics that might otherwise be impossible. Here, nonmembers join in the rhythm of the Command, since any prisoner who fails to do so is considered an opponent, and the place for such opponents is solitary confinement or a prison run by a different Command. But the PCC gains recognition from unbaptized inmates only if the Brothers successfully build bridges to that general population. The Command's success is thus based on the repression of actions understood in a negative light by that general population. Only by eliminating mistreatment by guards, prohibiting the domination of one prisoner by another, and impeding the destruction of prison facilities do the Brothers acquire their authority to negotiate on behalf of others. And if they are successful in those negotiations, they gain recognition and successfully construct the PCC. Thus, the recognition that accrues to the Command is the fruit of a constant quest that is constantly at risk, primarily because what the Brothers seek to do is to establish a Command built out of equals. Or, put more precisely, they work toward a Command without command.

The need to minimize risk and the tension between the principle of equality and the Brothers' actions gives rise to a series of theories—or policies—that offer a certain coherence (or intelligibility) to the relationship between political practice and equality and avoid the exercise of power by some over others. This relationship will be the focus of the next section.

Political Theory

The tensions that are so much a part of prison politics are on the one hand accentuated and on the other smashed to pieces. As a result, they are little different from electoral politics as described recently by a number of commentators. Like electoral politics, prison politics are not determined by a supposed origin point of power that would dictate or manipulate practice.[23] Prison politics are thus, above all, the result of connections, interactions, associations, and dissociations wrought by all parties involved. They come together as a species of local dispute within which multiple other battlefields are present.[24] This makes it impossible to think of this interaction as being organized around hierarchies that separate the different locales or even as an overarching structure organized in a dimension above and beyond its components.

The PCC often appears to be spread thin everywhere but rarely takes form anywhere. This perspective comes close to what Bruno Latour (2005) argues in relation to "the social." For Latour, the social is not a context that embraces actors while acting as a force that would push them toward certain actions. Nor does it stand as an explanation for those aspects of scholarly analysis that remain unexplainable in relation to specific phenomena.[25] In making these claims, Latour proposes conducting a "sociology of associations" rather than reproducing what he calls a "sociology of the social." In this light, the "social" does not so much designate one thing that might be compared to another. It gestures instead at a type of connection between things that are not in themselves social but come to be a part of novel associations and regroupings. In this way, the discipline of modern sociology too often becomes a means of tracing associations rather than an enlightening science of the social.

Eduardo Viveiros de Castro (2002) takes a similar tack and abandons dichotomizing explicative models in order to argue that there exist no pure units of analysis, given objects, or concepts exterior to those objects. He thus pushes for an anthropology that looks at people, their problems, and their tools for dealing with those problems without foisting preconceived concepts onto things or the researcher's concerns onto objects of analysis. Viveiros de Castro thus engages the pitfalls of something akin to what Latour dubs the counterproductive "preformed social explanations" so essential to a sociology of the social. These dead ends, common in modern social science, are counterproductive because more often than not they interrupt analysis abruptly, limiting the form, the size, and the heterogeneity of combinations and associations.

Latour denies an affinity with what is usually understood to be postmodern thought and instead points out that dispersion, destruction, and deconstruction are not his goals but rather are obstacles that need to be overcome. From this perspective, it is most important to identify new institutions, procedures, and available concepts so as to reconnect the multiple strands of what passes for the social.[26] To do so, Latour suggests, as does Viveiros de Castro to a different degree, that the researcher grant actors the space to elaborate their own concepts rather than foisting on these subjects some preconceived order favored by the anthropologist. Indeed, to impose an external order on the Brothers and their theories and methods of uniting as what they call the PCC would be to reproduce the results of the "sociologists of the social," who, discarding data that contradict their ideas, understand the Command as but a poor imitation of the state or capitalist corporations. For this reason, I avoid a reliance on "punishment" or "leadership" and work instead with native concepts such as "consequence" (*consequência*) and what might be translated as "response/responsibility" (*responsa*), or yet another type of "resonance," in order to describe the content of the PCC and the reflections that permeate it.[27]

Prisoners engage in a continuous series of reflections on their practices and the practice of formulating policy that supports Latour's argument that, rather than subjects bouncing against some "structure" that might impede them, actors are indeed conscious constructors of the relations they weave together. This perspective recalls Gabriel Tarde's (2007) proposal to substitute the verb "to be" with "to exist" so as not to interrupt movements in and across relations. By using this approach directed at rethinking the social, Tarde engaged the "monadology" of G. W. Leibniz, opening the substance of the monad and making these figures mutually interpenetrable, connectable, and modifiable in relation to movements of cooperation and exclusion. Such substantive, non-Cartesian theories of influence in which desire, rather than resemblance, brings together different entities that are imagined as striving to possess one another provide a means of conceptualizing and making possible novel forms of association. Here stability is possible only through the repression of desire and ambition, and any movement may explode into new possibility. Order, then, is vulnerable and finite. According to Tarde, "to exist is to diffuse,"[28] and the "social" is thus a principle of connection among heterogeneous entities.

If mutual senses or tendencies toward possession make up the qualities par excellence of the forms of association that emerge in light of the thought of Gabriel Tarde, then the entities involved gain a transitory and fluid character whose analysis impels the researcher to define the mechanisms that make such reciprocal possession possible. For Latour (2005), this illustrates the importance of learning, along with the "natives," exactly what collective existence is for them and what methods they elaborate in order to construct their connections. Such an approach forces the researcher to concede to actors a measure of autonomy and rationality. In this sense, the linguistic practices prisoners draw on in order to think through the fundaments and statutes that gird the Command serve as important resources for investigating participants' attempts to develop a native explicative as well as pragmatic philosophy. This is especially true in relation to the meanings of the "Equality" added to the PCC's slogan "Peace, Justice, and Liberty" in a move that epitomizes the differences between the Command and more hierarchical institutions associated publicly with criminality, such as the Commando Vermelho of Rio de Janeiro.

Over the course of my fieldwork, prisoners altered certain terms they used to describe the figures who led cell blocks. In 2004, I encountered a relatively rigid hierarchy of terms used to describe clearly defined positions.[29] But in ensuing years the relation between unbaptized prisoners and the Brothers has shifted, and there has been a definite move toward suppression or denial of authority. The position of "Cell Pilot," for example, fell out of favor, and prisoners came to identify this individual as the cell's "voice" (*voz*). But today the Brothers deny the existence of any sort of leadership within a particular cell. They explain this change by pointing out the importance and diffusion of the "ideas of the Command" in today's prisons and thus argue that there is no reason to have a Pilot or a voice. On the other hand, the idea of a Pilot who speaks for an entire pavilion, which had also come to be described by the term "voice," has reappeared. When I inquired about this shift, one inmate exclaimed, "It's impossible to speak in a single voice . . . just look how many prisoners are in this cell. When there's only one voice, it's as if only one of us is speaking. And just look around you at how many people we have who need to speak!" For my interlocutors, the disappearance of the "voice" is related to their conviction that use of that word ended up supporting an overarching enunciative position that silenced the multiple voices that make up that voice. This makes explicit the extent of the Brothers' concern with the difficulty, or even potential absence, of consensus.

Instead of using the term "voice," many prisoners now employ terms like "Pilot" and "Command," even though they are aware that this implies that there are those who are subject to those commands. Their justification for this switch turns on the claim that Pilots and commanders (*comandantes*) need to assume responsibilities that go far beyond those faced by most prisoners, or those who simply follow. Thus, the status of Pilot is accompanied by assumptions about that man's responsibility to follow a correct path so as to inspire and carry along the other prisoners under his command. And such positioning, according to the prisoners with whom I spoke, carries with it everything necessary to arrive at the putative equality so much a part of correct comportment.[30] Such explanations, as well as prisoners' linguistic attempts to limit authoritarian tendencies, illustrate how they seek to rationalize their methods and practices in ways that may lead to a rather clear delineation of the mechanisms that give rise to their collectivity. These sophisticated techniques for producing knowledge, which stand as a type of reflexive metalanguage, are precisely the forms of knowledge and practice so effectively stamped out by "sociologists of the social."[31]

There are a variety of reflexive movements among the Brothers that give rise to important changes in the dynamics that make the PCC congeal and function. Examples include the shifting methods for allotting bunk space and for baptizing new members discussed in the previous chapter. Additionally, I would like to highlight the thinking that led to a revision in the ban on homosexuality. Before 2006, only gay prisoners who could claim to have "held up their end of things" in relation to criminal activity (*ter representado no Crime*) were accepted in the prison yard, with the majority being discriminated against and being forced to remove themselves from interactions with the Command and associated areas of prison life. Inmates tended to claim that "a real thief has to be a real man." And yet quite a number recognized that "there are lottsa gays who are better criminals than many of your thieves out there." By mid-2006, then, the Command had moved away from the demand that homosexual prisoners move to protective custody, and the Brothers came to establish a specific cell or cells for gay prisoners. And just a few months later, another communiqué emerged that declared that the Command had reconsidered the need to segregate in relation to sexuality. It recommended that gay inmates be spread throughout the cells since "if everyone's equal, you can't discriminate."

I do not know how prisoners across São Paulo reacted to the new instructions from the Towers. But I do know that the news was not well received in the CDP in which I conducted most of my fieldwork. Many resisted accepting gays in their cells, arguing that the new arrivals would take up scarce bedspace since no "real" man would agree to sleep alongside a homosexual prisoner in the head-to-foot doubling up commonly used to adapt to the jails' overcrowded conditions. Prisoners also claimed that gays could not sleep in the crowded spaces of the cell floor and that pushing them up into the bunks would be unfair to those prisoners who had suffered in silence while awaiting their chance to occupy a bunk. Many inmates thus argued that gays "are 'of' crime, but they are not crime itself, because crime doesn't give up its ass." In response, the cells set off for gay prisoners remained a part of prison life. And in spite of the small advance allowing gay inmates to move out of protective custody, they were not permitted to take part in decision-making or in the collective life of the prison. So, for example, on visiting days, homosexual prisoners were forced to remain in their cells and, since the "other" inmates would not share personal items with them, separate sets of plates and utensils were reserved for their use.

Even as participants in the PCC constantly elaborate theories about prison life and the workings of the Party, they develop additional practices and reflections that force a questioning of those theories. This ends up mitigating against a unitary prescription for serving time, as well as a single theory of prison life. This dynamic became especially apparent at the end of 2006, when the Housekeepers transmitted an important communiqué (*salve*) intended for all the prisoners in the unit in which I was conducting research.

Each morning, as cell doors opened, prisoners would seek to learn from the Housekeepers whether "everything was normal" that day and whether there was a message or speech that needed to be heard. My husband reported to me that one morning, upon learning that an important communiqué had emerged, the men assembled on the patio to see what the Housekeepers had to say. And since this particular communiqué was much longer than usual, my husband imagined that I might be interested in its contents. So as soon as the Housekeepers finished passing on the message, he requested a copy of the document that had just been read.[32] I thus gained access to a manuscript about twenty pages long that the Brothers encouraged my husband to carry back to his quarters, where his cellmates helped him copy the text.

The different colored inks and varied handwriting that make up the version that my husband passed to me on visiting day testify to the collective nature of the labor that produced the copy. And the laborers performed this task in November 2006, the year in which an initial series of "attacks by the PCC" on police and police stations electrified Brazil. The document thus came into my hands at a moment when all manner of "experts" came to formulate explanations and motives for the attacks, and for the PCC. Many of these interpretations centered on issues of responsibility as well as measures that would need to be put in place to deter future violence. And the document passed on to me is a part of these debates.

The copy of the communiqué from November 2006 is quite special because it is in effect a message from, or an expression of the viewpoints of, the authors of the attacks that rocked the nation that year. The text, dubbed a primer (*cartilha*) by its authors, is a self-reflexive document that evaluates the events and their effects while proposing directives for future actions as well as what the document describes as new "conscious generation." Addressed to "the entire prison population of the state of São Paulo," it begins with a description of its political and self-reflexive goals:

> I hope that this primer serves as a trampoline for a leap in search
> of tranquil waters but, given the presence of strong currents, I hope
> that this lesson in consciousness helps you all navigate in search of

a solution. And this is where the request that you all recognize the importance of debates and speak openly to the entire prison population about this document comes in. We ask that you all converse and express yourselves. By means of such learning we will all conquer a future. Thus we ask that you lecture even on visiting day so that even our families will understand the reasons for our struggle and come to support us consciously. And it is by means of this new text that we will begin, in a direct and simple manner and by means of a language that all should be able to understand, comprehend, reflect upon, and think about, to seek out the new path so that we can act and improve ourselves at this juncture in our lives. Only by starting this novel task can we continue our journey with faith and courage as we move toward the future correction of our deficiencies and the overcoming of our current failures.

The issue of education is fundamental. And, in the first place, we are going to open it up so that we gain a better understanding of our struggle.

Next, the document presents a history of the PCC that departs from each of the words that make up its motto. The primer also offers insights into the "May attacks," conceptualizing them as a reaction to the provocations of a state that, in the view of the document's authors, provoked rebellions so as to put them down in a demonstration of its own strength. According to this analysis, such incitements are part of a wider provocative government strategy aimed ultimately at voters:

The government of this state, the police department, the corrections department, and the public prosecutor's investigative unit, the civil police and its GARRA and DEIC units . . . what they all do is coalesce in a very direct and coordinated manner in order to work together to avoid doing away with injustice. They do nothing to improve the system. They seek only to make things worse. They do nothing but nurture violence and when they want something, like your votes, they provoke us by promoting even more injustice and oppression inside the jails and they await our reactions, our revolts. In this way they make themselves into the saviors of the motherland, always using power and uncontrolled violence inside the jails to end revolts; revolts that they themselves cause. And next they use the power of the media against us. We need urgently to learn how to fight against such provocations and come to know the subterfuges those authorities use against us. We will prevail only by coming to know their ways of acting.

The "attacks by the PCC" were markedly violent. And thus those citizens who do not have anything to do with the PCC typically know it only as a collective that expresses itself through violence. Indeed, the majority of my interlocutors committed some form of violence that caused them to go to prison and become involved with the PCC. Undoubtedly, many of these men will continue to commit violent crimes.[33] Nonetheless, those criminal or violent practices make up those men's means of obtaining money, and thus the enunciators of the document read that day in prison do not consider such actions to be within the realm of actions that make up the PCC. Earning money and surviving are considered "private" activities. This is true even in cases such as the attacks on homes in my neighborhood that, as I narrate in chapter 1, run contrary to the Command's imperatives. Meanwhile, all activities that can be linked to participation in the PCC are understood to stand in a fundamentally different register. After all, they refer to, and express the goals of, that collectivity. Here violence is simply one of the manifestations of the PCC. And it is precisely its expression that confers visibility on the Command.

Although the PCC is intermittently present across a gamut of spaces and institutions, and is fundamental to the capillaries that connect prisoners, it gains visibility only when it expresses itself through violence. Violence is one of the ways in which the PCC acts politically, and it is customarily employed when there is a need to be noticed.[34] The primer produced by the PCC in 2006 offers evidence about such consciously deployed tactics, and it proposes other means of gaining visibility: "How can we fight and overcome our difficulties and achieve our rights as prisoners? By using the same weapons that they use against us, including propaganda and the media. We are going to move massively to express ourselves to Society and reveal overlooked scenes of injustice and violence.... We have to make everyone understand that we are not the monsters that the media depicts. We urgently have to show Society that we are used by politicians and that we only want what is within our rights. We want to be treated as human beings, and not the animals they treat us as now." In fact, Marcola, speaking to Congress, attributed the use of violence to his predecessor, Geleião: "He's also a much more un-cultured person, no? That's it. He always believed completely that vio-lence would be the factor that would resolve all problems. But we know it's not like that. By using violence we often bring violence back to us. The repercussions return to us. And that was my view of the situation: The violence he wanted to put in place would cause us much more harm than good."

The demands presented in the primer read in 2006 are quite similar to the demands enunciated by the Command in other contexts, whether public protests or as part of the everyday life of the jails. These demands are related to what inmates call "a dignified serving of time." And, in-deed, this is a right guaranteed by Brazil's national Law of Penal En-forcement (Lei de Execuções Penais, LEP). As the authors of the primer pointed out, "Our objectives and goals involve establishing, by means of our unity and with the help of our families, a humane jail system that would guarantee our rights. . . . We don't want privileges within the sys-tem; we want a humanized system with active, efficient professionalizing and educational opportunities. We want our families near us and we want adequate and necessary healthcare. We have those rights. But we don't get them. The only rights that the system imposes upon us are punish-ments, persecution, the abuse of power, violence, and mistreatment."

Since demands for the enforcement of the LEP by the state govern-ment appear continuously in the discourse of PCC participants, a de-fense of the fulfillment of the promises of the LEP may be understood in prison as a sign of membership in the PCC. This is true of prisoners as well as employees and visitors. To this effect, the rebellion I described earlier in this chapter shows that criminality is not the only thing ex-pected of the Brothers.

After the rebellious prisoners returned to their spokes, I walked, cu-rious, toward the door that opens onto a large patio that separates the jail's buildings and houses the metal detectors that scan visitors upon arrival. Suddenly I found myself face-to-face with a group of police of-ficers from the elite Group for Special Tactical Actions unit (Grupo de Ações Táticas Especiais, GATE). They carried shields and hid their faces behind visors while pointing heavy weapons directly at me. As they entered, they yelled, "How many are in there?" Immediately I raised my arms and replied calmly that they would find only visitors on the spoke. Unsatisfied with my answer, they repeated the question, "How many are they?" I responded calmly, with my arms still raised, "Please be calm. You don't need to come in like this [so brutally] because right here there are only visitors."

I was alone in the tight space of the doorway with ten heavily armed members of an elite unit. They repeated their question a third time without moving their firearms away from my head. Since I understood the question to be rather broad, I emphasized that all present in that area of the prison were visitors. I wanted to be sure that they would not misinterpret my words and invade the building violently. "Visitors?" they shouted again. "I'm not sure how many," I answered. "I think we're about forty in number."

They came closer, still without lowering their weapons. One group cornered me and pushed me up against the wall while their fellow officers went off to see if I was telling the truth. Slipping in, taking cover against walls, they encountered the other visitors crouching in a mass in a corner. The GATE officers then pushed us into a line and sent us across the yard to await permission to leave the jail. I was one of the last to leave, and when I reached the street, I found an unexpected group welcoming me: The area in front of the prison was filled with people, and they surrounded me, asking if I was a "sister-in-law" (*cunhada*) and thanking me for my courage in "facing down" the police. The members of the group—almost as if they were telling a heroic story—also celebrated the escape of seven prisoners, and they pointed out to me an elderly man who they believed had informed on those prisoners. I understood that they wanted me to reproach him since, owing to my dialogue with the police, the crowd had come to see me as a defender or a representative of the group. Such actions are characteristic of those who make up the PCC.

The sense that belonging to the PCC means defending the weak or demanding human rights is quite foreign to common, popular understandings of the Command. But the group of visitors milling about the front of the prison did not confuse me with a member of the PCC because I had committed a crime. Rather, they had confused me with a "Sister" because I had appeared to speak in the name of the collectivity while seeking to guarantee others' safety. Such attempts to gain rights for the general population on the part of Brothers who engage guards and the prison administration push the envelope of criminality and suggest how the PCC takes on a political tenor that is, as I have sought to illustrate, the result of constant theoretical and practical reflection.

In this chapter, I have sought to describe PCC politics in prison. These politics are put in place by means of political positions that are not tied to those who occupy them but that do carry with them serious responsibilities. At the center of this process are techniques aimed at directing the prison population and putting into practice the ideals of the Command without establishing any hierarchical relations. The tension between political action and the practice of equality thus gives rise to an incessant assembly of often-competing political theories that speak not simply to the goals of the PCC but to all aspects of the existence and survival of all prisoners who "walk alongside" the Command. This political production is directly related to the lability of the PCC's discipline, something I understand as being intrinsic to the functioning of a group that seeks to eliminate from its networks any hierarchies and thus become a Command without commanders. In relation to this potentially confusing state of affairs, I describe in the next chapter how those who walk alongside this Command arrive at their destinations.

CHAPTER THREE

The Politics of Immanence

> Not only for scientific reasons do biologists recoil at this idea
> [of immanence]. It runs counter to our very human tendency
> to believe that behind everything real in the world stands a
> necessity rooted in the very beginning of things. Against this
> notion, this powerful feeling of destiny, we must be constantly
> on guard. Immanence is alien to modern science. Destiny is
> written concurrently with the event, not prior to it.
>
> —JACQUES MONOD, *Acaso e necessidade*

As we saw in the previous chapter, the PCC added "Equality" to its motto, and the Command began to employ the concept in guiding its most important relations. This conjuncture generated a certain tension that coursed through the capillaries and across the relationships that make up this collectivity. The attempt to forge a Command without command thus carried with it a variety of implications for the development and functioning of the Family. And this relationship forces us to rethink the pertinence of claims about the PCC as "organized crime" or a "criminal organization."

Attempts to define organized crime and criminal organizations have forced legal professionals, sociologists, political scientists, security analysts, and anthropologists to work overtime. In 1998, the United Nations created a committee charged with developing an international treaty that might allow member states to face down "Organized Transnational Crime." The result of this effort, the United Nations Convention against Organized Transnational Crime—known also as the Palermo Convention—was adopted in 2000. Brazil ratified the agreement with Federal Decree 5,015 on March 12, 2004.Article two of the Palermo Convention defines an "organized criminal group" as "a structured group of three or more persons, existing for a period of time and acting in concert with the aim of committing one or more serious crimes or offences established in accordance with this Convention, in order to obtain, directly or indirectly, a financial or other material benefit."[1]

However, according to legal scholar Getúlio Santos, Brazil still needs to elaborate a legal definition based on the United Nations recommendations.

Faced with this omission, Guaracy Mingardi has suggested five characteristics that reappear throughout the literature on organized crime. These ostensibly defining characteristics are hierarchy, expectation of profit, division of labor, entrepreneurial planning, and symbiosis with the state.[2] Nonetheless, a number of authors have questioned such designations and the concepts that prop them up.

Michel Misse, for whom such forms of knowledge and their associated approaches encourage serious errors, argues that the terms hide more than they reveal about "the minor nuances and great differences among the diversity of actors, networks, and practices that are swept up in accusations (and the resultant process of criminalization) about their regularly-occurring and clearly articulated violations of articles of the Brazilian Legal Code."[3] Meanwhile, Gustavo Barbosa, in his examination of the segmented nature of the drug trade in Rio de Janeiro, reveals how, in spite of the statelike or entrepreneurial aspects of different Commands in that city, there also exist a number of mechanisms that displace these forms. The result, Barbosa argues, is a modification of the Commands and a series of tensions that force them into motion via relationships that mitigate against entrepreneurialism or a mimetic engagement with state forms.[4] By translating the "organization" of Rio's drug-dealing associations into a "process" or "movement," Barbosa resituates the supposedly efficient and brutal "organization" commonly attributed to drug trafficking.[5] In addition, this forces a rethinking of the frightening figure, or ghostly image, that follows the notion of "organized crime" so closely in accounts of a "parallel power" capable of subjugating and terrorizing populations and "against which the only strategy left is war."[6] This specter is related to the image, as criticized by Misse (2007), of an "omnipresent and omnipotent subject called 'Urban Violence' that flattens and conflates the most disparate of crimes, conflicts, quotidian offenses, behaviors, facts, and events."[7]

The PCC, when examined through the prism of so-called organized crime, gains form and renown as a phantasmagoric figure that, in addition to revealing little about its actual workings, ends up veiling and misrepresenting a variety of names, faces, histories, gestures, words, and desires, as well as practices, collisions, struggles, strategies, plans, and wars. This is in great part because such a focus encourages sanctioned experts to put together the sorts of analyses that square with the characteristics of the "organized crime" described here (hierarchy, expectation of profit, division of labor, entrepreneurial planning, and symbiosis with the state). As a result, many commentators focus on a parallel (to state) power or a capitalist corporation as the model for understanding groups like the PCC.

My ethnography suggests something different, that solid hierarchy and entrepreneurial planning are not what enable the PCC to mobilize so many people. There is something else at play, and close analysis of this something illustrates the flimsiness of so many current claims about hierarchy, fear, organizations that step into the void when the state is absent, and entrepreneurialism. How, then, does an "organization" without a command, without a hierarchy, without a leader, and without planning become possible? Ultimately, what makes the Command work?

Projects, Random Possibilities, Strategies, and Improvisations

Adalton Marques, in an article that examines piloting and housekeeping as "prison devices capable of a singular power that reorganizes prison," offers another perspective on the birth of the PCC. From this vantage point, the PCC seems to have arisen as part of a generalized demand catalyzed by the lack of skill of the Housekeepers who negotiated with prison authorities in the name of previous generations of prisoners. Thus, when a new generation of Housekeepers, operating under the new directives enunciated by the PCC, began to mediate quarrels among prisoners and to engage prison administrators, they put into effect a double policy of "war with the police" and "peace among thieves."[8] And the previous chapter illustrated how these activities are not simply central to the activities of imprisoned Brothers but come to occupy central places in the existence of the PCC. It seems, then, that there exist two projects that orient the existence of the PCC within prison. These are internal peace on the one hand and war against those outside the group (or, at a minimum, a select group of those outsiders) on the other. But in pointing out these two foundational projects, I would like to pause to distinguish between the words "project" and "strategy" as I employ them in this analysis. The terms are not interchangeable. And far from taking the first as a representation and the second as a practice, I understand them as being characterized by very different intensities, velocities, distributions, and scopes.

"Strategies," as employed here, are media that suggest a certain extension or reach. In other words, strategies activate chains of everyday practice. Projects, meanwhile, are orientations essential to the very existence of the PCC. They are closer to what, drawing on military technologies, one might call "the battle as the means towards the attainment of the object of the war."[9] Projects, then, are open to any and all types of strategies. They are able to absorb as many strategies as can be creatively offered.[10] It should thus be clear that projects exist independently of strategies, which are not constitutive elements of such projects. So, for example, without any modification of a PCC project of "war with the police," the heterodox strategies deployed by the Command may range from an agreement with a government minister to attacks on military police installations, rebellions, escape attempts, and everyday verbal duels (*debates*). Similarly, and without fundamentally altering the project of "peace between thieves," PCC strategies may oscillate between shutting down an argument between two prisoners and perpetrating a war intended to conquer and maintain control of particular spaces within the prison system.[11] Strategies—which, again, are not subunits of projects and are therefore not necessary for the existence of projects—thus take form here as plans for putting projects into practice. And in turn these strategies include innumerable tactics, or what I define here simply as methods for putting strategies into operation. Nonetheless, the shifting nature of the soil on which we all walk does not permit the crystallization of the border between strategies and tactics. As we will see, it is not difficult for a simple tactic to begin to shape or organize planning practices and thus transform into a strategy that, from there on out, will organize a multitude of other tactics.

A rebellion, in light of my approach to projects, strategies, and tactics, might be approached as a strategy that looks toward, and thus supports, the project of "war with the police." An example would be the rebellion that broke out in the São Bernardo de Campo CDP, part of which I described in the previous chapter.

Months of careful planning and practice runs preceded the rebellion.[12] The goal was to escape, but in order to do that, the prisoners would need to mobilize the confusion sowed by a rebellion to cover up their actions. The first move was to get hold of four firearms, one for each of the cages that determine access to a hub that leads to a spoke. The plan was to have a prisoner feign illness and faint on visiting day. When medical help arrived, one of the guns would be used to immobilize the guards gathered around the "sick" inmate. For months beforehand, the plotters practiced this maneuver, with one of the Housekeepers pretending to faint as the other members of the group worked out the precise maneuvers through which they would summon aid, overpower the guards, and take the jail. Yet the inmates did not plan out what would come next:

"We spent about two months practicing," one man told me.

"No! Seriously?"

"Seriously. I'm being serious. Really practicing so that it'd come off perfectly. We practiced."

"But only as far as the part about taking hostages?"

"No, our practice runs went as far as the medical post."

"And did you work out what you'd do next?"

"No."

What would come following the plotters' takeover of the prison would arise out of a still-unpracticed conjuncture. Since it was impossible to predict what would happen, the plotters realized that their next steps would be dictated by the still-unknown outcome of their designs. Yet they knew that, if the attempt went as planned, they would have relatively little time to chart their next moves. Anything was possible. Hostages might die, or the prisoners might find themselves free. The Brothers described their approach to such unstable situations as "sliding into the craziness" (*metendo o louco*), or leaving things to chance and risking everything.

While strategies disappear at the moment actors face the unknown, there is yet another factor that haunts the tension between detailed planning and "insane" risk. This factor is chance. On the eve of the execution of the escape attempt, the prisoner charged with faking illness found himself transferred to another jail! And one of the hidden guns had already been confiscated during a routine police sweep of the jail. Additionally, this discovery of a firearm increased the likelihood of additional police incursions and transfers of prisoners. Yet the date of the attempt could no longer be changed. The response to these twists of fate and seemingly random occurrences was to "look (further) into the craziness." Nonetheless, the Brothers did try to take concrete measures to improve their chances. They told me that very few on the cell block knew of their plans.[13] Such secrecy is a mechanism against betrayal. In spite of the rigor with which prisoners choose Brothers and Housekeepers, and a continued emphasis on transparency among inmates, suspicions abound. As the prisoners put it, they resist pressure to "put our hands in the fire for anyone" because it is always possible to come across a "rotten apple."[14]

At about noon on visiting day, one of the Brothers received a phone call from a compatriot on another wing: "We've taken the prison employees hostage—they're all in here and I'm already dressed in clothes I took off one of them. I'm off to the spoke. Grab that guy there, too. Grab that guy!" Almost immediately after hanging up, the Brother received another call: "We've got the middle cage [*gaiola*] already. We've got the guards' clothes and we're here in the middle. Now it's you. It's time!" Taking that second spoke was critical because of its proximity to the main doors (*chapões*) of the building, broken up into multiple spokes, that held the prisoners.

Without having practiced it, one prisoner cut his lips with a razor and pretended to faint. His cellmates, as they had planned, carried him to the door of their cell block and summoned authorities. "Medic! Medic!" they shouted urgently. When the guard opened the door, they exited the wing, carrying their comrade, and found themselves within the extremely strategic hub. When the guard asked them to go back to the spoke, they created a scene of confusion (*perrecaram*) that they had practiced diligently:

"We're not leaving the Brother alone; no way! When he comes to we'll leave him here, but not till then!

"You can leave him here."

"No, sir, we're *not* leaving him! We're not leaving him. We're not leaving him. . . . If anything happens to him I'll lose my head, sir. Are you crazy, sir? They're gonna beat the crap out of me if I leave him here. I'm not leaving him."

In this way, the actors convinced the guard to accompany the "victim" to the first aid post. By reaching that spot, they would have made it through the first of the building's main, exterior doors. There all plans, forecasts, and dry runs would butt up against their limits as they stepped into an unknown where they would need to react rapidly to each new wrinkle.

Brothers continuously sharpen their abilities to improvise. The most successful prisoner is precisely the one who is able to react adequately to unexpected situations. This generates a certain security when sliding into craziness (*metendo o louco*) since the prisoner has confidence in his ability to rise up to unforeseen challenges. Prisoners also often refer to such abilities as being necessary for success in a life of crime. In a positioning akin to those of the boxers studied by Löic Wacquant, even in the wake of repetitive practice sessions and a long apprenticeship, the execution of a fight, a robbery, or an escape attempt means that "everything takes place based on reflex, in fractions of a second. The head is in the body and the body is in the head."[15] This ability to improvise rests on a simultaneous domination of the body and discourse, of sensory perception, and of the capacity to reason.[16] Body, mind, and sentience become essential to the construction of an artfulness that is reactive as well as learned, imitative, carefully improved on, the product of intense training, and yet permeated by creativity and intuition. Or, as put forth in the aforementioned PCC primer that circulated across São Paulo's prisons, "Without preparation and the struggle to improve ourselves there will be no novel responses to moments of crisis."

The first aspect of the CDP escape attempt that required a creative initiative on the part of the plotters involved opening the main door of the entire building: "There's a guy who stays on the other side of it [*the chapão*]. When the guy went to open it up he got scared, seeing so many people . . . but he cracked it open. That's when I stuck my hand in. Next I slipped my whole arm in so he couldn't close it again. That's when my Brother pulled his gun, 'Now it's all ours! Shut up! Not a sound.' Then we pulled the guard inside and took his clothes."

The guard's shirt was given to a Brother, but this move generated a further problem. As one prisoner explained, "This guy was like Santa Claus. The Brother put the shirt on and it didn't even cover his bellybutton. 'Shit this isn't going to work!' I thought, 'I'm not gonna say anything' but there was a big chunk of tattoo sticking out from under the shirt."

Differences in girth were not the only unexpected occurrence. Earlier, before they had even left the spoke, another problem had come up. There was a group of visitors waiting to enter the spoke from outside the door that secured the building:

"There's a bunch of visitors out there."

"If a visitor gets shot we're fucked. Shit!"

"So let them in."

"Fake it, fake it!"

Dressed as guards, the Brothers sought to act the part, and they opened up the spoke to us.

"Good afternoon."

"But you're a prisoner!"

"Come on in, ma'am."

"But I need to sign in first."

"You don't need to sign anything, ma'am. Come on in. Please. Enter, enter. . . ."

"But I don't know where my son is."

"It's okay, come on in. . . ."

After letting the visitors in, the prisoners opened the gates within the hub that links one spoke to another. This is when they realized that a Brother from Spoke 7 had let all his cellmates know about the plan: "Brother Lucas opened the door from Spoke 7. . . . Everyone flooded out into the hub, which was completely empty of visitors. The only pavilion full of visitors we had expected to take was our own, and that was because it was up front and we needed it to get out of the prison. And then everyone—every last prisoner—from Spoke 7 rushed out. What the fuck! So the Brothers started in, 'Back, back, back!' Then even the Brothers from 7 ran back inside. We yelled out, 'No, not you, Brother. Let's go!'"

The Brothers told me that they could not allow everyone to flee since they were planning to wear the guards' clothing and, in addition to the fact that there simply was not enough clothing to go around, that mass of prisoners would draw too much attention to their attempt. In this case, the dominant ethos of equality was damaged by the details of the escape plan. So was the emphasis on transparency. But both these ruptures with PCC ideals were supported by the ideal of liberty, and unexpected events made these transgressions necessary. But this does not mean that the people involved will remain untouched by potential future repercussions should anyone—and here it would not matter if it were a Cousin or a Brother—decide to stretch the bubble gum because they felt they had been disadvantaged by the escapees' actions. Nonetheless, and even though they were conscious that they might be called to account later on, the Brothers maintained confidence in their plans, motives, and justifications. They continued with the escape, opening the other main building door and stepping into the yard surrounded by high walls topped by heavily armed guards. By crossing this open space, they could make it to the unit in which guards searched visitors, a building that also housed the prison office. This in turn offered a path to the prison gates (*portaria*), which also offered protection to the armed guards who surrounded them.

While still inside the spokes, the escapees agreed that they would break into groups of six and then, in pairs, seek to move slowly across

This view of a prison yard at the Santo André prison shows visitors on a visiting day coinciding with Children's Day in Brazil. Although cameras are normally prohibited in the jails of São Paulo, the prisoners negotiated with prison officials to allow the entry of two cameras on Children's Day. Photograph by Karina Biondi, 2005.

the prison's last exposed area without spooking the guards. But the members of the second such group that attempted this maneuver found themselves under fire from guards atop the walls. This forced the Brothers to remain inside the building reserved for processing visitors. There they abandoned the escape attempt and began the negotiations I described in chapter 2.

The unexpected is always present, and is thus seen as inevitable when inmates put strategies to work. Random events become confused with tactics, becoming a part of those devices in ways that mean that improvisations are put together strategically. And approaching the escape as a strategy and examining what unfolds as predicted reveals that most of the attempt involved rapid reactions to the unexpected. Nonetheless, these adaptations, to a certain extent, are ordered by the initial project and the strategies brought to bear on it. Hence, the strategies do much to anticipate or call forth the revisions put in place later. We might conclude, then, that strategies and improvisations are co-constructed since strategies especially are endowed with improvisations, and improvisations are adopted strategically. This makes it clear that, to a certain extent, chance includes strategies. And uncertainty and chance, when brought into the political model based on equality, generate a dynamic for the PCC that is remarkably different from what is typically understood as "organization." But such coincidences also produce effects in the Command's other project, peace among thieves.

The PCC's emphasis on maintaining peace among thieves is directed at prisoners who are in the general population and who are thus seen as having exhibited—and hence to possess—the all-important *proceder*, or history of proper conduct.[17] As I discussed in chapter 1, to be recognized as someone who carries himself properly, the prisoner must do more than follow the guidelines of the Command. Correct comportment as defined by the PCC turns also on a vast series of quotidian orientations that impact the subtlest of gestures, words, and bearings that permeate existence in the jails where the Brothers hold sway. Such an emphasis on self-control that prisoners refer to, and carry with them as a testament to proper bearing—and thus even a type of "procedure" or formula for conduct as suggested by the term in Portuguese—has been interpreted by some analysts as but a dislocation of the panoptic gaze of the prison regime: The "Command, just like the solidarity of the prisoners involved in that organization, does not arise as part of a collective interest or the free association of individuals, but by means of threat, fear, and imposition."[18] Yet my fieldwork highlights situations in which the diligent researcher might make out an enormous flexibility of discipline. Again, I trace this to the addition of Equality to the PCC motto and ethos, something celebrated in a communiqué that circulated across the prisons: "Equality also means the valorization of human life (among those who belong within the criminal element). This is because it was only through Equality that the right to speak and be heard, the opportunity to expose what is correct and true, and what is wrong and a lie, was conquered."

The Command's discipline is a strategy that aspires to the establishment of peace between thieves. But in the name of this peace, a large number of prescriptions and imperatives thought to maintain peace are blended into the disputed, improvised actions adopted strategically by the Brothers. In other words, the project of establishing a peace that brings together participants in the Command is not simply a part of

PCC discipline, but also an impediment to the crystallization of this discipline.

As the escape attempt illustrates, PCC discipline within prisons is remarkably labile. Another example of this flexibility involves the ways that prisoners debate whether an issue should be taken to the House-keepers (in accordance with the principle of transparency) or be resolved within a particular cell (in accordance with the premise that "what happens in the cell stays in the cell"). Such a debate was catalyzed when a prisoner known as Túlio struck his cellmate, Carlos. Such aggression is usually taken as an affront to the Command and is condemned by prisoners, since it recalls the "bad old days" of violence before the rise of the PCC, when privileges were conquered through force. Hence, this challenge should be reported to the Housekeepers, who, as representatives of the Family, guarantee the existence of the current order. At the same time, it also makes sense that prisoners follow the ethos of the Command and be granted a bit of autonomy in resolving their differences. After all, freedom is tied tightly to the practice of liberty, something central to the PCC precepts and motto. To compound things, it would be impractical to have each aspect of the life of the prison brought to the attention of the Housekeepers. Such moves would also create an environment rife with intrigue and misunderstandings. Thus, the discussions surrounding Túlio's aggression offer help in understanding the valences and contradictions of PCC "discipline."

During the debate in Túlio and Carlos's cell, prisoners focused on the reasons for the attack on a cellmate, or a member of a social unit that prisoners often refer to as a "family." According to witnesses, Túlio had hit Carlos only after the latter provoked him continually, testing him. Such behavior, understood as an incitement to violence, is commonly associated with police, guards, and prosecutors and judges. As a result, it is censored by the Command. This meant that, although Túlio had no doubt disobeyed the Command by striking a fellow prisoner, Carlos had also violated conventions by needling his cellmate. Given this double bind, the residents of the cell concluded that denouncing the incident might bring down a reaction from the Command, and perhaps even result in their cell being "seen poorly" (*malvisto*) by others. They agreed that Carlos had already suffered the "consequences" of his actions and that in the future he should agree to avoid testing the mettle of his fellow Thieves. He would have to be placed under observation by his peers. Meanwhile, Túlio would be punished by relinquishing his bunk and sleeping on the floor, or "beach," and cleaning the bathroom for a week.

Túlio was the third member of this cell to be taken out of the bunks as part of the analyses and discussions that make up the sort of debate encouraged by the PCC. But when Eduardo, one of the members of the cell who had suggested the punishments, was taken out of prison to attend a court hearing, Túlio joined the two other cellmates who had lost bunk privileges to plot revenge. The three—Túlio, Vinícius, and José— went to the Housekeepers and argued that Eduardo wanted to be the "sheriff of their cell" and was "trying to be a tough guy" (*pagando um de malandrão*) like certain common prisoners who had acted like bullies before the rise of the PCC.[19] So when Eduardo returned from his court date, a Brother named Hugo called him over to talk:

EDUARDO: What's going on here, Brother? You told the other
    two they couldn't have their bunks? That sure is old school,
    my friend!
BROTHER HUGO: A badass malandrão, Brother? How can you
    use a word like that on me, Brother? Malandrão? Listen up,
    who's stretching the bubble gum in here?

Hugo replied that it was the "guys in the cell" who were talking. Eduardo began immediately to sketch out a defense that, although improvised, also demonstrated shrewd strategizing:

EDUARDO: So ask him why he got taken down off the bunk,
    Brother. After he tells us we'll move on to this.
BROTHER HUGO: Tell us why you came down from the bunk!
VINÍCIUS: (Silence).
EDUARDO: The guy asked him to pass the pair of sandals that
    were under his mattress and so he threw them in the guy's face.
BROTHER HUGO: Really? Who is the other guy, Brother?
    Call him here.

With the aggrieved man before them, Eduardo continued, "Here's what happened, Brother. The two of them were fooling around, right?[20] So he put toothpaste on the guy's face while he was sleeping. So in the morning he goes and pushes it a little further. He keeps on toying with him. So the other guy gets down off his bunk to hit him. Those of us in the cell had to break it up so they wouldn't go beating each other up; you got it? Things get resolved right here in the cell, Brother."

Upon hearing this account, Brother Hugo commented, "That's not the story I got." Eduardo responded, "See, Brother? Call the other guy here." When Túlio arrived, Eduardo continued with his defense: "Okay, good, Túlio's here. Here's what's going on. The guy came in and started up with Túlio, so Túlio went after the guy. The guy was looking for trouble so Túlio went and reacted and hit him. He said he was a *malandro* and all that, and he hit the guy. And that was that. So, there, just like you guys say, 'Whatever you can resolve in the cell should be resolved in the cell. And we resolved it, right?' "

In the wake of this explanation, Hugo commented, "But that stuff about getting down off your bunk is not really right." This provoked the following exchange:

EDUARDO: Listen up, Brother. What I learned, I learned with your Brothers. What I'm telling you is exactly what your own Brothers told me.

BROTHER HUGO: But what Brother told you that stuff?

EDUARDO: Write down their names. . . . I even know where they are right now, so you can make a call and figure out what makes sense in here and what doesn't.

BROTHER HUGO: That's what used to happen.

EDUARDO: No, not in the old days, Brother. That's what's happening now in Dakar 7, in Pinheiros, in São Bernardo.[21]

In the wake of this short debate, Hugo moved to rein in the prisoners who had complained about Eduardo's attitude: "You see that, Túlio? You're a fuckup, boy! You came to me trying to start trouble. You said that this guy [Eduardo] is an old-school *malandrão*! But the guy's a real bandit, you hear me? You see, Vinícius? I admire you, you badass; I really do.[22] Serving your time and beating on your cellmates, is it? That doesn't work in here. You're no fucking badass! Why don't you guys come hit me? Beat me! Hit me with your sandals! Why don't you get into the ring with me?"

Brother Hugo then went to the cell occupied by the prisoners involved in the incident and discussed the "journey that went down" while confirming with the Family, or all the members of the cell, the version of events recounted by Eduardo. Hugo then emphasized that, "This is not going to work. This kinda thing is twisting the Command's word," even as he added that "what the Brother [Eduardo] did in there, that stuff about giving up your bunk, that's not right. It's *malandrão* stuff!" The

Brother's affirmation of Eduardo's supposed return to actions reminiscent of the *malandrão* of the old days forced the discussion back into the realm of the Housekeepers once again:

BROTHER GILSON: What happened, Eduardo?

EDUARDO: The guy back there, calling me a *malandrão*, and in front of my "Family" [cellmates] to top it off!

BROTHER HUGO: No, I said it was *malandrão* "stuff," not that he was a *malandrao*!"

EDUARDO: If I'm doing that, then I am what I'm doing, right? *Malandrão*. The thing is, the people who told me this stuff are your Brothers. So I'm gonna put them on the phone, right?

BROTHER GILSON: What is it you're trying to say with these here words, Brother?

EDUARDO: Well, if he's calling me a *malandrão* it's only because I did some stuff that I learned from his Brothers. So he's calling your Brothers *malandrões* [plural] too.

BROTHER HUGO: I'm not saying that. I didn't call any Brother a *malandrão*. Watch your words!

EDUARDO: Brother, like I already explained, the people who taught me all this were your Brothers. Dakar 7 works like that. Pinheiros too. São Bernardo is the same way. It's only in here that things are different. What do you want me to do? I already told your Brothers here, if you want to go your own way and follow your own ideas, so be it. But that word *malandrão* doesn't fit me. For a long time I've been running with the Command, side by side. I'm representing and you guys don't even recognize it!

Following the discussion just presented, Brothers Hugo and Gilson went back to the cell where Eduardo lived and, altering their original determination of responsibility, "took back the word" (*retiraram a palavra*). Eduardo even managed, with the support of his cellmates, to have the three prisoners who had complained about his conduct transferred to new cells. He then confided to Hugo that,

Brother, like you said, whatever we can resolve in the cell, we'll resolve there even if it's a thousand degree issue! We'll resolve it in the cell, right? It's all cool. You guys have problems to resolve that are even hotter than a thousand degrees. It's not like I'm not gonna be taking every little problem to you. And then that other guy had to get involved. I'd already given him the chance to fix things without carrying it outside. It was already over! That way it wasn't gonna cause him any problems.

What if he [Túlio] gets tagged as the guy who did wrong and the other guy [Carlos] asks for his pound of flesh? You know what I mean, Brother? The guy got socked. And the guy is a bandit. You hearing me? He's a criminal. Did you understand, Brother? The guy gets punched in his own cell and then we've got to face the possibility that he's gonna demand the correct kind of retribution. It's a right he has, Brother. After all, everyone's an equal, right? So the guy takes a few slaps . . . and next comes payback in full . . . but the guy's a bandit too, Brother. And he ends up getting slapped around? It's not something he's gonna like. So we resolved it among ourselves; we dropped a stone on top of that shitpile and that was that. But then some guy goes and stirs things up by telling you I'm a big *malandro?* I can't be comfortable living with a guy like that.

Hugo replied, "Me neither," and Gilson added, "I don't trust a guy like that either!"

Eduardo was skillful in dealing with the tangled knot that some refer to as the "discipline" of the PCC. His experience suggests that abilities similar to those that prisoners rely on in dealing with the surprises that arise during an escape attempt are also powerful tools in operationalizing the forms of discipline developed by the Command.

As should be clear, Eduardo had been surprised by the accusations when he stepped off the trolley (*bonde*) that brought him back to jail from a court date. He had no time to prepare his defense, and consequently he had to improvise. In this case, he managed to transform the situation by placing the Brothers in charge of housekeeping in a delicate position in relation to their Brothers in other jails. And, like Eduardo, these Brothers improvised novel responses in the face of the spiraling reconfigurations in which they found themselves. In doing so, they skated atop the discipline of the Command and were successful in maintaining peace among thieves.

The Command, far from constructing a rigid center of power through its disciplinary efforts, pulverizes that power since it permits articulations of its collective power only in relation to a prisoner's capacities.[23] The flexibility that a commitment to improvisation grants to PCC discipline does not interfere with the diffusion of its codes of conduct, which inmates accept as paradigms. But it does mean that these codes are constantly manipulated, adjusted, disputed, and twisted, not simply to protect larger projects but also in order to guarantee that they are put into practice. Again, then, we come face-to-face with a strategy (the discipline of the Command) endowed with, and mixed into, a panoply of improvisations. And as I will analyze, the co-construction of strategies and improvisations is possible thanks to a very different element in the PCC toolkit that, by means of its slipperiness, fortifies them both. This something else is what inmates refer to as disposition (*disposição*).

Desires, Appetites, and Dispositions

In November 2007, a nongovernmental organization from Presidente Prudente, a city in the interior of São Paulo State, sponsored a demonstration in front of Congress in Brasilia, Brazil's national capital. Those who were assembled demanded improvements in Brazil's penitentiary system and, above all, the application and fulfillment of the letter of the national Law of Penal Enforcement (Lei de Execuções Penais). In the midst of the demonstration, a commission composed of lawyers and relatives of prisoners delivered a petition to the National Congress's Committee of Parliamentary Investigation of the Carceral System. The document described conditions within Brazilian jails and presented the demonstrators' demands.

The event in Brasilia brought together pilgrims from the states of São Paulo, Rio de Janeiro, Espírito Santo, Minas Gerais, Mato Grosso, Mato Grosso do Sul, Paraná, Santa Catarina, and Goiás. From the São Paulo metropolitan region alone, twenty-two buses and a larger number of automobiles departed. My journey to Brasilia in one of those buses was punctuated by changes in date, negotiations that allowed me to be accepted onto the bus, a shortage of seats, the reappearance of open seats, police checks, long waits, debates about the contents of my research, changes in the vehicles used, and issues that arose owing to questions of gender. In fact, it appeared that the event would never take place. To begin with, as soon as a date for the demonstration was proposed, for the demonstration it would be cancelled, forgotten, and then altered again. There was no centralized source of information. I became nervous about the fact that there was no one to ask about the details, since no one knew them. All the information was fragmentary, discontinuous, contradictory, and often incoherent.

On the day we were to depart, I still did not know where I should go to board my bus or who the person was who would serve as an intermediary and let me in on the knowledge necessary to make it to Brasília. And even after I finally encountered this person, I still harbored strong suspicions that the event would never come to fruition. No one knew who would go, where, and when. At one point, hundreds of people milled about, awaiting the buses on a narrow, forgotten street in São Paulo. And those buses never arrived. Instead, we were divided up between other buses that departed from diverse spots across one of the world's largest and most traffic-choked cities. And I found myself spending hours moving between different parts of the city until I finally found a seat on one of the vehicles.

At long last, we began to accompany other groups headed for Brasília. Passengers from some of the buses in our convoy were less lucky, as the police prohibited two of the vehicles from leaving the city. Those of us on the twenty other vehicles in the convoy worked to avoid drawing attention to ourselves, since we feared that if we drew suspicion the police would find some way to stop our journey. None of the passengers had outstanding arrest warrants. In fact, this was one of the prerequisites for signing up, since we knew that this might give the police yet another excuse for stopping us. And participants made a great effort to delink the manifestation from the PCC. But since the Command is present in 90 percent of the prisons in São Paulo State, and since the people assembled were overwhelmingly the relatives of prisoners and former prisoners (most of whom probably served their time in institutions controlled by the PCC), our group came to be linked to "organized crime." This was the result of individuals having maintained relations of some sort with the PCC at some point in their lives. Even if none of the participants were baptized members of the Party, they found their path pockmarked with fears about the criminalization of their political activities. Ironically, this concern with police repression ended up encouraging the group to add my name, like that of Adalton Marques, who was at the time studying at the University of São Paulo, onto the list of passengers. As one person who was busily signing up people who wanted to participate in the demonstrations scheduled for Brasília commented to us, "The police think twice before bothering students."

In spite of the many roadblocks, the demonstration came off. Even better, I was able to join in. Upon returning to São Paulo, I commented to a friend, "With everything that was going on, I figured there'd be only a few dozen people in Brasilia, but two thousand showed up!" Her response was eye-opening, "There's really no secret to it. Think about it. Every one of those people really wanted to be there!" Today her words resonate across the present text and my thinking about my research. That simple statement illuminated a variety of perspectives and understandings that my naturalized ways of thinking had covered up. It forced me to reevaluate my analysis and recognize a type of immanence that, bound to so many other instances, contributed to the formation of the PCC. In response, I began to focus in on those moments when my attempts to make sense of my experiences had covered up the potential that emanated from the desires and impulses of those who make up that multitude that we often gloss as "prisoners."

Those desires, expressed by prisoners through terms such as "disposition" (*disposição*) and appetite (*apetite*), nourish their actions and permit the elaboration of strategies, designs for projects, and the definition of objectives that, when executed, are not abandoned in the face of errors, unforeseen events, and impasses. "Disposition" and "appetite" are words used by prisoners to indicate the intensity and the reach of their broadest desires, in their most varied forms. The two enable the production of outlines, twists, and improvised solutions that so often rest on chance for their success. And once they gain speed, they are capable of offering resistance to the power that bears down on bodies to modulate or limit possibility.

One prisoner's account of the conjuncture that led to a small number of inmates "winning the prison for the PCC" (*ganhar a cadeia para o PCC*) provides evidence about these dispositions as motivating forces for prisoners' actions and thus for the construction of a Command without command. This man told me that he was advised by the Housekeepers that he should gather up his things because the bus that was to transfer him to a new jail had arrived. Immediately, he phoned his family to inform them about the transfer and to advise them not to worry. But, as is so common, the vehicle that was to carry him arrived late and was overcrowded—word about what was happening had been passed down by housekeeping at 6 A.M. Yet the bus did not arrive at its destination and drop off the last of its occupants in the new facility until late at night, despite the fact that the prisoner being transferred was being moved to another institution within the city of São Paulo's metropolitan region.

My interlocutor described the ride in the following manner: "Then they're like 'get on the bus.' Inside there were a ton of people standing, with no place to sit. Keeling over, fainting, vomiting. . . . My God! It was horrible. A pack of wild animals. . . . They treat us as if we were animals. Then the guard lost it: They put us in that old can parked in the sun and started pepper spraying us. Shit was crazy . . . coughing everywhere. . . . It burns like hell. It was ugly. Then the guys started screaming, 'Open the door, we can't breathe in here' and we got 'Shut up' from the guards. Our response was 'Shut up, my ass; son of a bitch!' " Then the insanity—something that becomes understandable only in light of the fact that the "trolley" sent out that night to move men between prisons contained no Brothers, only Cousins—started for real.

The "insanity" that my interlocutor identified seems a common, and even constitutive, part of prison life in São Paulo. For example, during his deposition to Congress, Marcola also described such a trip, suggesting that the violence suffered by prisoners during their transfer between institutions was an important incitement for the May 2006 wave of attacks by the PCC: "In there, the use of gas was like playtime. . . . If the guy gets on the bus and he's already sick, he's gonna die. It's pretty simple. You can't even breathe, do you understand what I'm telling you? . . . And the heat. Metal all around us. The sun beats down and it becomes a frying pan."[24] Thus the man understood by Brazil's national legislators as the Command's "leader," like the prisoners with whom I conversed about the transfer process, expressed a sense of revolt and a willingness to engage in drastic actions in the face of the "craziness" and brutality of the transfer process. Marcola's testimony thus reveals how although something as seemingly trivial as the process whereby prisoners are taken to their court dates might be approached as but a sidebar to the story of the construction in prison of a Command without commanders, it may in fact be critical to the shapes taken by that Command. And what took place in relation to my interlocutor's transfer between facilities that night reveals much about the workings of power and about the PCC.

When prisoners arrive by bus at a new CDP, they pass through an arrivals area, where they answer a questionnaire and guards register their possessions. As the assembled group moved through this triage process, João, one of the Cousins being transferred from the CDP who recounted his story to me, found himself in front of a guard who declared that he could not enter the new facility with his toothbrush because its color violated the arbitrary codes of his new "home":

JOÃO: What's this? That can't come in?

GUARD: No, it can't come in because it's blue.

JOÃO: So what?

GUARD: It's simply that this is a blue prison, so you can't have blue things with you.

JOÃO: No way. If I want paint in this place I'll find a way to get my hands on it. Come on, sir, stop it.

GUARD: No, it's not coming in.

HEAD GUARD: Hey, Thief, what are you complaining about?

JOÃO: I'm not complaining, sir. I just want my stuff. This thing was tough for my family to bring in, to get to me.

HEAD GUARD: You're talking too much. Do you want to be the first to baptize this place's new solitary?

JOÃO: I don't want to baptize anything, sir. I want my stuff, see? It's mine. . . .

PRISON DIRECTOR: What's he complaining about?

GUARD: His toothbrush.

PRISON DIRECTOR: Come on, give him his toothbrush. Go ahead.

A bit taken aback, I asked João if it was the lack of a toothbrush that really had motivated him to create such a clash with guards. He answered, "Logically! I wanted the brush. How am I gonna brush my teeth? I needed the brush to brush my teeth." But the issue here was not necessarily, or solely, the exact object being confiscated. It was also an attempt to resist the circumscriptions of freedom being perpetrated during the transfer process.

Resistance to what prisoners considered excesses augmented the already tense situation surrounding the prison bus. In the midst of that process, João and his colleagues being transferred out of a prison run by the Command overheard another prisoner reporting his profession as "security guard" in response to the guard's standard questionnaire. The other new arrivals looked at each other in surprise, since security guards are typically thought to work closely with the police, and this admission on the part of another prisoner generated great suspicion. Such a man is usually configured in PCC prisons as a "thing." João and Rodrigo, another of his busmates, thus furrowed their brows and looked at one another worriedly. "Oh shit," one blurted out, "But we're gonna have to figure this out later. We can't debate it in front of the guards. We'll talk later. Leave the chicken alone, for now." At that point, the two, who had been the first to get off the bus, found themselves being ushered through the doors that gave access to their new spoke. João described the experience to me as strange because, at the time, he said, "I kept thinking, where're the Housekeepers? At moments like that we look for help from the House-keepers. Then the 'widow' (the *viúva*, or doors to the spoke) opened up, and I stepped in while the guards went and closed the door on me. You know what I mean? They pull on that thing and the door closes. But when I looked inside, the guys inside were from the CRBC!"

The CRBC, or the Brazilian Revolutionary Command of Criminal-ity, is one of the few commands that battles the PCC for control of São Paulo's prisons. Its members, like the prisoners who find themselves in the facilities it controls—and who thus "run with" the CRBC—are con-sidered things by the PCC and its associates. Thus, even though there was not a single Brother in the bus transporting João and Rodrigo to a new jail, and there was not a single official member of the CRBC pres-ent at the time, the situation unfolded as a clash between prisoners from the PCC and CRBC. Such an encounter could easily carry all involved into a war since, just as prisoners associated with the CRBC are not ac-cepted by those who walk with the PCC, the CRBC does not accept prisoners allied with the PCC. They are in turn, in CRBC eyes, things. Thus, the situation for the two arrivals was delicate. They were out-numbered, and they surmised that, if they entered the spoke, they would be killed. For this reason, they confronted the guards who had pushed them into the widow:

"What's this? I'm going to get the knife! I'm going to die in this shit-hole, do you understand."

"No way, I'm not going in. No way!"

"There you go, you're going . . ."

"No, no, no, I'm not going in!"

"No, no way; you're *not* going to close the door. Are you crazy?

"You're crazy, son of a bitch!"

Before the door could be closed completely, João stuck his arm into the remaining space and shouted, "You can break my arm if you want, but you're not going to lock that piece of shit! No way!" Meanwhile, Rodrigo punched the boxed-in video camera from which the guards watched the action and ordered, "Open up this piece of shit!"

At that moment, the two men noticed some brooms nearby. Rodrigo grabbed one, snapped it in two jagged-ended halves, and shouted out to

João, "You can let that thing go. I'm gonna kill a half dozen just for me!" Addressing the guards, he yelled, "Close it. Go ahead. Close it! I'm gonna die but I'm gonna KILL! I'M GONNA KILL!!!" João also grabbed and broke a broom, and both began to move down the spoke toward the cells filled with prisoners allied with the CRBC.

The prisoners screamed, "Goddamnit, they're going to kill us! Guaaaaaaaaaaaaaaaaaaards!!" João advanced and tore down a CRBC flag, growling, "You're all gonna die." According to João and Rodrigo, the prisoners were terrified and wouldn't stop screaming, "No, they're not coming in here! Aaaah! Guards!!

At that point, a guard entered the widow and asked what was going on. João and Rodrigo told him, "Sir, what the fuck is this? We were in a jail run by the Command and now you put us in a CRBC? Open that door, let us out! If you put us inside, we're gonna kill. WE ARE GOING TO KILL! I'm not afraid, sir. I've got a thirty year sentence. And if I can take thirty, I do fifty, playing. I'm not even counting the time."

Neither João nor Rodrigo were facing anything near thirty years in prison. They claimed to be facing such high sentences solely to intimidate the guards or, in their own words, to "play psychologist." But this does not mean that they were unprepared to kill their enemies if necessary. But before that possibility became necessary, their actions bore fruit. The guard who had stepped into the widow took them back out of the spoke. Safely outside and surrounded by guards with nightsticks, they dropped the broom handles and spoke with the director, who promised to place them in a wing without CRBC prisoners.

João and Rodrigo had to return to the processing center. When the other prisoners asked them what had happened, João's report that, "There's a ton of CRBC in there. They even have a flag. This is nuts," initiated another tumult. "Sir, what's going on?" they screamed at the director, who needed to promise that all CRBC prisoners would be removed from the spoke before they were brought in. The new prisoners agreed that when they were taken to the spoke, the first ones in would scream, whistle, and cause a ruckus if there was anything amiss. Rodrigo and João were the last to walk down the spoke. There they found the cells empty except for the Cousins who had been brought in on the buses with them. They had "won the jail" for the PCC.

In spite of what an outsider might imagine, winning a jail for the PCC is not always the result of a plan. João and Rodrigo had not acted in an attempt to take control of space. They had not planned to take the prison, nor had they even thought of it during their battle to protect themselves in the new space. Instead, the end result seemed to arise from their burning desire to remain alive.

Disposition and appetite are drives that do not necessarily imply any sort of teleological movement or any end result. Their reach varies along with their intensities, and these are modulated by the encounters put together along the "walk" that both draws on and builds up the dispositions and appetites so important to João and Rodrigo's survival. This modulation so important to the ways subjects become something else takes form in a dynamic through which certain drives are built up by encounters even as others are tamped down in slightly different encounters. And any such overcoming of potential barriers depends on the intensity of actors' movements as well as the power of the barriers faced. This dynamic exists wherever the PCC exists. Thus, for example, the encounter at a roadblock between the police and the two buses filled with prisoners' relatives headed to the National Congress ended up blocking those pilgrims' attempt to make it to Brasília and agitate for inmate rights. Meanwhile, the encounter between the Cousins being transferred and the prisoners "belonging" to the CRBC potentialized an intensity of flows that gave rise to the conquest of a new space. And the "point of view" put forth by Marcola in relation to the 2006 PCC attacks on symbols of the state appears to support this interpretation:

> I think it all began with that revolt by [the prisoner named] Wenceslau. In my opinion, it began with Wenceslau, with the prisoners asking for help from the bandits on the outside. And then the thing started gaining uncontrollable proportions, precisely because there was no leader. Do you understand, sir? Because there was no person there who could say "stop" or "do this" and "do that." So, the thing became generalized. This is my own view of it. I may be wrong, do you understand? But that's how I see it, spilling out and escaping everyone's control, precisely because there was nothing to control it. It was really something.... One guy called from here, another called from over there, and yet another from another place. There were multiple telephone calls to various people who started in.... That's my opinion.... The impression left by the way it was done, by the way it began and then stopped, was that it was an orchestrated revolt. Only I guarantee you, sir, that it wasn't, and precisely because it was a generalized uprising.[25]

In the relationship between two prisoners, there also arise multiple intensities, including the attempt to "play psychologist" (*dar um psicológico*) and thus "invade the mind" (*invadir a mente*) of another so as to win a debate or influence someone as part of the work of producing consensus. And while a prisoner tries to invade someone's mind, he tries also to shield his own mind so as not to have it invaded. This play of possession and resistance spirals along in accordance with the appetites and desires of those involved in the struggle, and the end result is in great part a function of "disposition." Here a disposition is not simply an orientation but also an agentive welling up that orients. Brothers who are considered to be "without disposition" (*sem disposição*) are not usually respected by their peers or even by Cousins, who accuse them of lacking a "future" because they are soft and lazy and actually enjoy prison life (*gozam a cadeia*). So although, as I indicated in chapter 2, there are a variety of factors that play into how a Brother is judged by other inmates, judgments about a Brother's success are in the end evaluated in relation to desire, "appetites," and "dispositions."

The dynamic that emanates from variations in appetite and disposition bears remarkably little resemblance to more standard concepts of "*crime organizado.*" The role of the PCC, as we have seen, even though it includes baskets of strategies and projects, is permeated instead by chance and is made real and powerful by the dispositions of its participants, who make do in relation to that chance. There exists, however, a force that ensures that such an apparently fragile formation endures in its instability. This suggests that the PCC make take form as an exteriorized force capable of producing dispositions and unexpected associations.

CHAPTER FOUR

The Politics of Transcendence

> For me, you were, along with much else, also something like
> a window through which I could see the streets. I could not
> do that by myself.
> —FRANZ KAFKA, Letter to Oskar Pollak, September 6, 1903

Throughout this book, I have worked to understand the animating contradiction that the PCC belongs to no individual, but gains definitive form in relation to what individuals do. And the Command also takes on what I refer to as a transcendental form, or a life and function to which participants ascribe a particular durability and agency. Such an exteriorized, autonomous version of the PCC is what makes possible the group's presence, and the authorization of my work, in a space where there are no baptized Brothers. One such institution is the Fundação CASA, or São Paulo's infamous penal and rehabilitation facility for youthful offenders. The transcendental form of the PCC is also what made it possible for me to gain authorization for my research without turning to all participants or relying on the authority of a few atop some hierarchical structure. This is partly because messages (*salves*) put forth by the Towers are decoupled from their enunciators and passed across prison units in ways that grant them a certain impersonal character as they become the property of an autonomous PCC. Something similar takes place when the PCC begins to gain what participants come to see as its own discipline, or as one Brother put it earlier in this book, "Respect the Command and its discipline!"

Nonetheless, the Brothers do not hold onto the Command's discipline as though it were a thing or entity. Instead, they base their actions on their Command's discipline and serve as examples for other prisoners as to how one lives in accordance with that discipline. As I describe in chapter 2, because this discipline is not the property of any one of the participants in the PCC and is seen instead as independent of their actions and desires, when one Brother felt an urge to rip off the head of the fellow inmate I refer to as "Silas," he restrained himself out of respect for what he took to be the Command's impersonal discipline; or, in the Brother's words, because "Silas was getting a serious break [*pegando o maior axé*] from the Command." So, in order to control Silas, the Brother turned to the Towers, whose decisions are considered manifestations of the collective will.

Whether Brothers find themselves in CDPs, in penitentiaries, or in the Towers, their task is to instill in and make prisoners follow the ideas of the Command. But the fact that the existence of the discipline and the ideas of the Command depend on more than individual Brothers is helpful. Otherwise, prisoners might very well lean on Brothers in order to resolve any type of dispute.

What makes possible the theorization of the practices and politics at play in the Command is the resonance of desires, in their most varied expressions, on the part of bodies that mix together to run side by side (*correm lado-a-lado*) and in tune with one another. This running side by side, as opposed to simply alongside, means that an initiative, idea, action, or enunciation by one subject activates an entire imitative chain of responses and additions. The resulting braided, semiotic space of attunement, which is not without its chokepoints that may become nodes of resistance and adaptation, resonates among those who share the walk called life in a jail run by the PCC. Since this process and this enunciative space unfurl without claims to individual authorship or authority, it becomes resolutely public and collective. The walk becomes the Command. So even though the "discipline of the Command" never comes to the fore as an inflexible center of power but is instead predicated on articulations of prisoners' agentive force, it never belongs to a particular prisoner. On the contrary, the discipline always belongs to the Command. Thus, the PCC possesses an ideal, or a form of discipline that disciplines the very concept of discipline, which is capable of supporting and expanding on the actions of its participants.

If it is true that dispositions, as part of their varied reaches and intensities, nurture my interlocutors' actions, then other questions arise: What produces those dispositions? What leads thousands of people who typically do not know one another to participate in the same walk? A focus on interpersonal relations alone does not do much to clarify this issue since the relationships developed between participants are for the most part transitory and circumstantial. They do not suggest any stable or enduring bond among individuals. Thus, on the one hand, what permeates and passes through the bodies of the multitude are precisely the forces that make up the PCC. On the other hand, the Command, as an entity moved by the forces of its elements, is what maintains those bodies in harmony, side by side and mixed together. How, then, is such a formation able to arise as the product of those dispositions? What takes place so that a formation whose links are so fragile and composed as prisoners share a "walk" endures?

At issue in understanding the reach and coherency of the Command are the ways that we as social scientists work to define the PCC, an entity that becomes visible as an outside force that gives off the appearance of acting autonomously. Here, and rather than inventing some novel concept that might begin to describe the crystallizations so much a part of but not necessarily definitive of the Command, I prefer to rework a concept that has much in common with the PCC that I examine here. This is the issue of transcendence, or what I approach as the conditions of possibility for making claims about the world, and thus the deployment and construction of knowledge itself. An ethnography of the PCC that attends to the real details of the group's movements and development is thus also a wager on the possibility of novel anthropology. Such an anthropology might follow the PCC and turn on the possibility of reconceptualizing transcendental and "social" scientific knowledge claims, a project that unfolds here in sympathy with contemporary attempts to produce a postsocial social science as put forth by thinkers such as Bruno Latour, Gilles Deleuze and Felix Guattari, and anthropologist Eduardo Viveiros de Castro.[1]

Deleuze and Guattari remind us, in a discussion of their model of rhizomes and roots which is nonetheless not quite a model of distinct entities but rather of unexpected communication, that, "The important point is that the root-tree and canal-rhizome are not two opposed models: the first operates as a transcendent model and tracing, even if it engenders its own escapes; the second operates as an immanent process that overturns the model and outlines a map, even if it constitutes its own hierarchies, even if it gives rise to a despotic channel."[2]

Followed to its logical conclusion, this argument forces us to consider the possible existence of transcendence within immanence. Yet my point here is not about trying to conceive of the two in dualist terms but rather to understand their interpenetration and how the two tendencies interact to create or describe a special space with an important role in politics. It should be clear also that it is impossible to suggest that there is but one model for transcendence. In fact, transcendence has been debated by philosophers for centuries.[3] However, the version of transcendence and a transcendental concept usually criticized, and thus avoided, by "postsocial" anthropologists is that which relates to the Durkheimian concept of "society." The social as transcendental refers to a preexisting totality proposed by the individuals that make it up.[4] This is the version that I aim to twist in order to account for the PCC. Or, put another way, I seek to deform this type of transcendental claim by means of the interplay of native theories and anthropological repertories.

In arguing that there exists a certain type of transcendental claim in the dynamics of the PCC, I am not claiming that there is some explanatory process that arises from beyond the PCC, or my object of study. The issue is instead one of identifying a force that cannot be confused with the participants in a particular social formation but that is nonetheless responsible for their associations, movements, and dispositions even as it is produced by those elements. In performing such an analysis, we move close to the explanations put forth by Leibniz when he attributes to God the propulsive force of his monads. Yet what I propose in relation to the PCC is not really related to Leibniz's move. This is because even as I posit the existence of such an animating force, I describe its construction in detail. This leads me to envision transcendentals as products and producers of dispositions. But this form of transcendence is nonetheless capable of acting autonomously and independently of the dispositions that make it up, even as it exists thanks to the participants who produce it. And for this reason the present chapter is aimed at examining how a form of transcendence that functions as a producer of dispositions is capable of pulling people together in a sympathy that depends on the very forms taken by those transcendentals.

Deindividualization in the Service of Transcendence

Discipline and Punish, Michel Foucault's well-known work on prisons, suggests that the individual is not a pregiven, existing entity but rather an effect of the forms of power and knowledge characteristic of disciplinary societies that arose in the nineteenth century. For Foucault, to study the change-inducing effects of punishment means examining political technologies of the body and thus the emergence of an individualizing form of power that includes the careful production of obedient bodies as well as a series of knowledges that arise from and nourish such disciplinary practices. In this way, the individualization of punishment and the play of new, modern knowledge-producing disciplines aimed at the human gave rise to a new conception of the human body as a unity. The individual becomes neither a causal agent nor an explanation but rather an idea that arose at a specific historical moment as a result of mechanisms present in a variety of settings, including prisons—the individual "is no doubt the fictitious atom of an 'ideological' representation of society; but he is also a reality fabricated by this specific technology of power that I have called 'discipline.' . . . In fact, power produces; it produces reality; it produces domains of objects and rituals of truth."[5] From this perspective, the modern disciplinary regime, or prison, is a key place for such productive power.

Although we do not necessarily find ourselves today within the same disciplinary regime described by Foucault, individualizing projects are still an important part of prison life, and the influence of the individual permeates social science. But I am not interested in arguing about some sort of epistemic succession or in establishing correspondences between different historical formations. Such a project would lead me to examine in detail prison life and its apparatuses and effects. Instead, I have sought to draw attention away from institutions and their operators and focus instead on fields of struggle that make up prisons. Such a move does not focus on the issue of histories as much as it does on perspectives.

What interests me most is a consideration of how the fictional nature of the individual posited by Foucault permits us to take disciplinary practices as a starting point for specifying with greater clarity a series of phenomena that run contrary to the production of individuals. And I hope to do so even within, or in relation to, existing (and persistent) individualizing discourses. This supports a critique of the concept of the individual that draws on a description of "deindividualizing processes" that emerge from resistance to modern individualizing techniques. Quite a number of practices encouraged by the PCC make individualizing practices visible. Especially salient is the expression, uttered continually by Brothers, Cousins, and even visitors, that "we are together [alongside one another] and mixed up," or, in more idiomatic English, something a bit different from, but akin to, "we stand together as one" (*estamos juntos e misturados*). When I first heard this expression, I asked what it meant, and I was told, "It's like this. You know when you're more than simply together? When you're so close you mix, kind of like coffee and milk?" The phrase thus describes a situation in which it is unclear where one entity ends and another begins.

The boundary between prisoners and their wives is one place where a blurriness between two actors becomes visible. As I foreshadowed in the introduction, prisoners' partners must submit themselves to an array of demands, recommendations, and restrictions. Wives are advised not to attend events where they might attract the attention of men who do not know who their husbands are. This is because men who know their husbands, and especially those who know they are in prison, will adopt a respectful stance toward the women. And it is assumed that such respect will be an essential part of any context that includes ex-prisoners, since those men will be familiar with expected codes of conduct that give rise to mutual respect. This explains why I would often overhear women planning an outing saying things like, "There are going to be a bunch of Brothers there, so he'll probably let me go." What is at play here is not the woman herself but rather her relationship to the prisoner: Any violations of accepted codes of conduct are seen more as an affront to the woman's husband than to these women's ostensibly "sacred" status.[6] The practices that surround taboos directed at visitors are thus a relationship between Brothers and Cousins that is organized through, or around, the prisoner's wife.[7]

I experienced this type of relation during my fieldwork when I visited prisons with my male colleague Adalton Marques. It was fascinating to note how prisoners took care to avoid me so as not to offend my husband. On many occasions, messages directed to me were transmitted to my anthropological colleague, while I stood there listening. The use of such a "member of society" as a mediator was a solution to the impasses created by the gendered impositions associated with the Command's codes. And this suggested how my relationship to my colleague was of a fundamentally different order from my relationships to those men; or, put better, from those men's relationships to my husband. And yet my partnership with my colleague was never made into an issue. After all, our professional relationship was understood as foreign to regnant forms of prison sociality since it could not be fit into the prisoner-wife-prisoner triad.

Experiences such as these revealed a certain disaggregation of me as a subject. I never stopped being a "wife of a prisoner," but I was also a "student of society" and was disaggregated, differently at times, in relation to the relationship at play at a particular juncture. This disaggregation led me to experience a certain desubstantialization of the individual tied to a body in ways that led me to feel how that desubstantialization was produced: What I saw at play was not a singular individual, or Karina the researcher or Karina the wife of a prisoner, but the relations in which I participated or that crisscrossed me. This insight supports the arguments offered in chapter 3, since the prisoners' behavior was not rigidly prescribed but was adopted circumstantially. This required calculations, evaluations, and valuations between what was pulled apart or, put better, those phenomena that entered into relations with one another.

Equally interesting were the differences in perceptions that marked my colleague Adalton's and my own fieldwork experiences. Usually because of differences in gender, things that I failed to notice were nonetheless clear to Adalton, and vice versa. In fact, the gendered distinctions that permeated my fieldwork permitted me to make out deindividualizing tendencies present in the PCC's political work: While issues of gender disaggregated the individual, the resulting fragments began to mix into the collective. Thus, my experiences with Adalton made clear two processes—one that fragmented and another that mixed things up—that also came to blend into one another.

In chapter 2, I described how the addition of "Equality" to the PCC motto of "Peace, Justice, and Liberty" gave rise to a tension that has become constitutive of the PCC itself. With this switch, a series of mechanisms and strategies were put in place in an attempt to construct a "Command among equals" in ways that generated tensions that become clear when we observe the political dimensions so much a part of the PCC. We also saw how the activities undertaken by the Brothers inside prisons are linked intrinsically to demands or attributions of responsibility for the workings of the prison. And these are supposed to be undertaken in consonance with the ideal of equality, or without claiming any authority, superiority, or power over another. In this sense, the Brothers gain equality to the extent that they speak and do things for the Command, which is, in itself, over and above everyone else. In order to get rid of differences that emerge in the multiple spaces of prison life, participants in the PCC take advantage of mechanisms that tamp down any expression of individuality on the part of Brothers (whether they are acting as Housekeepers, Pilots, or Towers). "Individualities" cannot appear if the Brothers are to put into practice ideas like "no one is more than any other" or "one for all and all for one."

As I mentioned also earlier in this book, decisions cannot be undertaken by only one Brother since, as prisoners tend to claim, "decisions can't be isolated." This is why each prison always boasts more than one Pilot and why Brothers look to the Towers at important moments. This is a way of avoiding "isolated attitudes" that might indicate someone wants to be "more than the Command." But for those who participate in the PCC, the fact that Brothers and the Towers are not considered individual actors when they perform their duties conjures up the Command as a real formation. If, ideally, nobody can try to be more than one's Brothers within the Command, then a process of deindividualization is brought about on two fronts. On the one hand, it takes shape in the name of equality among prisoners, and, on the other hand, it comes into being in the name of the superiority of the Command. In the end, as prisoners say plainly, they are "all alongside one another, and blended tightly" (*juntos e misturados*).

In his testimony to Congress, Marcola pulverizes the individuals his questioners attempt to describe as the leaders of the PCC. He argues that the former leaders of the PCC were "repudiated" not by its current leaders but by "the rest of the prison population," or what he describes as "the penitentiary system." When, in a reference to the PCC as a group of people set off from the rest of the prison population, Marcola's questioner then asks whether this censure came from the group, Marcola responds, "No, because the group symbolizes the system since the system is a group. . . . Because what the group does is not just done at random. Everything the group does is in conversation with the system. Because the group favors the system. You can be sure of that, Sir."[8]

Marcola denied that he was in charge of changing the PCC leadership, since "the whole system repudiated that yellow uniform [they tried to make us wear]" while also affirming that there was no one who "decides who dies," since this is a decision made by the "prison population." Marcola attributes decisions, whether the prohibition of crack inside prison or the decision to unleash the May 2006 attacks on police, to the "system" and the "population." Such decisions are the result of consensus. Here there are no individuals, and there are no groups. What is present is a mixture.

I am not really interested in whether Marcola's statements were attempts at avoiding responsibility or incrimination. What is most important to the present discussion is the effects that such moves produce. Even if in his testimony Marcola is trying to avoid responsibility, he acts as one of the pieces of this process of deindividualization and depersonalization of decision-making. At the moment that the individual is removed in favor of the "system" or the "population," the question of leadership stops making sense. In fact, the Brothers claim that they do not lead but instead "support the fulfillment of the ideals of the Command." Acting in the name of the Party, they work as "operators" for the PCC, which in turn takes form as a force that is reified and that gains autonomy and superiority in relation to its producers. This reification becomes even more evident when we note that before the rise of the PCC, each prisoner was the only person responsible for his actions. Prisoners held property in jail, and they could exercise their power over others or dominate spaces in their own name. But today no initiatives can be taken except in the name of the PCC, with its authorization, and in accordance with its orientations. One does not look to persons for authorization but instead looks to the Command. Although there are of course people who operate this machine, they are necessarily autonomous.

This same relation is reflected in issues of property and ownership. Cells, which were once property of certain prisoners and as a result something that could be sold, are today conceived of as collective property. As Brothers are fond of saying, "Everything is ours, and nothing is ours" (*Tudo é nosso e nada é nosso*). Or, looked at slightly differently, if everything belongs to the system and the population, nothing is the property of the individual. Thus, all these processes of deindividualization are put into play by the possibility of drawing on the "ideals of the PCC," or the "discipline of the Command."

The addition of Equality to the PCC motto reinforced the Command's attempts to restrain robbery, extortion, rape and other types of aggression, or practices that express the power of one prisoner over another. This functions to guarantee the mixture produced by processes of deindividualization as well as to make real a certain crystallization of hierarchies. It means also that the PCC prohibited attempts to force repayment of moral and financial debts that occurred on the outside, in the *Mundão*. Many of my interlocutors interpreted this as a negative development, since the attempt to "keep peace among thieves" meant that some prisoners were relieved of certain responsibilities. In other words, one result of the attempt to guarantee peace was that certain acts that previously would have generated internal disputes now came to be accepted or at least ignored. For some prisoners, this meant that the

PCC became a "mother," a guardian of inmates, and thus a "factory that produces little brats" (*fábrica de moleques*).

Even though the PCC might be considered a "factory that produces little brats" when the Brother making such a claim is considered a stand-up guy (*firmeza*), looked at from a different perspective, that Brother might be considered "without a future" or "without vision" and the PCC as without fault. In certain cases, this becomes possible through individualization.[9] One example involves the post hoc attribution of misdeeds within the Party to the Command's founders. So, rather than arguing simply that the Command needed to be rethought, a number of those who came to play active roles after Geleião's demise as the earlier, more hierarchical PCC's leader began to single out earlier leaders as lacking in vision. One man who had been imprisoned for a number of years and had been baptized during Geleião's reign told me, "Those guys had no future. Thank god we were able to clean house and get rid of those rotten apples. Our new, renewed Command ["the Fifteen"] is much more than they ever were. The PCC never should have been in their hands."

According to Marcola, "People linked to that leadership team got drunk on their success. They ended up committing atrocities, even worse things than those they fought against.... It was an abuse of power." The exclusion of the old leaders, however, does not guarantee that today there are no more "vain" Brothers who "want to show off," "run the show," and "be more than the Command." So if equality leads to mixture, those who are not considered equals are no longer considered part of the "population" or "mixed in" with the rest. Instead, they are individualized and are declared personally responsible for their positions.

For my interlocutors, to follow the discipline of the Command is in no way an imposition, and it has nothing to do with obligations. It is simply something that goes with running side by side and finding oneself "within the same system." But to join up or enter into agreement and "close" (*fechar*) with the Command does not mean one necessarily joins up with every Brother. Many Brothers point out that there do exist other Brothers who do not fit in with the precepts of the Command. In this way, even in the face of dissensus between Brothers, the Command is never to blame. If things don't go well, the fault is not with the Party but with the Brothers who fail to represent the PCC correctly. As a result, even when faced with what might seem to be poorly managed PCC territory, those who are part of that node never stop "running side by side" with the Command.

If someone is not a "real man" (*sujeito homem*) and lacks disposition or *proceder*, it is not the Command's fault. The Command retains a bit of autonomy in relation to its adherents, who see it as a higher and, in some senses, superior force. This observation may contradict my earlier arguments and make the Command appear to exist independently of the Brothers. But that is precisely the contradiction at the center of this text: The PCC takes on the form of an autonomous entity independent of its Brothers even as their actions sustain it. Each of these Brothers considers himself responsible for the Command and argues that it is his responsibility to set an example because the Brothers are the Command. They are the voice of the Command, which speaks through them and thus depends on them in order to be heard. They are also the instruments that put the Command into action and secure its existence in space. In other words, there cannot be a Command without the Brothers. As a result, their activity cannot be denied or quashed. After all, the Command is only recognized as such by prisoners and only plays a role in those prisoners' and the guards' everyday actions if the Brothers successfully build up this relationship. This relationship *is* the PCC.

The success of the Command, then, is the result of an ongoing struggle to successfully manage the relationships between prisoners and the prison even though that activity is not usually recognized as emanating from those prisoners, its agents. In this sense, the fruits of success are gathered by the Command and not by the Brothers. The Command are not—and here my iconoclastic verb form is intentional—seen as people blessed with individuality and their own self-centered qualities. The Brothers are the PCC's operators, or something like an operator at a telephone company. As a result, the process of deindividualization takes place in the name of the construction of a superior entity. This building up of the PCC as a transcendental entity takes place through the deindividualization of its members. Thus, the PCC exists autonomously, or as something that cannot be boiled down to the sum of its membership even though it is produced by the Brothers. Even more specifically, the PCC is produced by the *mixing* of its members.

Nonetheless, we should not confuse the making of the PCC with the founding of the modern state and associated theories of sovereignty.[10] The advent of the modern state is coeval with the appearance of the individual and "society." So, in addition to offering up the conditions for the appearance of these figures, the existence of the state requires that both society and the individual be interdependent. And this state establishes a power that unravels from and is concentrated in the sovereign, who sits above his subjects. In the PCC, there is no sovereign and no subjects but rather only the collision of forces that arise immanently within the association itself. In this space, power is not hierarchized. The ligaments that hold together the PCC are unlike a social contract theorized by Hobbes, whereby individuals give up personal prerogatives to the state. And power can never be ascendant, since the PCC-as-transcendence is never really localizable or even capable of being touched. The Command exists only as the (de)individualization of those who are together as well as mixed. And since the Command is what pushes the process of deindvidualization, it is both a result of and a guarantee of its own existence. Thus, even though the Command gains a certain status or positioning over and beyond its members, it can never be dissociated from its producers. Here immanence and transcendence meet as well as mix.

"PCC" is the name of both a transcendent entity and a collectivity that does not permit individualizing processes within its structuring relations. More specifically, the PCC is based on a transcendence that is born as the effect of deindividualizing processes but which—and this will be the topic of the next section—also guarantee the persistence of the collective without territorial links or stable subjects or persons.

Transcendence as a Component of Deterritorialization

Since the existence of the PCC is conceived of independently of individual manifestations and is grafted onto the transcendental plane, it can also be conceived of as lacking any links to territory. This explains why the PCC can be present even in the absence of Brothers or defined physical territories, and even though conquest of territory and the attraction of new prisoners for baptism are among its goals. Insofar as the PCC represents a transcendental entity as a producer and catalyst for an incredibly varied array of desires, stable territorial links are unnecessary for the effective sharing of those desires. Thus, participants are free to pass through any spaces as long as they remain a part of the "walk" (*caminhada*). In support of these points, Brothers know one another only in relation to the extent that their destinations overlap, whether as a function of their activities in the world of crime (*correrias*), their neighborhoods, or because of their constant, painful movement between prison units.

Nonetheless, two Brothers who come out of the same neighborhood or serve time together may not know one another. This seems applicable to the case of Otávio, one of the Brothers who supported my research and with whom I lost contact after my husband was moved to another jail. Since Otávio was fundamental to my research, I tried to track him after my husband was transferred. I traveled to Otávio's home region and reached out to the Brothers there. Since he had been the Pilot for that region of the city, I was surprised when the first Brother with whom I talked claimed not to know him. Then, trying to be helpful, the Brother introduced me to two more Brothers:

> Hey, I need to follow the trail of Brother Otávio. He served time with my husband, but they ended up losing touch.
> Brother Otávio.... Damn, could that be him? Daniel, do you know Brother Otávio?
> Brother Otávio? Hmmmm.... I can't put a face to a name.
> Could it be that Brother Otávio, may he rest in peace, who blew up with that arms shipment?
> You're right. That's him! He's a big fat guy, full of tattoos, isn't he ma'am?

I didn't really know what Otávio looked like since when I spoke with prisoners I often made a habit of not asking individuals their names. I would only come to know their names subsequently, when my husband made a reference to one of them for a specific reason.

On the day I set out to find Otávio, the two Brothers I encountered seemed convinced they had identified the man I was looking for:

> Look, ma'am, he got killed doing a really crazy job on a boat.
> I heard something about heavy arms and then they exploded.
> But are you sure it's the same Brother?
> If it's Brother Otávio from [name of neighborhood omitted], then it can only be that guy!

On our next visiting day, I let my husband know about the death of Brother Otávio. He asked me if I was sure, and I answered, "Wasn't he heavy, with lots of tattoos?" My husband responded quickly, "No! That's not Brother Otávio. He's a little skinny guy!"

Even though Otávio had been a Pilot in their home neighborhood, the local Brothers seemed not to know him. Meanwhile, on another occasion, I mentioned his name in a small city 400 kilometers from his home, and the Brothers recognized him immediately and reported that it would be very difficult to find him since he had escaped from prison and was a wanted man. Thus, I never heard anything from him, and I have no idea whether he remains free or has passed away.

Something similar took place with Sister Maria, who, after we made some initial contacts, gave me her phone number and expressed interest in helping with my research. Ten days later, I tried to contact her again. The person who answered the phone told me that the number I had dialed no longer belonged to the woman I sought to contact. Yet loss of contact is not simply a function of things like phones being cut off. Sonia, a sister-in-law (*cunhada*), or like me the wife of a prisoner (who served as a Tower), and someone who had accompanied me on the pilgrimage to Brasilia, gave me both her landline and cell phone numbers. We spoke a few times by phone and agreed to meet, but after a few frustrated attempts caused by our busy schedules, I found that both her devices had been cut off. Two different recordings informed me that the numbers did not exist.

These missed opportunities and failed meetings are as common as unexpected meetings in the universe of the PCC. When a prisoner I call "Sebastião" left prison, he moved with his family to a city in the interior of Sao Paulo State. He told me that he was walking down the street in his new neighborhood and heard "Salve" followed by his nickname and realized he had just been hailed by someone using his prison moniker. No one out in the wide world beyond prison walls knew that he went by that name. The man who had recognized him was Bernardo, with whom he had served time in the state capital and who had traveled to the countryside to wait for a "thousand degree problem"—or the fallout from a crime—to die down. Bernardo and Sebastião exchanged pleasantries and caught up for a bit, never to see one another again. Such stories are extremely common in the universe of the PCC.

To add to this portrait, after my husband was released and we bumped into people I knew in "the street," I began to learn that some of them had served time with my husband and that some of them even had links to the Command. But I had never learned of such potential ties. The linkages between us had never been activated because those people had no idea I was a prisoner's "visitor" and there was no reason to relate to me on those terms.

Here we encounter situations in which people who know one another lose all contact, in which former inmates who had lost contact find one another by chance, in which Brothers lack knowledge of fellow Brothers whose biographies indicate they should know them, and in which Brothers know other Brothers they never imagined they would know but never needed to recognize as Brothers because the situation did not demand it. It's as if a line—at one moment coupled to another (when mixed with) and at another moment uncoupled (when individualized)—lost its way and disappeared from sight without leaving a trace. And yet, often and without any apparent explanation or motive, such lines return and move adjacent to one another, braid, or cross at some distant future point.

What permits people who live in different places and who often do not know one another to come into contact is the PCC as a transcendental organization. This transcendence, established by those who participate in it, guarantees the presence of the PCC. This occurs even in places such as the CDP I described in the previous chapter that was run by a rival command and was "taken" by recently transferred prisoners who identified with the Command but were not baptized Brothers, where there are no official "members" present. The Command had not been present previously in that prison, but the actions of prisoners who "won the jail" for the PCC activated and actualized the PCC's transcendental qualities.[11]

My interpretations are supported by the ways in which the unbaptized prisoners from a PCC-controlled facility who had "won" the new jail for the Command reflected on their actions during their first night in their bunks. As they told it to me:

It was like this. Check it out: We got there and there was a boatload of things [prisoners attached to a rival command] in there. Then the shit hit the fan. We got into their minds and we got rid of the things. But the "[big] boys" [members of the rival command] were there too, it's just that they were in segregation at the time. Think about that. . . . The whole cell block and all its residents there, open before us. Bunch of little brats, first-offenders in there. No problem. No balls at all. They [prisoners already on the cell block] had no Housekeepers. So they grabbed the guards and said, "Hey, put us back in there so we can talk with the boys [new arrivals]." So the guards put a bunch of first-timers, young kids, with us again, out there in the first pavilion. They had no idea how to debate; they didn't know shit! So what happened? At night we started in, communicating across the cells:

Salve [hail].

Salve!

We've gotta set up Housekeeping.

Yeah, you see what went down [when the new arrivals got off the trolley]?

That's it! We saw it!

Have you seen Luiz?

Hey, Luiz, what's up? Here comes a message!

Speak!

Salve, Thief!

What do you have to say?

Luiz, we've gotta see about this housekeeping stuff.

What stuff?

Housekeeping. We've gotta set up housekeeping. The guys are saying we need you for housekeeping here!

Not me!

And then the guys go jumping around, talking about each candidate.

We're gonna resolve this tomorrow!

I asked my interlocutor whether and why anyone would agree to join Housekeeping in the newly taken unit. "The guys didn't want to, but he ended up going for it. Think about it: You lose the prison for the Command?" The next day, the new prisoners approached the guards as they distributed breakfast and claimed that no food could be passed out until they completed the *rapa*, or initial cleansing of the pavilion. To do so, they needed to set up a Housekeeping squad, or the leaders who would make sure that their area of the jail was clean before the arrival of any food. And once the new prisoners set up their PCC, they invoked the PCC to argue to the guards that their special cell should be left open all day long. They did this by waiting until the guard came by to lock them in after breakfast. Luiz approached him:

Hey, leave this thing open. . . . Housekeeping has to be on top of everything. . . . Because when we got here there was a shitload of "things" [non-PCC prisoners, or *coisas*] around, right? So you're gonna leave this thing open so we can keep an eye on who you put in here with us, Sir. Imagine what will happen if you put a

busload of things in here with us? We don't know either. And
we'll have to settle it with the knife. So we need to be up front
here and keep an eye on who is who here in this jail, boss. . . .
This prison belongs to the Command.
No, I'm not leaving it open.

The guard took them to see the chief disciplinary officer. There, Luiz
and Adolfo said to him:

Sir, we've been locked up now for a short time in here, in your
jail. At the very least the housekeeping cell needs to be kept
open because if you lock us, who knows, maybe you'll put us back
on the trolley and send us away. If you shut us in and then put us
on the bus it's gonna get real bad, trust us. We've already got a
group chosen to back us up if that happens. And they're gonna
take the same position we do.
No, don't worry. What I want is cooperation. I just don't want any
rebellions, stuff like that.
So then open up that space for us. Because when you drop someone
in here we need to know who they are, right? If he's a first-timer
we'll give them instructions. We'll need to know their criminal
records, right? If you put a guy in here and we find out he's a
rapist, we'll kill him!

Through this action, the prisoners were able to install the Housekeepers
and keep their cell open so the squad could engage in the sort of political work that emanates from and supports the Command. Here the existence of the PCC as a transcendent force made it possible for a whole
series of actions to come to fruition and thus to turn the new prison
into a PCC territory that nonetheless lacked Brothers.

In the eyes of my interlocutors, the PCC is not located in the people
who participate in its actions or populate specific territories. It is above
them, and their linkage to or articulation with that higher force is what
makes possible the ties that bind the prison population. As they state
frequently, "The Command is above all else, and we are here together and
mixed up."[12] The existence of political positions that do not depend on
the presence or charisma of specific people contributes to the durability
of the PCC in the face of the intensity of life in prison, in impoverished
neighborhoods, and as part of the Crime. Prisoners are subject to, and
insert themselves into, these flows for a variety of reasons. They may find

themselves hustled onto buses or may become highly mobile as a means of protecting themselves in a world of crime characterized by police persecution or the constant movement necessary to search for new targets of opportunity. In this context, it seems clear that the transcendence or transcendentalism discussed here is a component of a deterritorializing process because it makes life possible in the face of the frequent need to abandon territory on the part of people who enter into a "contract with Crime" (*um compromisso com o Crime*). This agreement requires invisibility, of "not being seen so as not to be remembered" and so as not to be investigated or captured.

In the eyes of the Brothers, identity documents, working papers, and jobs are appropriate to the lives of "Joe Citizen" but not necessarily their own ways of being. This is why one former inmate, spotted following release in his new "on the books" job when an old cellmate passed by, asked his friend not to tell anyone about his new status. "It's because I don't want to be pulled through all that bile again," he exclaimed. Another ex-prisoner caught in a similar position pretended not to recognize the person who noticed him. Such incidents highlight the extent to which it is frowned on for someone from the world of crime to establish links to the System (*o Sistema*). This is such a powerful ethos that, upon baptism, Brothers must say that they are establishing a covenant with "the Crime" (*o Crime*). This Crime lies outside of society in a relationship that underscores how citizens who inhabit "society" march to a different beat because they do not participate in the system of relations that constitutes the PCC.

In spite of the importance of deterritorialization to participation in the world of crime, entrance into the life does not mean that those involved give up all links to territories. Nonetheless, it is often necessary to be ready to flee at a moment's notice. So it is not always wise or convenient to set down roots or establish strong ties. Even one's *quebrada*, or home neighborhood, and thus a nexus of different types of affiliations, may need to be abandoned in spite of the fact that the person involved may intend to return someday. As the Brothers told me, if a person is involved in the race, then he needs to run, take what he can, and get out quickly (*vazar*). He cannot remain in place. The participant in the Crime needs to be a nomad in relation to territory, as well as personal relations and material possessions. But that nomad can never forget about his covenant with the Crime.

Those who participate in the collectivity I map crisscross the territories through which they pass. At times, they do so imperceptibly, whereas at other times they leave enormous scars. Their tracks melt away as they move forward. Often they meet up again. But even if this does not happen—reencounters are never guaranteed, after all—they rely on the support provided by the transcendental form of the PCC, which keeps them in tune with one another, alongside one another, and even mixed together. And it is this specific form of linkage that permits enormous mobility without the dissolution of the collectivity.

Conclusion

> I didn't paint the war, because I am not that kind of painter that
> goes like a photographer in search of a subject. But there's no
> doubt that the war exists in the paintings that I did.
>
> —PABLO PICASSO

Over the course of this book, I have sought to describe how the PCC
works. I began with its composition and means of occupying territory.
This illustrated how, largely because the bodies that populate it are
not tied statically to defined political functions as is typical of state institutions, the PCC's territorial disposition is tied intimately to the
Command's mutating composition and shape. And because these relations strike me as so completely transitory, or circumstantially occupied
through micropolitics such as those described by Pierre Clastres (2003)
in another context, I have treated them as "political positions." This
confers on the participants in the PCC the possibility of passing through
territories without establishing any link that might tie them definitively
to that territory. Hence, under certain circumstances, a first offender may
become a resident. At other moments, the first offender in one prison
might be dubbed a resident in another, as the situation demands. And
someone who is a Pilot today might lose that stamp of approval tomorrow. Even more indicative of how the Command functions, we have
seen how there may be no Brothers in a jail that belongs to the PCC. To
this I add that in the PCC today there exist Towers without the territorial units—or prisons—that are also referred to as "Towers." And a prison
that is considered a Tower today may fall in status and lose that role.
When such an alteration takes place, the prisoners who serve as Towers
stop exercising their roles as Towers even though they may come to occupy such a position again at a later date.

A synchronic analysis might find the PCC animated by a power that
comes down from above. In such a portrait, the Towers would stand
atop a hierarchical structure and the Pilots, just below them, would help
out. Next would come the Housekeepers and, eventually, the prison
"population." To be fair, such an approach to the Brotherhood would
not be completely incorrect if the image it produced were not frozen, if

we were not working to understand a movement put together by protagonists who are in the midst of living and performing their "walks" (*caminhadas*). Indeed, if one is to understand the PCC, one cannot cast off this constitutive fluidity in the face of what takes on the appearance of hierarchy. The Command is in flux. It is circumstantial, transitory, situational, and in motion. And thus it can be understood only diachronically, or, even better, as an event.

In this book, I have pulled together the diverse planes from which politics become operationalized in and by the PCC. The planes possess different intensities and velocities. At times, they act as lines of flight in the face of other lines, those along which prisoners move so intensely. The ideal of equality crosses all these planes and might be understood as a major factor in keeping the PCC in motion, in part because it grants participants a certain liberty in manifesting their desires. This is because it removes from relationships put together at moments of crisis or lack of liberty precisely those obligations that might limit creativity. Hence, a commitment to avoiding any sort of weakening of the central ideal of equality motivates practices that ensure ferocious resistance to any new situation in which a few inmates might curtail the actions, and freedom, of fellow prisoners. This gives rise to a powerful, ongoing deferral of authority. Nonetheless, and in intimate association with this deferral of the closure that limits freedom, there arise mechanisms that blur those differences that never cease to boil over.

One mechanism involves the deindividualization of decisions, since decisions, as I described in chapter 2, "cannot be isolated" as belonging to or authored by specific persons. Here we see a certain type of slippage at work. This involves a separation of political positions and the people who occupy them, or recourse to a technique to compensate for the expressions of difference that never cease to appear. The importance of distinguishing the office from the person becomes especially clear when decisions are attributed to Towers or to the Command, rather than to a particular Brother. In these cases, the ascriptions of authority make clear the extent to which decisions emanate not from individual initiatives but from collective manifestations of the Command made public and operational through communiqués (*salves*). We might thus argue that the Brothers work as "operators" for a PCC that is greater than they are and that mirrors their actions but is nonetheless much more than a collection of individuals.

One important effect of the mechanisms examined throughout this book involves the production of a particular type of power that should not be confused with the actions of participants in the PCC and that is imbued with a certain autonomy that I have come to refer to as "transcendence." Even though this transcendence is produced in immanence, or as a part of the PCC, it is nonetheless what maintains the collectivity. This is because such a transcendence calls forth and joins all participants by linking them to an autonomous—hence my recourse to the term "transcendent" or even "transcendental"—figure, apparently free of interpersonal ties and unrelated to stable territories. Nonetheless, transcendence is possible, and endures, only when nourished continuously by the molecular forces that work incessantly in its production.

Indeed, throughout this book, I have detailed multiple references to the Command that present it as a force detached from any individuality. We have encountered situations that lead back to a PCC capable of acting autonomously and independently of the individual men who hold the Party's political positions. And at each juncture that permits a partial glimpse of the dotted lines and fragmented images that make up the PCC's immanence, we have also come across powerful references to the transcendent PCC. Thus, it seems that the Command's immanence works only to the extent that it wards off its transcendental forms. Concomitantly, the PCC-as-transcendence exists only because that transcendental identity base is an immanence that guarantees its counterpart. The one does not just create the other. Instead, the immanent and the transcendent may each come to function like the other owing to the intensities of the ways they call out, soliciting one another mutually and incessantly.

The transcendence so important to the Command brings about processes of de-individualization even as it arises from those processes. In chapter 2, we saw clearly how, when one prisoner makes demands of another or claims an ability to correct his peer, all decisions related to those pressures are depersonalized in the name of the discipline associated with the Command. This method deindividualizes the transcendental— here manifested as a crystallized hierarchy that "belongs to" or characterizes a group and would place one Brother in a position of power over another—as a potential, but unrealized, state. The dynamic is the result of antistatist mechanisms activated by the force of the equality so central to PCC ideals.

The state to which I refer here is not a simple bureaucracy or even the "System" (o Sistema) that the PCC opposes in its "war against the police." It is instead the potential interiorization of the forms of knowledge—the prejudices—and practices of the state, or the risk of adopting for oneself precisely what the addition of "Equality" to the PCC slogan was designed to ward off. This emphasis on equality serves to counter those practices that would obscure or deny creative, immanent impulses. This is precisely what the adoption of equality by the Command was intended to avoid. Nonetheless, the PCC remains at risk of adopting the state form. Although attempts by the PCC to consolidate a counter-state formation reminiscent of the practices among indigenous peoples documented by French ethnologist Pierre Clastres (2003) are clear, the borders between the Brazilian state and the Brotherhood that controls São Paulo's prisons are porous. Incursions by one form into the other are constant, and the seeds of the state form never cease to sprout within the PCC. At the same time, new mechanisms for inhibiting their rise are created. This generates a constant and curious tension between a state that is ready to grow within the PCC and that collectivity's resistance to that state that I approach, building on Clastres (2003), as a means of thinking through and facing particular forms of rationality, superorganic forms, and hierarchies. One facet of this engagement involves the care dedicated to choosing the Cousins who are invited to undergo baptism. After all, the fight against the exterior, empirically apparent state as well as the entailments of that state that grow within, in a mimicry of the external state, depends on the political capacities of the new Brother.

Although the "primitive" societies engaged by Clastres may not have known the modern nation-state intimately, prisoners in São Paulo know this entity all too well. After all, "One is never deeper in the state than when one is in a prison."[1] And we should not forget that, in its earlier, hierarchical manifestations, the PCC lived in this "interior state," particularly under the leadership of Geleião. The form of transcendence that took root at that moment lacked its immanent counterpart, and the regime established by Geleião never relied on the counter-state for its existence. Perhaps this is why it depended so heavily on a hierarchical rigidity.

Participants in the PCC are well aware of the effects of the internalization of the state form. This is apparent in the following passage extracted from the primer that I discussed in chapter 2, which circulated across São Paulo's prisons: "Where there is domination there will always be struggles for liberty. Where there is human exploitation there will always exist contests to end that oppression. Where there are human rights violations, there will always be resistance, in the name of dignity."

The primer explains rather well why the PCC arduously elaborates mechanisms to rid itself of a state form that Deleuze and Guattari, in their elaboration of Clastres's work, understand as bundles of state- and counter-state-like forces that coexist in conflict. The Command was born as a poor imitation of the state, in that case a state composed of actual institutions and empirically available processes. Yet the dissolution of the pyramid-like structure promoted by Marcola and the addition of equality to its basic ideals generated a change in the assemblage that once pushed the PCC to take shape as a "parallel power," or by mimicking the state structure all too perfectly. The destruction of that old regime has led to a new regime that contains an internalized counter-state. Nonetheless, and to complicate things, it has become clear also that even as the PCC manifests itself against the state today, it continues to operate in relation to forces that simplify and overdetermine. But these forces are no longer concrete dams but rather flows that spew out lines of flight and accelerate their movements. After all, the specificity of the formation put in place by the PCC's new regime lies in its reliance on immanence, and the guarantee that this state form confers a certain immanence on the existing counter-state. In other words, at the same time that the transcendental PCC is the product of and the producer of desires, it also constitutes a form of power that shines down on its participants, who, in turn, overdetermine these relations.

To a certain extent, we have not escaped a situation in which the state serves as a tonic against the state. But even this troubling relationship is capable of gaining velocity in order to inscribe a singularity in the PCC. For the Command, this involves holding onto, and producing and being produced from, a transcendence or transcendental that is not cut off from immanence. Neither is anterior to the other. On the contrary, each functions in relation to the other. It is as if everything has come together. And everything stands together, as one.

Author's Afterword to the English-Language Edition

In 2012, the state of São Paulo became the scene of what soon came to be called a "wave of violence." Indeed, homicide rates, which had been dropping steadily over the previous decade, increased by 40 percent relative to 2011, with authorities in the capital city registering 1,495 of the state's 4,836 total murders. Among the dead were 111 police officers and 19 prison guards.[1] In an attempt to explain, or at least comment on, what was happening, the press looked swiftly to a series of experts who might provide reasons for the upward trend in homicide rates. These analysts offered an array of explanations, with the majority pointing to a dispute between police forces and the PCC.

The wave of violence rose to new heights while I was in the midst of a new phase of fieldwork related to the PCC. This research required that I pass through regions of São Paulo and its working-class suburbs that commentators were identifying as sites of confrontation between forces of the state and those associated with Crime. Yet what I witnessed was so disparate, so filled with heterogeneous and at times mystifying events and relations, that I often found myself unprepared to offer any unified analysis of what was taking place around me. This afterword is an attempt to illustrate the scene then unfolding in my home state and its capital city while also helping the reader understand better how the PCC's motile politics and forms of becoming play out to make the Command present. I present five ethnographic scenes, all stitched together on the basis of fieldwork experiences and snippets of news reports from 2011 and 2012. I then close this book by engaging this newer material as part of an attempt to review certain key points from previous chapters while also offering a slight extension of that analysis. In this final section, then, I am most interested in how my newer experiences and observations may support additional more detailed and thus more insightful perspectives on the constitutive engagements between the PCC and the Brazilian state and its scientific apparatuses and knowledge.

First Scene: Police Stories

I began my research in a city near the coast of São Paulo State in December 2011. There I conducted sporadic visits to different locales in an attempt to get to know the Thieves (*ladrões*) who belonged to, and made up, a specific neighborhood or region's Crime. My goal was to negotiate with the Thieves in order to see whether it would be possible to begin a fieldwork project there that would shift my focus more toward the actions of the PCC outside prison walls.

But, by April 2012, the local press had begun to raise an alarm about a wave of violence that was supposedly cresting in this particular region, since, "on the 10th of this month, military policeman Rui Gonzaga Siqueira, age 46, was shot to death while moonlighting as a security officer in the Jardim Castelo neighborhood. After the officer's death five residents of the surrounding region, or the Northwest Zone . . . were killed by hooded men on motorcycles or in cars with tinted windows. . . . According to detectives, the five assassinations may have been part of some sort of retaliation for the death of the police officer."[2]

However, the executions did not cease. The media began to comment regularly on homicides in the region, focusing especially on the deaths of local funk musicians.[3] Nonetheless, and in spite of the intensity of the news reports, the rhythms of everyday life did not change radically in the impoverished neighborhoods in which Brothers live and work (*quebradas*). These were precisely the sites in which I conducted, or sought to conduct, ethnography. In fact, around the time of the outset of the news coverage of the wave of violence, I found myself speaking with a PCC Brother I will call "Edvaldo." One of my fellow researchers commented on the news reports that had begun to appear each day, asking, "So, what's up with all this death?" Edvaldo smiled as my companion barked out, "It's the police doing the killing! Isn't it?" In response, Edvaldo looked around at the group and commented, "Well, if you're charging it to the police account then, by all means, it's all cool."

Second Scene: The Communiqué (*Salve*) Has Come Down!

In July 2012, news reports began to coalesce into a relatively unified narrative about a wave of violence that had supposedly begun its movement across the state of São Paulo in mid-June even though, as illustrated in the first scene, by April the same media outlets had already

begun referring to a "wave of violence" associated with a struggle between the PCC and the police:

> The tally of assaults that make up the wave of violence that has
> hit São Paulo over the last 20 days does not stop rising: As of this
> Tuesday afternoon 17 buses were burned in different parts of the
> state and 11 police bases—10 of them belonging to the military
> police and the last a unit housing Municipal Guards [Guarda Civil
> Municipal]—were attacked with small arms fire. . . . Ongoing
> investigations have not ruled out the possibility that these assaults
> represent attempts by criminal factions of the PCC (Primeiro
> Comando da Capital) to avenge a May military police action against
> the group that left six supposed members dead, one whose body
> bore clear signs of torture and another shot at point-blank range.
> The police are also considering the possibility that the attacks are
> payback for the transfer of a PCC leader to a new penitentiary.[4]

New but related versions of this story began to appear daily, lamenting
an ongoing "wave of violence" and presenting numbers that, even
though they often diverged wildly, gestured at the gravity of what was
taking place. And even though the news reports never offered a precise—
or even collectively agreed on—date for the beginning of the purported
wave, all sought to count up "losses" attributable to the struggle while
suggesting that the PCC authored the attacks. The situation troubled me,
and I thought briefly about giving up this phase of research. But I decided to continue on, and I planned to begin ethnography in the *quebrada*
on July 14. I would move into a small house in the community and spend
several months in this urban region that, over the course of my nearly
daily visits before my intended move-in date, continued in its normal
everyday rhythms.

Later, as I read through the figures reported by the press, I noted that
television news reports were claiming that on that July 14 the PCC had
begun an offensive directed at São Paulo's police institutions. But I
know that the images exhibited to back up such claims on television were
older, stock footage. They were not from the fourteenth. Something
seemed wrong with the account, its origin stories, and its fundamental
unity. So I was a bit surprised when I telephoned the person who had
agreed to meet me when I got to the *quebrada*. Her immediate response
when she heard my voice was, "Don't come! Don't do it! You can't come.
Trouble's here!

Confused, I asked, "What do you mean? Is it what I'm seeing on TV right now?" She elaborated, "Yeah, that's it; the communiqué [from the PCC] has come down. Things are gonna get hot!"

Still perplexed, I pressed, "But what's happening is not something new. It's been going on for a few days, right?"

To this, the woman replied, "No, it's not just that. What I mean is that it's arrived here. It's not just the television now. It's that, well, I've learned something about what's happening here. The communiqué [*salve*] has come down!"

Third Scene: Fifteen Days of Exception

As news reports about the wave of violence continued daily, the number of attacks and the number of victims attributed to the PCC grew also. However, facing deadlines, I found it frustrating to sit around waiting while listening to official reports about what was going on in my intended field site. This, together with my interlocutor's refusal to receive me as planned, convinced me to set out in search of a new research site. Luckily, a friend soon introduced me around in another *quebrada*. There residents welcomed me, and began to support my project, with great interest. During initial discussions of my goals and research undertakings with the Thieves active in the region (*a correria*), and thus either participating in or associated in some way with the PCC, I began to ask about the attacks that, as reported by the press, appeared to be continuing without a break. One man responded as follows:

AUTHOR: And the communiqué authorizing the attacks?
MAN: It's no longer in vigor.
AUTHOR: But did the communiqué [*salve*] ever actually come down?
MAN: It did, but it's over. It lasted only fifteen days.[5]

Fourth Scene: The Brothers Disappeared

In yet another *quebrada*, I found myself making small talk with a member of the *correria* who was nonetheless not a full Brother. I commented to the man, "It seems like the communiqué about the attacks has made it down here." His response was, "Yeah, but you see, I think the communiqué made it only as far as 'X' *quebrada*—it never made it here." This left me musing about the source of the communiqué, as well as the details of its transmission and path. But I soon realized how confusing any answer might be, especially in an age of cell phones. So I continued the conversation:

AUTHOR: You mean the communiqué never arrived here?
MAN: Ah, not quite: Before it arrived the Brothers disappeared. They knew that it would get here, sooner or later. And they knew it'd already gotten to "X" *quebrada*. So they flew the coop.

Two months later, with the Brothers still missing in action, and apparently without ever having permitted the message to be passed on, the press reported that a police officer had been killed in the *quebrada* in which I had conducted the interview.

Fifth Scene: It's Personal

At the end of May 2012, newspaper headlines blared, "The Special ROTA Patrol Kills 6; Military Police Jailed, Suspects in Executions."[6] Then, in late June, newspapers reported that police officers had been killed in the same region: "Three military policemen were shot to death in the eastern region of the state capital over the last seven days.... Sources suspect that the three deaths were perpetrated by the criminal faction known as the PCC in retaliation for the May police operation, also in eastern São Paulo, that resulted in the death of six men."[7]

Two months later, I learned that a man I knew from the same neighborhood would soon be released from prison. When we met, I asked him to comment on the violence that had taken place in his home *quebrada*:

So, listen up doctor [*doutora*]![8] I got there and I asked, "What happened, what sort of shit came down here when the guys got killed?" They told me that the police were already shooting when they rolled up. It was nuts....
But I was told that there was a communiqué put out about killing police.
No, that's not from the Command. No way. There was no communiqué. It was some guy, some individual, who decided to take his pound of flesh. It's a personal thing, something invented by a guy who thinks he's got it right, that he's the correct one, because he's disgusted by the police. The police are killing like crazy, *doutora*.

But they told me that the communiqué arrived as part of a network
that passes through neighborhood (*quebrada*) X, and then
neighborhood Y.

Yeah, but it never got here. No way.

HERE WE COME face-to-face with an unfolding historical trajectory
marked by deaths chalked up to the police, murders tied to the PCC in
communities in which the Command's communiqués seem to have failed
to have been delivered, Brothers who flee in the face of a possible message from the Towers, and a communiqué that arrived only after a
month-long delay or only after it had expired. In the face of these five
scenes, which stand as illustrative, communicative events within the
present text, it becomes increasingly difficult to put forth a nuanced
ethnographic explanation. This difficulty is related to the national debate about the PCC that even today still presents those events as part of
a war between two cohesive forces or monolithic entities. Indeed, in
2012, after completing the first, Brazilian edition of *Sharing This Walk*
(Juntos e misturado), I found it extremely difficult to piece together in any
definitively sense-making way the fragments of information to which I
was privy during the so-called wave of violence. As had been the case
years earlier when I sought to put together the often alienating as well as
seemingly contradictory experiences of visiting my husband in prison, I
found it difficult to weave into a coherent narrative the information I
had collected over the course of the investigations begun as part of the
follow-up project after the publication of the Brazilian edition of *Shar-*
ing This Walk. At the core of my difficulties lay the fact that I had gathered
a disparate array of data, and much of my information clashed rather con-
cretely and directly. Such a situation is not unknown in anthropology,
or in any investigation. But as I have been arguing since the introduction
to this book, the contradictory mess of information made a special sort
of sense in relation to the PCC.

My first move in the attempt to make sense of things was to make clear
to myself that the principal issue at play was not the simple claim that
the Brothers with whom I spoke lacked detailed knowledge of what was
going on. My fieldwork suggests not only that they did know what was
happening but also that they were precisely the actors who lived out
what afterwards became headlines and news reports. In other words,
and as illustrated by the following police exchange transcribed and pub-

lished in a São Paulo newspaper, they put in motion and produced what would take place:

CIVIL POLICE OFFICER: Explain, from the beginning, the "walk" [the missions you were supposed to complete].[9]

FAT LEO: The *salve* [order] came down to me. I knew already that there was a communiqué circulating. I was aware of it. I had received it and passed it on so the Brothers could carry it out [to kill others]. The communiqué was related to the injustices that were going on since the ROTA military police patrols began to increase their killing and planting of evidence so as to charge us with crimes. So the path we're involved in now involves, as its goal, knocking off a military policeman in every one of the microregions under our control.

CIVIL POLICE OFFICER: What was the timeframe you were given to execute the police officers?

FAT LEO: It was ten days. But then the communiqué was cancelled because the guys were killing off too many innocent people. There was even a police officer who worked in the bureaucracy, in the administration, who was killed. They shot into a vehicle and he got hit. That wasn't supposed to happen.

CIVIL POLICE OFFICER: So what was supposed to take place? What was your mission?

FAT LEO: That wasn't the goal. Our idea was to react to the ROTA Unit's injustice. We weren't out to avenge isolated errors or to attack moonlighting cops. Our struggle was about getting to the ROTA. We weren't after police working in station houses, guys trying to earn a little extra cash on their days off, or even any old uniformed military police officer.

CIVIL POLICE OFFICER: When you go talking [on the telephone, which was bugged] about how the time period is expiring and that you're gonna be held to your quota and you go and suggest, "let's go get any little guy out there. . . ."

FAT LEO: I remember that plan, but I wasn't the one who said that! That concern came to me and I even stopped it. I spoke, but not the way you're making it out, no way.

CIVIL POLICE OFFICER: Wasn't it the plan that the Brothers in each *quebrada* would kill a police officer?

FAT LEO: No. I was part of the correct communiqué. That's what came down to us. That was the one.[10]

This dialogue can be read alongside multiple—perhaps thousands—of similar communications in São Paulo in 2012. Read in relation to those communications, it reinforces much of what appeared in those other reports published during the same time period. Nonetheless, among the claims it would seem to support, there emerges one slightly different interpretation.

Even though the press—and, in case it is not clear in the preceding transcription, the police—extracted from Fat Leo a confession about the lack of a PCC command structure, it also made clear that the witness was conscious and self-assured in his actions. For Fat Leo, the confusion surrounding the communiqué was not some result of a lack of command or direction. It pointed instead at the circulation of divergent ideas. In fact, there do not appear to have been holes or contradictions in the information passed on through this man interrogated by the police. Such a lack would make sense only in light of a search for cohesive wholes. But the Thieves who walk (*caminham*) with the PCC do not live or work within that type of totality. Rather, they make up a *movement*.

Movement

In contradistinction to the police interrogators of Fat Leo, who focused in on a "mission" that was supposed to have been transmitted through a communiqué, those who run with, and alongside, the PCC often refer to it as a "movement." As a movement that lacks a defined origin or endpoints, the PCC does not fit easily into specific, delimited spaces or temporal intervals. Hence, the PCC-as-movement is never limited to the trajectories traced out or encouraged by particular people, not even the Brothers themselves. It is composed instead by the simultaneous crossing of several movements. These traverse territories, times, and people in a motility that erases and leaves behind, even as it establishes powerful traces. This is one result of a PCC composed of disparate phenomena that do not reveal any definitive corresponding identities. Or, put slightly differently, people and things do not come together— all together—in order to take up shared, definitive paths in realizing a common goal or participating in a cohesive mission. Far from making up a monolithic unit, the movement called the PCC does not behave solely like the type of movement I am working to describe here since it is also constituted by various "minor" movements. These promise to provide the movement called the PCC with diverse shapes, calibrating resources, velocities, and pathways.

It should not be entirely surprising that over the course of researching and writing this book I was never able to see in their entirety any of the movements I seek to describe here. In spite of all my struggles to put together ways of accompanying different or even divergent strands, I was never able to get to them fully. It really did not matter how and where I positioned myself. The feeling that I had missed some part of the story or that what I had was partial and badly told because I possessed only partial data arising from poorly executed research dogged me. This disquiet pushed me to search out other modes of ethnography and to develop iconoclastic ways of sensing my field site. But rather than filling in lacunae and calming my fears, the data that arose from these sites and novel methods only increased the confusing panoply of partially perceived movements arising from my engagement with the PCC, its settings, and its effects. But if this was, at least initially, a motive for despair, over the course of writing and continuing with the research I began to understand that, like me, my interlocutors did not understand the totality of their movement.

In the view of each of the Brothers with whom I conversed, the scene presented itself in a singular manner. It did so in ways that permitted that person to understand the movement to the extent to which he was capable. The different scenes presented here are symptomatic of this process. Each is a description of a movement that, together with the others, makes up the so-called wave of violence. But from my interlocutors' points of view, their understandings of relations that police and the media ossified curiously as a "wave of violence" were not partial visions of a whole, or even representations dependent on contradictory or incomplete data. What the Thieves expressed to me over and over was that they were in the presence of a movement that they were at times able to glimpse, if only partially, at the same time that they made it up.

The nature of the composition, the form, and the extension acquired by a movement depends on perspective, or how one views that movement. Movement is not, in itself, something natural that might be apprehended partially or in its totality by the anthropologist or by the anthropologist's interlocutors. So because interpretations of the PCC as a movement depend on the perspective adopted by those who would claim to perceive it, the portraits here are much more than fragmented representations of a supposedly ultimately unavailable totality. They are testaments to an ethnography that follows as a movement that interests me and that lacks a definitive beginning or end becomes what one makes of it on the basis of the view it presents. Even more, and independently of the ways in which it is perceived, the type of movement I encountered during fieldwork gained consistency because of the efforts of those who constituted it. Each of those actors sought to act in his own way, thus imprinting the association with a particular sense and direction. Thus, it is not only the "wave of violence" but also any movement composed in the manner I have begun to outline that warrants characterization in relation to the effects of such imprints, or plays of force. And this is why my interpretation of movements is neither more nor less encompassing than the perspectives offered up by any of my interlocutors.

It is impossible to put together visions, understandings, and complete—or totalizing—perceptions on the movement called the PCC precisely because there is no totality to be perceived. And in the time that has expired since *Sharing This Walk* first appeared, this has become even clearer. I have begun to refer to this quality, which some analysts might reduce to something ephemeral, as "movement." I am thus keenly interested in how the application of the concept of movement to the PCC-as-movement permits a clarification of what is described throughout this book's chapters. This is especially true in relation to the transitory nature of what I refer to as "political positions"—as in, for example, the apparent authority of the Towers discussed in the preceding chapters—and thus the lability of the "disciplines" and even the "ideas" of the PCC.

Ideas

A variety of dynamics discussed throughout *Sharing This Walk* come to light in relation to something present in each of them—ideas (*ideias*). Far from standing as just components of the movement, these ideas typically become confused with the movement itself. We might understand this entwinement and differentiate movement and idea by approaching a movement as the idea coupled to whatever it mobilizes, or everything it mobilizes and everything to which it couples, including *quebradas*, the Thieves in prison and on the outside, objects, words, openings and gaps, other movements, and other ideas. Since, invariably, these elements come coupled with ideas (or towed by ideas), they are constantly produced and mobilized by Thieves so as to maintain, nurture, drive, strengthen, propagate, and alter the movements.

Attention to the dynamics of what Thieves refer to as ideas may also offer another perspective on what I characterized in the Brazilian edition of chapter 1 as collective amnesia, or what I described as "debates that burbled and boiled would cool down and disappear, across just a short time. For reasons as diverse as the impulses that first generated them, these debates would be closed down, as if they had never existed." This depiction referred to the ways that multiple histories of the birth of the PCC were erased and gave rise to only one version, as well as the appearance of a victorious version that left the impression that it had always been the only account and that alternatives had never existed. I have also employed the expression to describe the way that equality came to take hold in the prisons controlled by the PCC:

> After "Equality" was added to the slogan I still came across brothers who made reference to "soldiers" and "generals" in talking about the Command's organization. But "Equality" soon became a definitive part of the PCC motto, its symbolic repertoire, as well as the quotidian dispositions its members should, ideally, enact. And in what seems like another example of the "collective amnesia" mentioned in the previous chapter, an emphasis on equality very quickly became a part of the group's official positioning. This took place in a manner that effectively erased mention of the previous hierarchies. Even the hybrid, transitional period during which Brothers in different prisons emphasized, and failed to emphasize, equality as part of a heterogeneous set of positions seemed to disappear.

Over the course of subsequent research, I noticed the same phenomenon occurring in other movements: Ideas treated as burning issues (*mil grau*) at one point simply disappeared the next day. This disappearance was the result of forces poised to make the idea die (*a ideia morrer*). I noted also the efforts put forth by the Thieves to keep an idea alive, to make it win, and to take on greater force. But I also witnessed multiple strategies directed at deactivating, as well as reactivating, an idea. My experiences suggest that, among the Thieves, an idea had nothing to do with thought, formulation, or invention. For example, in the company of Thieves, one never says, "I have an idea." Instead, ideas gain existence only when they manifest themselves, detaching from enunciators and, as they become movements, taking on their own diverse directions. In other words, ideas only exist when in flux in the world or when shared. At that point, they become both centers of convergence for the forces that struggle over their directions in the world and sites or sources that provide the movement with direction, temporal orientation, and form. In this sense, ideas gain their very own existence: Although they result from forces that bear in on them, they are also capable of constraining these forces.

In the scenes sketched in this afterword, and especially in the statement given in the interrogation of a Thief that police authorities turned over to the press for republication, one comes across ideas at their moment of collision, or before their stabilization. And at the juncture so often described as a wave of violence, there was no single winning idea. The ideas that made up the movement died (*morreram*).

It is important to emphasize that if ideas gain importance through their manifestation, it is in their repercussions that they avoid death or remain alive. As a result, interested actors need to direct their efforts at engendering repercussions so as to keep ideas alive—no idea survives by inertia; not even the PCC. As is the case with ideas, the PCC and its members make constant reference to each of its movements (and thus also each of its ideas). It is therefore fed continuously, and made real, as a movement in everyday, even seemingly trivial, speech and action. Or, as I have attempted to describe throughout this book, the PCC is immanent in its own production.

Rhythm

The existence of an idea is tied to its repercussions. With each expression, an idea is marked by the juncture at which that expression takes place and thus by all that it mobilizes or gathers around in composing its movement. Additionally, forces that influence the maintenance, transformation, and strengthening of an idea intensify around that idea, thus indicating that the idea itself is one result of the collisions. Given this situation that emanates from the importance of becoming manifest in the generalization of ideas in the world, ideas must thus always contain within themselves shifting arrays of, or possibilities for, change. Ideas carry with them a possibility of transformation. Key to this immanence is the process whereby any manifestation of an idea guarantees that the idea will be imprinted by the situational conditions of its emergence.

If, at each moment that it is manifested, an idea is clad with the circumstances in which it occurs as an event, then it must vary in relation to its previous manifestations. Thus, even the most general of ideas, including "peace," "equality," and the PCC itself, are inscribed by and with the local conditions of their emergence, in relation to which they vary. Thieves refer to these variations as "rhythm." They also employ this term to refer to the occurrences or often fleeting qualities that attach to the idea and make it differ. Rhythm, then, refers to the specific states of affairs that attach to and reconstitute the ideas differently, as well as the resulting variation, which in turn becomes a new set of conditions of emergence. And these shifts mean that ideas must vary.

The five scenes described earlier illustrate the importance of paying attention to the coexistence of various rhythms. And this variation is not exclusively the result of the means by which an idea is incorporated into a local rhythm. It is also a function of the particular ideas that couple with that rhythm. Some ideas make it there, whereas others do not. In other words, the very conditions of possibility of the arrival—or not—of an idea reside in rhythm. But rhythm, at least as lived by the Brothers, is not quite a structure. It is a configuration of ideas and bodies trying to guarantee that some resonate and live whereas others die or become deactivated. But this confused set of impulses and practices grants a certain character to a territory or temporal period. In this light, and as part of such a syncopation, it becomes possible to understand in new ways the differences identified here in relation to the flows and interpretations of communiqués like the one described here that came down or failed to come down, or came down and was unable to be picked up because of the absence of Brothers.

In working to understand better the particular nature and function of the PCC communiqué, as well as the PCC's constitution in relation to movements, ideas, and rhythm as presented so far, I avoid claims about errors, disorder, and lack of command. And, as I argued in chapter 2, my ethnography leads me to reject definitively the characterization of the communiqué as an order or "law." I approach the PCC proclamation put forth in relation to the attacks not as a single message received and interpreted in light of sets of relations reified as local conditions, but rather as a rhythmic bundle or accretion of motile signs that is transformed as it resonates.

Hierarchy

The impulse to avoid characterizing PCC proclamations as codes or commands raises the issue of hierarchy, a concept discussed throughout this book by means of forms of ethnographic analysis that we might expect to be received poorly by the social scientist or politician interested in what the PCC "really is" and how it appears to take on the form of an organization characterized by tight discipline and rigid hierarchy. Thus, I emphasize again that, since the PCC never ceases to become real or to congeal at certain moments of intensity, it would be ridiculous to argue that the Brotherhood lacks a hierarchy. Yet, whenever a hierarchy arises, so do forces that inhibit its crystallization. Therefore, my assertion that over the course of fieldwork I came face-to-face with pivots or sites of hierarchies that became loci of conjecture—and thus for a dismantling or frustration of hierarchy—is rather different from the argument that there exists some relatively fixed structure. Hierarchy, in relation to the Command, does not look toward or invoke ranked structures. And a conceptualization of the PCC as a movement, expressed alongside or in dialogue with the dynamic play of ideas that are imbricated in that movement, supports this claim.

Once entangled in a movement or movements, ideas take on new valences, mobilize greater or lesser numbers of people, become objects of debates waged at varying intensities, face off against assorted forms of resistance, pass through moments of stabilization, and may even gain force and permanence by defying their own death. Whatever the particulars, the idea comes to resonate in relation to the forms through which others embrace it or not. At such moments, the idea is transformed from something associated with someone into a collective entity. Its resonance, or the way that it stays alive, is strengthened in this collectivity. In the process, the forces exerted across this trajectory blend into or forcibly engage the idea's movements. This repurposes the power and projection of the Thieves who engage ideas.

Even as Thieves gain power as their ideas reverberate and acquire force, those ideas partake of the power of those men. However, if Thieves involve themselves in what prisoners usually call "wrong" ideas (*ideias erradas*), they lose power. So do their ideas. In this sense, the Thief's power and ideas' force always go hand in hand: The power of the actor who manifests an idea is written onto that idea itself as it gains force and continues to resonate. On the other hand, a Thief who is unable to encourage his idea's reverberations loses his power. Thus, it is not uncommon to observe an actor, fortified by the same ideas that he sought to support, taking on a position of renown that is in turn not dissociable from his ability to enter into and engage ideas. Here, what is so often misidentified as hierarchy becomes less fixed and may, in opposition to its more traditional social scientific meanings, come to gain a form that is tied intimately to the dynamics that loop around to reconfigure ideas.

That said, those involved in the Crime recognize full well that there are certain Thieves who are able to enact cadences and carry their ideas forward in ways that mean that other prisoners end up following rhythms imposed on them, even as they struggle not to. Yet this arrangement is never stable: There are Thieves who, after getting mixed up in incorrect ideas like the attempt to impose order, lose their power and, as a result, the force of their ideas. It is therefore important to emphasize that the imposition of a rhythm has nothing to do with the imposition of ideas but rather with the successful planting of ideas at the heart of a then-dominant rhythm. This is because an idea needs to be attractive and advantageous in order to be embraced (*abraçada*) so that it reverberates. Put slightly differently, an idea needs to be launched in relation to specific conditions so that it is seductive because of some apparent advantage. Not every Thief has the ability to put this in motion, since it requires knowledge of specific local conditions. But the Thief who is successful in engendering repercussions in relation to his ideas gains notoriety.

In order to stay alive, ideas must keep resonating, and this takes place only when they are interior to the specific circumstances in which they become manifest. Any imposition of ideas from outside—or those that do not speak to the specific conditions of the rhythm—is taken as unsuitable to the Thieves' embrace, and those ideas end up being rejected. This activates dynamics that only ideas immanent in the rhythm itself are capable of altering. The result is a rejection by Brothers of any attempt to boss or control another, since this action is taken as indicative of a reliance on ideas that are external to the forms of circulation and alliance in rhythmic sympathy.

The suggestion, drawn from my ethnography both inside and outside of prisons, that for Brothers there is no hierarchical figure capable of imposing ideas, such as sending out communiqués presented as orders to which Brothers must submit, makes clearer what actually took place during the wave of violence. In addition to the impossibility of strengthening ideas through imposition, each new manifestation of an idea implies an additional transformation so that it may be incorporated into local rhythms. The effort to impose an individual or hierarchical, organized, and univalent will on another weakens the Thief who attempts that maneuver. It thus raises serious doubts about the possibility of a single PCC communiqué being transmitted with a unified meaning.

Anthropology

My perspectives on fieldwork and the PCC—as well as movement, power, and ideas—are unlikely to satisfy readers who seek explanations. Yet, as anthropologist Jorge Villela argues in the original, Portuguese-language preface to this book, it is "not a legitimate move for an ethnographer to affirm, or even postulate, a problem that fails to afflict those who are the sources of the data that gird a research program."[11] And formulating global explanations as to what was going on within a putative wave of violence was not part of the scope of activities of my interlocutors in 2011 and 2012. Thus, my resistance to an overarching explanation of the sort that found little purchase among the people I engaged during fieldwork finds sustenance in their own approaches to the life of an idea. And this support is backed up by a long tradition of anthropological praxis.

Back in 1958, as part of a postwar attempt to specify how anthropology and sociology differ as disciplines, anthropologist Claude Lévi-Strauss argued, "While sociology seeks to advance the social science of the observer, anthropology seeks to advance that of what is observed."[12] Lévi-Strauss's disciplinary intervention has important implications, or, as Thieves would argue, consequences (consequências). On the one hand, it suggests that the people about whom I write here weave rich reflections about their existence and put together theories that support and orient their lives. On the other hand, it means that I must focus on the PCC without working to point out mistakes or imagine that as an anthropologist I am somehow empowered to dictate public security policy. This is especially true in relation to the reach of the modern, liberal nation-state, or the dominant contemporary vessel for democratic participation. I thus appreciate how Lévi-Strauss encourages the ethnographer to avoid accepting categories and ethics supported by that state in assessing who and what institutions are the norm and thus rational, moral, and correct.

If one were to accept the assumptions and sense-making activities of the Brazilian state, as well as the predictions that so often accompany them to congeal around issues of policing and public security, one would most likely produce the "social science of the observer" against which Lévi-Strauss agitated to formulate modern anthropology. Such a social science based on the prejudices of the observer would say much more about the liberal democratic state—the modern State of Right—and "public safety" than it would reveal about the PCC. But that is not my goal. Most of all, it is not what my experiences and my interlocutors have permitted me to do.

If I were seeking to propose solutions to the problems of crime or the PCC, I would have to treat the PCC as a statelike entity, or precisely what ensues when it is classified in legal, journalistic, or even academic writings as a "criminal organization." Only in this way is it possible to fix a statelike gaze on the Brothers and their collectivity. To make matters worse, to criticize or to denounce the practices of those about whom I write would mean comparing the data produced about their practices and aspirations to my own assumptions as to what democracy really is rather than how it is practiced in the places and by the people under consideration. In one way or another, then, such an anthropology involves inserting into ethnographic analysis concepts that do not really fit the relations that the researcher struggles to explicate. One result of such investigative agendas and orientations is explanations that arise in tighter relation to the observer than to the people at the heart of the research. Put simply, the end result is a form of social criticism by and about the observer.

Inside and Outside

Ironically, the assumed neutrality and sense of objectivity that accompany a "social science of the observer" do not mean that the products of such knowledge fail to be picked up on, and even employed as building blocks, by the PCC. It is as if, at a certain moment, these knowledge practices are harvested and then digested by the Command in ways that transform those nuggets so they make up part of the PCC-as-movement. In this sense, public security initiatives that social-scientific "observers" often characterize as applied or even helpful interventions—whether initiatives to toughen sentences by making them longer while advocating greater recourse to solitary confinement, palliative reforms based on adherence to laws, or even ad hoc measures such as the transfer of prison leaders—are both activated by and activate the creation of new movements. This may encourage orientations that are rather different from those that preceded them. Hence, more "traditional" approaches to knowledge of the social, as well as putatively marginal citizens, may not only mold rhythms but may also contribute to the realignments of the PCC, from which those movements in turn emerge. Adding to this scenario of creative and necessary appropriation is the fact that what is said and written about the PCC also enters into the choreography of movements. This is what is illustrated in scene 2 as well as by the centrality of Jozino's book *Cobras e Lagartos* to the stabilization of ideas (*ideias*) about the birth of the PCC.

Perhaps surprisingly, even police invasions of working-class communities or prison yards end up helping to compose movements. This is because they lend direction and mold rhythms. A number of my fieldwork encounters in October and November of 2012, a time when stories of PCC- and police-imposed curfews on peripheral neighborhoods filled the news, exemplify this issue. For example, once, while in an impoverished neighborhood, I listened as residents recounted how violent police were invading their favela community multiple times each day, and not simply as a means of enforcing a curfew or apprehending specific lawbreakers. Often these incursions resulted in what local people described as a "humiliation of those who live here." According to the citizens, during one of the raids, the representatives of the state forced a group of young men from the community to strip naked. Police then paraded the nude prisoners through the neighborhood, beating them. Four of the prisoners had large Xs inscribed across their backs with knives. Pointing a machine gun at one boy, the "forces of order," as they are often referred to in Brazil, forced him to kiss a male neighbor on the lips. Finally, the police decided to strip search a twelve-year-old girl, lingering in their review of her genitalia.

The Brothers had fled this hot spot and could not do anything, at least not immediately, in the face of the police offensive. Meanwhile, in an adjoining *quebrada*, the Brothers remained and, in the face of their presence, that favela took on a tranquil feel. As one put it to me, "Here it's safe. We even go to sleep with unlocked doors. The police pass right on by, sticking to the main streets." In other words, in the first case described, police action produced a hot spot, or a neighborhood in tumult. In the second, the form of policing imposed on the community gave rise to a much more tranquil situation. This gives some idea as to how the police also contribute to rhythms. As a result, when one is analyzing a movement composed of innumerable smaller movements, the borders that separate inside and outside are no longer evident.

WHEN I SAT DOWN and engaged the material that I had collected about the wave of violence, I began, finally, to believe my earlier intuitions and feel a bit more comfortable with my ongoing attempt to deal with contradictory, fragmented data that seemed to confound attempts to control that information and its narrativization. In fact, facing this material productively meant that I would finally abandon the attempt to offer explanations and instead linger in my fieldwork-based descriptions. Most basically, this approach has enabled me to realize that the attempt to write an ethnography of a movement that arose in a field site that is in motion requires an ethnography that is also in motion. In effect, by conducting research in various parts of São Paulo where the PCC was active, I had come up against multiple PCCs. These different PCCs revealed diverse characteristics that challenged, and thus added to, the version of the PCC that emanated from my work in the state's prisons. Additionally, the preeminence of description in this book meant that I found it necessary to pay close attention and confer significant analytic importance to disjunctures and differences. This helped me avoid distilling into a single identity the different PCCs that came into view as I took different positions over the course of my multisite fieldwork that focused not on a collection of individual groups or manifestations, but on the agreements and disagreements that connect supposedly heterogeneous spaces in ways that a social science of the observer misidentifies continuously. So if in this book I have worked to illustrate how the PCC comes into being only as this coming into being unfolds, or in the specific experience of taking on presence and form as part of a series of rhythmic associations, what I have ended up realizing is that there exists a PCC for every point of view that permits a focus on the movement. And each of these points of view corresponds, in itself, to the PCC.

Notes

Note from the Editor-Translator

1. See the 2014 *Levantamento Nacional de Informações Penitenciárias* at http://www.cnj.jus.br/files/conteudo/arquivo/2015/11/080f04f01d5b0efebfbcf06d050d ca34.pdf, last accessed January 24, 2016.

2. Boiteux and Padua, *A desproporcionalidade da lei de drogas*; Gay, *Bruno*.

3. See Amnesty International, "Brazil: 'Trigger Happy' Military Police Kill Hundreds as Rio Prepares for Olympic Countdown," https://www.amnesty.org/en/latest/news/2015/08/brazil-trigger-happy-military-police-kill-hundreds-as-rio-prepares-for-olympic-countdown/; and the *Economist*, "Serial Killing," March 20, 2014, http://www.economist.com/blogs/americasview/2014/03/police-violence-brazil. On contemporary realignments between police as maintainers of public order and police as assassins of those who are perceived as disturbing such order in Rio de Janeiro, see James Armour Young, "The Murder Rate Is Down in Rio—But Its Cops Continue to Kill," Vice News, January 28, 2016, https://news.vice.com/article/the-murder-rate-is-down-in-rio-but-its-cops-continue-to-kill.

4. Viotti da Costa, *The Brazilian Empire*, 77.

5. Schwarz, *Misplaced Ideas*.

6. Hobsbawm, *Bandits*.

7. Deleuze and Guattari, *A Thousand Plateaus*.

Foreword

1. Abu-Lughod, "Writing against Culture," 137–54.

2. Jullien, *Fundar o moral*.

3. In fact, to talk about the PCC in the singular is to cover up its particular singularity, namely that it is resolutely multiple.

4. Leach, *Pul Eliya*. See also Foucault, "Le mailles du pouvoir."

Introduction

1. Located in southeastern Brazil, metropolitan São Paulo sprawls for 7,943.82 square kilometers. It is made up of the capital city of the same name and thirty-eight municipalities. Today, it concentrates nearly one-fifth of Brazil's gross domestic product, a sum that corresponds to approximately US$350 billion, or $17,852 per capita.

2. The designation "the Family" did not appear until 2007, at least in terms of my fieldwork experiences. Today, São Paulo State has 147 prison units. These are overseen by the Secretaria de Administração Pentenciária (Secretary of Penitentiary

Administration) and hold roughly 150,000 people (www.sap.sp.gov.br). The figures cited in the present study are the fruit of estimates put together with and by prisoners, ex-prisoners, visitors, and some journalists and legal sources. For work on the PCC presence in urban areas, see especially Biondi, "Tecendo as tramas do significado" and two works by Feltran, "Trabalhadores e bandidos" and *Fronteiras de tensão*.

3. Nietzsche, "On Truth and Lies in a Nonmoral Sense," 83.

4. The many distinctions between, and resultant implications of, imprisonment in CDPs, or what theoretically are short- and medium-term institutions for prisoners awaiting or in the midst of a trial, and penitentiary-type units for the condemned whose cases have already come before a judge, are discussed at length in chapter 1.

5. The punishment meted out to *talaricos* is death. Nonetheless, it is not possible to generalize this prescription (as is true of all other prescriptions we come across in the universe of São Paulo's prisons) and create a broad law concerning people's actions. For example, I came across the story of an ex-Brother (a former member of the PCC) who was "excluded from the Party" (*excluído do Partido*) because he killed a man who pursued his wife but he did not request permission from the PCC for the execution. In yet another case, the *talarico* was imprisoned alongside the husband he had cuckolded, and when the aggrieved party requested that the PCC take action, the Brothers decided that the *talarico* would be executed by the woman's husband. This prisoner refused because he had been jailed on a minor offense and was unwilling to face the additional prison time such a murder would have brought down. He and his rival thus served their sentences together.

6. This history—almost an origin story that nonetheless extends into the present and future—will become critical to the discussions of authority and disposition developed throughout this book.

7. For a discussion of how the appellation "Presinho da Silva"—(a diminutive that refers to an imagined prisoner "da Silva," or what would in English be something like "Prisoner Smith" or "Prisoner Joe Blow") or the version of "Zé Povinho" used in Brazil's Northeast—leeches into everyday working-class, and even ludic, vocabularies in the city of Salvador, Bahia, see Collins, *Revolt of the Saints*.

8. Biondi, "Tecendo as tramas do significado," 303–50.

9. Marques and Villela, "O que se diz, o que se escreve," 17.

10. Vargas, "Uso de drogas," 584.

11. Marques, *Intrigas e questões*.

12. The importance of considering silence, nonstatements, and nonevents is elaborated in Leirner, *Meia volta volver*.

13. The *Mundão*, or in Portuguese the "Big World," is one term used by prisoners to describe the spatial outlines of freedom or escape from incarceration. Other terms include *rua* (street) and *pista* (highway).

14. Even when these people are not criminals, they tend to fear the possibility of being stigmatized as criminals because of their social positions or association with lawbreakers.

15. Wacquant, *Body and Soul*, viii.

16. But such an action might open him up to accusations of "taking an isolationist stance," an issue discussed at length in chapter 2 and aids in producing what I argue is the PCC's nonhierarchical functioning.

17. Within the PCC, if a Brother is called on to locate another Brother he does not know personally, he activates a complex network of interpersonal relations. This is something I explore in chapter 1.

18. Favret-Saada, "'Ser afetado,' de Jeanne Favret-Saada," 157.

19. Latour, *Reassembling the Social*; Strathern, "1989 Debate"; Toren, "The Concept of Society Is Theoretically Obsolete"; Wagner, *The Invention of Culture.*

20. Wagner, *The Invention of Culture.*

21. Peel, "1989 Debate."

22. "The Crime" (*O Crime*) is a "native" concept used to refer to actors who practice crimes but also refers to an ethic and certain forms of prescribed conduct. The concept of "World of Crime" has been explored at length in Ramalho, *Mundo do crime.*

23. For an example of such an argument, see Peel, "1989 Debate."

24. For Deleuze and Guattari, "collective assemblages of enunciation" (*A Thousand Plateaus*, 7) are regimes of signs, or forms of expression, that express incorporeal transformations that are 'attributed' as such (properties) to bodies or contents" (ibid., 504) that do not stand as objects in a causal relation with the subject. Instead, they "have their own formalization and have no relation of symbolic correspondence or linear causality with a form of expression: the two forms are in reciprocal presupposition, and they can be abstracted from each other only in a very relative way because they are two sides of a single assemblage" (ibid., 140).

25. Deleuze and Guattari claim that their concepts such as "rhizomatics," "stratoanalysis," "schizoanalysis," "micropolitics," and "pragmatics" are lines of thought and practice, and they do so without recognizing these concepts as scientific or ideological. For these two thinkers, they are instead assemblages that provide researchers with methods for dealing with multiplicity rather than standing as dualist concepts or models, which would supercode the connective figures they dub "rhizomes" in ways that end up structuring, neutralizing, stabilizing, and essentializing the multitude of associations they dub—perhaps unsurprisingly—"the multitude."

26. According to Deleuze and Guattari, the "map is open and connectable in all of its dimensions; it is detachable, reversible, susceptible to constant modification" (*A Thousand Plateaus*, 12), whereas the more commonly performed practice of tracing "has generated, structuralized the rhizome, and when it thinks it is reproducing something else it is in fact only reproducing itself. That's why the tracing is so dangerous. It injects redundancies and propagates them" (ibid., 13).

27. Strathern, "1989 Debate."

28. Viveiros de Castro, "O Nativo Relativo."

29. Deleuze and Guattari, *A Thousand Plateaus*, 7.

30. Ibid., 13.

31. Ibid., 20.

32. As we will see in subsequent chapters, even the attempt at producing a relatively transcendental PCC is a mechanism that attempts to undo certain arboreal formations.

33. In the language used by Deleuze and Guattari in *A Thousand Plateaus*, the bulb, although linked to the rhizome, serves as an image of stabilization.

34. On mid-twentieth-century anthropological approaches to states, their ostensible absence in "primitive" societies, and political systems, see, for example, Fortes and Evans-Pritchard, *African Political Systems*.

Chapter One

1. The actual number of prisoners killed remains the subject of much controversy. Prisoners who survived "the Massacre" speak of a much larger number of victims, whose bodies were supposedly removed by garbage trucks before the official count and investigations by state and human rights authorities. For an early history of Carandiru and a comparison of penal institutions, see especially Cancelli, "Repressão e controle prisional no Brasil."

2. Law 8,209 of January 4, 1993.

3. According to Wacquant, such growth in prison populations is part of a worldwide tendency in which Europe and Latin America have tended increasingly to follow U.S. approaches to incarceration. For example, in the United States, the prison population tripled over the course of less than fifteen years (from 740,000 prisoners in 1985 to nearly 2,000,000 in 1998). See Wacquant, *As prisões da miséria*, 81.

4. Barros, "A construção do PCC."

5. Sacramento, *O prisioneiro da grade de ferro*.

6. Souza, *PCC, a facção*, 9.

7. Ibid., 16.

8. For an example of official state pronouncements about the existence of the Command, see Milena Buosi, "Presidente da Assembléia reconhece existência do PCC," *Folha de São Paulo*, February 19, 2001, http://www1.folha.uol.com.br/folha/cotidiano/ult95u22527.shtml.

9. Souza, *PCC, a facção*, 56.

10. Jozino, *Cobras e lagartos*, 143–44.

11. Souza, *PCC, a facção*, 226.

12. Edited by Alfredo Bosi, the "Dossiê" appeared as a series of articles in *Revista de Estudos Avançados* 21, no. 61.

13. Adorno and Salla, "Criminalidade organizada nas prisões e os ataques do PCC," 9.

14. Durkheim, *O suicídio*.

15. Foucault, *Il faut defender la société*.

16. Bosi, "Dossiê crime organizado," 24.

17. Adorno and Salla, "Criminalidade organizada nas prisões e os ataques do PCC," 24.

18. Santos, "A hora e a vez de derrotar o Crime Organizado," 100–1.

19. www.mj.gov.br/depen.

20. The word *chefão*, or "big boss," is commonly used by inmates to refer to prison employees.

21. The word *tatu*, or "armadillo," seems to be a reference to that animal's penchant for burrowing.

22. *"um compromisso com o Comando."*

23. The term *"noia"* is an abbreviation of the word paranoia, a description commonly used in Sao Paulo for the agitated and dangerous state provoked by crack cocaine use. On *noias* and *noia* in central São Paulo, see Heckenberger, "Marginal Bodies, Altered States, and Subhumans." On the related term *"saci"* as employed in northeastern Brazil, see two works by Collins, " 'X Marks the Future of Brazil' " and *Revolt of the Saints*.

24. As Deleuze and Guattari put it, the virtual is not so much opposed to the real or the existent as much as it refers to something that has not yet been actualized or made manifest in a particular manner. See Deleuze and Guattari, *A Thousand Plateaus*.

25. On the idea of *proceder*, or proper comportment, uprightness, and what might be translated as "getting it done" in a way that makes a lasting reputation in prison, see two works by Marques, *"Proceder"* and *Crime, proceder, convívio-seguro*.

26. Perpetrators of crimes that attract significant notice in the press often find their lives threatened even before they arrive in jail. In a majority of such cases, these prisoners are sent to protective custody. But sometimes even the inmates already in protective custody refuse to admit the new arrivals, and this constitutes a major issue for the SAP, which is charged officially with preserving their lives. For an analysis of one such case, see Marques, *Crime, proceder, convívio-seguro*.

27. The key concept of *proceder*, or what I approach as a "disposition" or "way of being," which is translated for clarity's sake as "comportment," has much to do with one's habitus, microinteractions with prisoners and guards, and thus one's history or reputation.

28. Marques, " 'Dar um psicológico.' "

29. Nonetheless, if a violation is particularly egregious, the Brother may be "repudiated" (*repudiado*) in addition to being excluded. This involves declaring that subject socially dead.

30. As used in prisons controlled by the Command, the verb "to resonate" (*repercutir*) is an important term since it indicates that an action may have consequences. These consequences may be unknown, but the fact that an act has repercussions indicates that the inmate may be evaluated at a future moment.

31. For Foucault, "technologies of the self permit individuals to effect by their own means or with the help of others a certain number of operations on their own bodies and souls, thoughts, conduct, and way of being, so as to transform themselves in order to attain a certain state of happiness, purity, wisdom, perfection, or immortality." See Foucault, "Technologies of the Self," 18. For a genealogy of the production of the modern individual, see especially Foucault, *Discipline and Punish*.

32. The noun *cabulosidade*, or a "hairiness," implies an ability to act danger-ously, impetuously, and thus in destabilizing and troubling manners. Marques emphasizes that a "hairy" (*cabuloso*) subject is one who frustrates any attempt at subjugation by another, or what is referred to in prison as "getting into the mind" of someone (*entrar na mente*). See Marques, "'Liderança,' 'proceder' e 'igualdade.'"

Chapter Two

1. And yet Adalton Marques informed me in a personal communication that, at least as recounted by a number of his interlocutors, this hierarchical structure was not present at the PCC's birth. These men claimed instead that it was put in place by a number of early members blinded by power. Such an origin story is fascinating as a retrospective construction that, independently of its veracity in relation to a previous period, illustrates how concerns and hopes in the pres-ent are projected on the past through the structures and contents of memory.

2. Marques, "'Liderança,' 'proceder' e 'igualdade.'"

3. According to my interlocutors, this concept of equality distinguishes São Paulo's PCC and the Comando Vermelho of Rio de Janeiro from other com-mands in Brazil. More recently, a female interlocutor in Rio de Janeiro told me that she preferred a situation in which a command would be "together and orga-nized" (*Juntos e organizado*) rather than "together and mixed together" (*Juntos e misturado*) since, in her words, "that which is mixed becomes a real mess" (*ba-gunça*).

4. Marques, "'Liderança,' 'proceder' e 'igualdade.'"

5. What is translated here as "standing up for" is, literally, "to take a frontline position for us" (*tomar a frente*). Such "fronting" is important to understanding PCC approaches to politics, since those who occupy political positions in the PCC are referred to as the "front" (*frente*).

6. For my interlocutors, to see or "to have vision" (*ter visão*) is the result of vari-ous qualities. These include intelligence, perspicacity, knowledge of prison life and the PCC, and a sense of justice. Prisoners who lack these qualities are de-scribed as "lacking vision" or "having the vision of a cherry [*jatobá*] tree," or a plant that when mixed with sugar cane liquor produces a cloyingly sweet, cloudy brown cocktail popular in Brazil's Northeast.

7. The phrase describing the delicate juncture at which Brothers found them-selves in that prison at the time was "*nós estamos no progresso*," or "we're in the middle of some progress." In this case, "progress" refers to an escape plan, such as the dig-ging of a tunnel.

8. Solitary confinement in São Paulo's prisons really isn't "solitary" because the transferred prisoner is simply kept alongside others punished in the same way in a smaller unit and denied what inmates call the "sunbath" (*banho de sol*), or the right to leave the cell and enter the prison yard for recreation.

9. See, for example, Adorno and Salla, "Criminalidade organizada nas prisões e os ataques do PCC."

10. Field notes, April 23, 2006.

11. Swartz, Turner, and Tuden, *Political Anthropology*.

12. Palmeira, "Política, facções e voto," 54.

13. For discussions of fear, perception, and resistance to the Shock Battalion's actions in the city of Salvador, Bahia, see two works by Collins, "'X Marks the Future of Brazil'" and *Revolt of the Saints*.

14. The absence of an exchange of material benefits means that the Brothers play a role that is rather different from that of the "brokers" social scientists have identified as important facilitators of the exchange relations so characteristic of patron–client structures. See Landé, "Introduction."

15. For references to the salience of such exchanges in prison, see Jocenir, *Diário de um detento*; Zeni, *Sobrevivente André du Rap (do Massacre do Carandiru)*. Also, for the city of Rio de Janeiro, see Barbosa, "Um levantamento introdutório das práticas de violência física dentro das cadeias cariocas."

16. Although prison employees control the supply of water, food, and medical assistance, prisoners hold the power to begin rebellions that break the fragile sense of order the jailors seek to establish.

17. Villela, *O povo em armas*, 269.

18. Over the course of her research, Camila Caldeira Nunes Dias witnessed the upholding of the "white flag" by Brothers who sought to maintain peace so as to influence prison authorities and obtain the transfer of PCC leaders from high-security, supermax-style prisons (*Regimes Disciplinares Diferenciados*, RDDs) to more "normal" penitentiaries. Based on this experience, she reports that the authority of the Command was recognized clearly by prisoners as well as prison authorities. See Dias, *A igreja como refúgio e a Bíblia como esconderijo*. Former PCC leader Marcola also supports this observation, testifying before Congress that the "Then-Secretary of São Paulo's Penitentiary Administration went and asked me to talk with other prisoners so that we could begin some sort of consciousness-raising effort. He indicated that if he were going to do something for us, we would have to demonstrate that we could encourage peace on the inside. That was when we went through a period of . . . I dunno . . . two years without a death." See http://www1.folha.uol.com.br/folha/cotidiano/20060708-marcos _camacho.pdf.

19. The word *"parceiro"*—literally, "partner"—is a powerful term among Thieves in Brazil since it denotes an individual one trusts enough to go out and commit crimes and potentially face police torture that might induce one or both of the individuals involved to "rat out" the other.

20. The word *"axé"* is typically used to refer to a quality of spirit, or an agentive density, related to the Afro-Brazilian religion known as Candomblé and centered in the northeastern Brazilian state of Bahia, a region that has seen substantial out-migration to more industrialized São Paulo. In São Paulo's prisons, the expression *"pegar o axé"* is used to describe someone who is offered a second chance or an attenuation of a punishment.

21. This happens to be the same prison unit that I was told failed to receive one of the communiqués that had been passed around to other units.

22. Marques, "'Liderança,' 'proceder' e 'igualdade.'"

23. See, for example, Bezerra, *Em nome das Bases*; Goldman, *Como funciona a democracia*; Marques and Villela, "O que se diz, o que se escreve"; Palmeira and Heredia, "Os comícios e a política de facções."

24. I thank Anna Catarina Morawska Vianna of the University of São Paulo for engaging me in the discussions that have led me to this point.

25. As is by now rather well known, Latour, like Gabriel Tarde, does not consider the social to be a thing in itself, and he offers a vociferous critique of those who would employ it as a black box to explain that which remains otherwise unexplained in academic analyses. See Latour, *Reassembling the Social*; Tarde, "Monadologia e sociologia."

26. Latour, *Reassembling the Social*, 11.

27. Marques attributes great importance to the notion of response in relation to Marcola's declaration to Congress that "the system" (or unbaptized prisoners) joins with the "group" (PCC) because the group represents the system as part of a resonant receptivity (a "responsivity"), or what interlocutors in the PCC call a *responsa*. See Marques, "'Liderança,' 'proceder' e 'igualdade.'"

28. Tarde, "Monadologia e sociologia," 98.

29. Biondi, "Tecendo as tramas do significado."

30. I mention the shift from "Pilot" to "voice" and back to "Pilot" not as an attempt to suggest that the PCC has settled definitively on the term "Pilot" as part of some evolving strategy but to illustrate how practices and commentaries on those practices are linked up in ways that produce knowledge about, and for, the Command. I fully expect the terms to continue to shift in relation to alterations in the PCC and the networks in which it takes form.

31. Latour, *Reassembling the Social*, 30.

32. Such communiqués, or *salves gerais*, are not secret. They are posted publicly in cell blocks, in full view of guards and the administration.

33. Marcola, in his testimony to Congress, claimed that he did not know any Thieves who abandoned a life of crime as a result of the punishment to which they were subjected, and he predicted an early end for them: "Life is really short, even for an arms trafficker. Don't imagine that he's gonna survive twenty, thirty years when he's involved in this sort of thing. The overwhelming tendency is for everything linked to violence to be taken down by violence."

34. For a complex consideration of the relationship between violence and drug trafficking, see Cunha, "A violência e o tráfico."

Chapter Three

1. See United Nations, "United Nations Convention against Transnational Organized Crime and the Protocols Thereto," http://www.unodc.org/documents /treaties/UNTOC/Publications/TOC%20Convention/TOCebook-e.pdf, last accessed August 28, 2015.

2. Mingardi, "O trabalho da Inteligência no controle do Crime Organizado," 56.

3. Misse, "Mercados ilegais, redes de proteção e organização local do crime no Rio de Janeiro," 140.

4. The description of a "segmented" status deployed by Barbosa is rather particular and is indebted to the discussion of Deleuze and Guattari's adoption of anthropological approaches to segmentation, since "the notion of segmentarity was constructed by ethnologists to account for so-called primitive societies, which have no fixed, central State apparatus and no global power mechanisms or specialized political institutions" (Deleuze and Guattari, *A Thousand Plateaus*, 209). To describe something as segmented in this sense is to attempt to account for relations between heterogeneous beings that are developed in multiple manners, without some orienting or determinative base.

5. Barbosa, "Segmentaridade e tráfico de drogas no Rio de Janeiro," 177.

6. Telles and Hirata, "Cidade e práticas urbanas," 187.

7. Ibid., 176.

8. Marques, "'Faxina' e 'pilotagem,'" 289.

9. Clausewitz, *On War*, 177.

10. Participants in the PCC see creativity as one of their weapons. In the PCC primer discussed in chapter 2, they conceptualize creativity as a mechanism capable of uncovering new ways of gaining visibility since, in the words of the Brothers, "creativity is infinite."

11. The spaces to which I refer here are precisely the "PCC jails," or those institutions where the PCC dominates and where it imposes what it defines as "peace" between all prisoners who walk with the Command.

12. Information about the rebellion is drawn from an account offered to me by one of the prisoners involved in the escape attempt.

13. This secrecy seems to contradict the emphasis on transparency apparently so central to PCC ideals. Yet, as we will see, in another wing of the prison, all residents of one of the pavilions had advance notice of the plan. Such variability in planning illustrates the lability of PCC discipline and the extent to which plans are formulated in relation to the highly variegated and yet often interlinked rhythms of prison life.

14. As I attempted to describe in the introduction, mistrust is propagated also among visitors, who are continually oriented to treat one another with respect but to remain ever vigilant and to trust no one.

15. Wacquant, *Body and Soul*, 238.

16. Prisoners, who often speak of "smelling evil" or "hearing instincts," are explicit about expanding the sensory faculties so that these perceptions go beyond the biological.

17. Marques, *Crime, proceder, convívio-seguro*.

18. Dias, *A igreja como refúgio e a Bíblia como esconderijo*, 285.

19. The term *malandrão*, which is an exaggeration of the positively valued *malandro*, or a quite common Brazilian designation for a trickster, tough guy, or slick character, is used in prison to refer to a prisoner who behaves in a manner reminiscent of the days before the PCC, when prisoners would extort, sexually abuse, and otherwise oppress others.

20. The verb used by Eduardo to indicate such playfulness (*mular*) is used in prison to indicate a form of play without sexual connotations. But, in prison, the

more common Portuguese designation for play, *brincar*, does carry with it certain sexual meanings.

21. These are references to other prison units across the state of São Paulo.

22. Here, Brother Hugo ironically draws on the term *malandro* to dress down his interlocutor.

23. For related reflections on the articulation of power and claims to truth in relation to the courtroom dramas that he approaches as ritual elements, see Marques, "'Liderança,' 'proceder' e 'igualdade.'"

24. Marcola's words can be found at http://www1.folha.uol.com.br, last accessed August 28, 2015.

25. Ibid.

Chapter Four

1. For an example of how the work of Latour and of Deleuze and Guattari factors into a project for a postsocial anthropology that draws fundamentally on new work in Brazil, see the discussion in Viveiros de Castro, "Filiação intensiva e aliança demoníaca."

2. Deleuze and Guattari, *A Thousand Plateaus*, 20.

3. Lalande, *Vocabulário técnico e crítico da filosofia*.

4. Related approaches to the Durkheimian treatment of "the social" can be found in, among others, Donzelot, *L'Invention du Social*; Latour, *Reassembling the Social*; Strathern, "1989 Debate"; Toren, "The Concept of Society Is Theoretically Obsolete"; and two works by Vargas, *Antes Tarde do que nunca* and *Monadologia e sociologia e outros ensaios*.

5. Foucault, *Discipline and Punish*, 194.

6. Prisoners commonly affirm that the "visitor is sacred." They argue that such sacredness arises in relation to the trials and tribulations faced by women seeking to enter the prison to visit them.

7. The mediation of the relationship between two men by people, animals, or objects is not limited to the Command. In *O povo em armas*, Villela illustrates how the destruction of property, theft of animals, and attacks on patrons' clients in rural regions of the northeastern state of Pernambuco are intended to offend, insult, or cause damage to the reputation of one's enemy.

8. http://www.1.folha.uol.com.br/folha/cotidiano/20060708-Luiz_camacho .pdf.

9. In *Entre o bairro e a prisão*, Cunha describes processes of individualization in Portuguese jails as prison house strategies for escaping the collective punishments meted out by that country's justice system.

10. Hobbes, *Leviathan*.

11. Even though the transcendence attached to the PCC needed to be activated, I do not approach this form as what some refer to as a "virtuality," which, as discussed by Deleuze and Guattari in *A Thousand Plateaus* is, like the concept as I use it here, not opposed to the real. But it may or may not be actualized. Additionally, the version of the transcendental with which I work is not only

susceptible to actualization but is itself agentive—for example, it may actualize itself because of dynamics that exist only because they draw strength from that transcendental.

12. When prisoners affirm that the Command is above them, they are stating only that the Command ranks higher than they do in importance. Such a relationship led to a situation I learned of in which a Brother was held responsible for the misbehavior of his partner on the line of visitors and was given two options: Either hit her or be excluded. His response in the ensuing debate was that "the Command is above all" and "you can always find a woman, but there's only one Command." He then went on to add, "A woman is like a cookie. You pull one out and eighteen come along with her."

Conclusion

1. Bailey, *Gifts and Poison*, 173.

Author's Afterword to the English-Language Edition

1. These figures are from the Comissão de Segurança Pública e Assuntos Penitenciários da Assembleia Legislativa de São Paulo, as reported in Sobrinho, "Três meses após promessa, famílias de PMs assassinados estão sem indenização."

2. Caramante, "Baixada enfrenta nova onda de violência."

3. Funk is an urban musical and dance genre popular with youths across Brazil. It is often associated with the pleasures, perils, and criminal commands of Rio de Janeiro. For English-language works that treat funk, see especially Moehn, *Contemporary Carioca*.

4. http://noticias.uol.com.br/cotidiano/ultimas-noticias/2012/07/03/em-20 -dias-17-onibus-e-11-bases-sao-atacadas-em-sp-30pms-e-suspeitos-sao-mortos .htm, last accessed January 23, 2016.

5. What is truly impressive here, in its contradictions, is that my interlocutor made this statement only one week after the communiqué had arrived in the region of the coastal city in which I was working to set up a new field site. In other words, by the time the *salve* arrived in my potential field site, it had already expired in at least some of the other regions in which I was conducting research!

6. The headline appears here as reproduced from the report by Jozino, "Rota mata seis e PMs são presos suspeitos de execução." Here it is important to note that ROTA is the acronym of the widely feared Rondas Ostensivas Tobias de Aguiar, or the Tobias de Aguiar Ostensive Police Patrols. This special police unit is generally employed to put down large public demonstrations as well as to police São Paulo's highest-crime neighborhoods and track down especially notorious criminals. It has thus acquired a reputation as something of a state-controlled death squad that even has its own Facebook page—"amigos da Rota" (friends of the ROTA)—maintained by a civic organization seemingly made up of family and supporters. See https://www.facebook.com/OficialRota?ref=stream, last accessed January 21, 2016.

7. André Caramante, "Tres PMs são mortos em uma semana na zona leste," *Folha de São Paulo*, June 22, 2012, http://www1.folha.uol.com.br/fsp/cotidiano /50327-tres-pms-sao-mortos-em-uma-semana-na-zona-leste.shtml.

8. Again, the title *doutor* (*doutora* in the feminine form) is frequently employed in working-class Brazilian speech to show respect, indicate social distance, and mark an interlocutor as a member of the lettered classes. It does not necessarily designate that the recipient of the honorific holds any advanced degree but rather that the person bears himself or is presented as having a social or professional position consonant with such a degree.

9. Note the rather instrumental deployment and textual clarification of the supposed meaning of the term "walk" (*a caminhada*), which is so important to my analysis of the PCC. The textualization of this interrogation that appears here in the form of a document coauthored by the press and the police presents what I have described in multiple situations as a "walk" and a broad, historicized disposition and ethos as an action directed at the strategic taking out of enemies.

10. Please note that the words added in brackets in the transcript of the interrogation of Fat Leo that I extracted from a newspaper and reproduce here were added by the author of that article, not by the anthropologist. See Delphino, "PCC também perde o controle dos comandados."

11. Villela, "Apresentação," 14.

12. Lévi-Strauss, *Structural Anthropology*, 363.

Bibliography

Abu-Lughod, Lila. "Writing against Culture." In *Recapturing Anthropology: Working in the Present*, edited by Richard G. Fox, 137–54. Santa Fe, N.Mex.: School of American Research Press, 1991.

Adorno, Sérgio, and Fernando Salla. 2007. "Criminalidade organizada nas prisões e os ataques do PCC." *Revista Estudos Avançados* 21, no. 61: 7–29.

Amnesty International. 2015. "Brazil: 'Trigger Happy' Military Police Kill Hundreds as Rio Prepares for Olympic Countdown," https://www.amnesty.org/en/latest/news/2015/08/brazil-trigger-happy-military-police-kill-hundreds-as-rio-prepares-for-olympic-countdown/, last accessed January 12, 2016.

Bailey, F. G. 1971. *Gifts and Poison: The Politics of Reputation*. Oxford: Basil Blackwell.

Barbosa, Antônio Rafael. 2001. "Segmentaridade e tráfico de drogas no Rio de Janeiro." *Alceu* 2, no. 3: 166–79.

———. 2007. "Um levantamento introdutório das práticas de violência física dentro das cadeias cariocas." In *Conflitos, política e relações pessoais*, edited by Ana Claudia Marques, 129–72. Campinas: Pontes Editores.

Barros, João de. 2006. "A construção do PCC." *Caros Amigos* Special Edition, 10, no. 28: 3–13.

Bezerra, M. O. 1999. *Em nome das Bases: Política, favor e dependência pessoal*. Rio de Janeiro: Relume Dumará.

Biondi, Karina. 2006. "Tecendo as tramas do significado: As facções prisionais enquanto organizações fundantes de padrões sociais." In *Antropologia e Direitos Humanos 4*, edited by M. P. Grossi, M. L. Heilborn, and L. Z. Machado, 303–50. Florianópolis: Nova Letra.

Boiteux, Luciana, and João Padua. 2013. *A desproporcionalidade da lei de drogas: Os custos humanos e econômicos da atual política do Brasil*. Rio de Janeiro: Coletivo de Estudos Drogas e Direito.

Bosi, Alfredo, ed. 2007. "Dossiê crime organizado." *Revista Estudos Avançados* 21, no. 61.

Cancelli, Elizabeth. 2005. "Repressão e controle prisional no Brasil: Prisões comparadas." *História: Questões & Debates* no. 42: 141–56.

Caramante, André. 2012. "Baixada enfrenta nova onda de violência." *Folha de São Paulo*, April 18, www1.folha.uol.com.br/fsp/cotidiano/37872-baixada-enfrenta-nova-onda-de-violencia.shtml, last accessed January 14, 2016.

———. 2012. "Tres PMs são mortos em uma semana na zona leste." *Folha de São Paulo*, June 22, http://www1.folha.uol.com.br/fsp/cotidiano/50327-tres-pms-sao-mortos-em-uma-semana-na-zona-leste.shtml, last accessed December 17, 2015.

Clastres, Pierre. 2003 [1974]. *A Sociedade contra o Estado*. São Paulo: Cosac Naify.

Clausewitz, Carl von. 1976. *On War*. Princeton, N.J.: Princeton University Press.

Collins, John. 2004. "'X Marks the Future of Brazil': Racial Politics, Bedeviling Mixtures and Protestant Ethics in a Brazilian Cultural Heritage Center." In *Off Stage/On Display: Intimacies and Ethnographies in the Age of Public Culture*, edited by Andrew Shryock, 191–224. Stanford, Calif.: Stanford University Press.

———. 2007. "A violência e o tráfico: Para uma comparação dos narcomercados." In *Conflitos, política e relações pessoais*, edited by Ana Claudia Marques, 173–79. Campinas: Pontes Editores.

———. 2015. *Revolt of the Saints: Memory and Redemption in the Twilight of Brazilian Racial Democracy*. Durham, N.C.: Duke University Press.

Cunha, Manuela Ivone. 2002. *Entre o bairro e a prisão: Tráfico e trajectos*. Lisbon: Fim de Século.

Deleuze, Gilles, and Félix Guattari. 1987. *A Thousand Plateaus: Capitalism and Schizophrenia*, translated by Brian Massumi. Minneapolis: University of Minnesota Press.

Delphino, Plínio. 2012. "PCC também perde o controle dos comandados." *Diário de São Paulo*, November 23, http://www.redebomdia.com.br/noticia /detalhe/38491/PCC+tambem+perde+o+controle+dos+comandados, last accessed January 22, 2016.

Dias, Camila Caldeira Nunes. 2008. *A igreja como refúgio e a Bíblia como esconderijo: Religião e violência na prisão*. São Paulo: Humanitas.

Donzelot, Jacques. 1994. *L'Invention du Social: Essai sur le declin des passion politiques*. Paris: Fayart.

Durkheim, E. 2000. *O suicídio: Estudo de sociologia*. São Paulo: Martins Fontes.

The Economist. March 20, 2014. "Serial Killing," http://www.economist.com /blogs/americasview/2014/03/police-violence-brazil, last accessed January 12, 2016.

Favret-Saada, Jeanne. 2005. "'Ser afetado,' de Jeanne Favret-Saada." Translated by Paula Siqueira. *Cadernos de campo*, no. 13: 155–61.

Feltran, Gabriel de Santis. 2007. "Trabalhadores e bandidos: Categorias de nomeação, significados políticos." *Revista Temáticas* 30, no. 15: 11–50.

———. 2008. *Fronteiras de tensão: Um estudo sobre política e violência nas periferias de São Paulo*. Campinas: Tese de Doutorado em Ciências Sociais, UNICAMP.

Fortes, Meyer, and E. E. Evans-Pritchard. 1940. *African Political Systems*. Oxford: Oxford University Press.

Foucault, Michel. 1988. "Technologies of the Self." In *Technologies of the Self: A Seminar with Michel Foucault*," edited by Luther H. Martin, Huck Gutman and Patrick Hutton, 16–49. Northampton, M.A.: Univ. of Massachusets Press, 1988.

———. 1994. "Le mailles du pouvoir." In *Dits et écrits*, vol. 4, 182–201. Paris: Gallimard.

———. 1996. [1975]. *Discipline and Punish: The Birth of the Prison*, translated by Alan Sheridan. New York: Vintage Books.

———. 1997. *Il faut defender la société*. Paris: Gallimard.

Furukawa, Nagashi. 2008. "O PCC e a gestão dos presídios em São Paulo." *Novos Estudos—CEBRAP* no. 80: 21–41.

Gay, Robert. 2015. *Bruno: Conversations with a Brazilian Drug Dealer*. Durham, N.C.: Duke University Press.

Goffman, Erwin. 1999. *Manicômios, prisões e conventos*. São Paulo: Perspectiva.

Goldman, Marcio. 2006. *Como funciona a democracia: Uma teoria etnográfica da política*. Rio de Janeiro: Editora 7 Letras.

Heckenberger, Michael. 2013. "Marginal Bodies, Altered States, and Subhumans: (Dis)articulations between Physical and Virtual Realities in *Centro*, São Paulo." In *Human No More: Digital Subjectivities, Unhuman Subjects, and the End of Anthropology*, edited by Neil Whitehead and Michael Wesch, 199–216. Boulder, C.O.: University of Colorado Press.

Hobbes, Thomas. 1982. *Leviathan*. New York: Penguin.

Hobsbawm, Eric. 1981. *Bandits*. New York: New Press.

Ingold, Tim, ed. 1996. *Key Debates in Anthropology*. London: Routledge.

Jocenir. 2001. *Diário de um detento: O livro*. São Paulo: Labortexto Editorial.

Jozino, Josmar. 2004. *Cobras e lagartos*. Rio de Janeiro: Objectiva.

———. 2012. "Rota mata seis e PMs são presos suspeitos de execução." *Agora*, São Paulo, May 30, http://www.agora.uol.com.br/saopaulo/ult10103u1097654.shtml, last accessed January 23, 2016.

Jullien, François. 2001. *Fundar a moral*. São Paulo: Editora Discurso.

Kafka, Franz. 2013. *Letters to Friends, Family and Editors*. New York: Random House LLC.

Lalande, André. 1999. *Vocabulário técnico e crítico da filosofia*. Translated by Fátima Sá Correa et al. 3rd ed. São Paulo: Martins Fontes.

Landé, Carl H. 1997. "Introduction: The Dyadic Basis of Clientelism." In *Friends, Followers, and Factions: A Reader in Political Clientelism*, edited by Steffen Schmidt, Laura Guasti, Carl Landé, and James Scott, 506–10. Berkeley: University of California Press.

Latour, Bruno. 2005. *Reassembling the Social: An Introduction to Actor-Network Theory*. Oxford: Oxford University Press.

Leach, Edmund. 1968. *Pul Eliya: A Village in Ceylon*. Cambridge: Cambridge University Press.

Leirner, Piero de Camargo. 1997. *Meia volta volver*. Rio de Janeiro: Editora Fundação Getúlio Vargas.

Levantamento Nacional de Informações Penitenciárias. 2014. http://www.cnj.jus.br/files/conteudo/arquivo/2015/11/080f04f01d5b0efebfbcf06d050dca34.pdf, last accessed January 24, 2016.

Lévi-Strauss, C. 1963. *Structural Anthropology*. Translated by Claire Jacobson and Brooke Grundfest Schoepf. New York: Doubleday Anchor.

Marques, Adalton. 2006. *"Proceder": "O certo pelo certo" no mundo prisional*. Monograph. Graduação em Sociologia e Política, Escola de Sociologia e Política de São Paulo.

———. 2007. "'Dar um psicológico': Estratégias de produção de verdade no tribunal do crime." In VII Reunião de Antropologia do Mercosul, 2007, Porto Alegre: VII Reunião de Antropologia do Mercosul—Desafios Antropológicos (CD-ROM). Vol. 1.

———. 2008. "'Faxina' e 'pilotagem': Dispositivos (de guerra) políticos no seio da administração prisional." *Lugar comum—Estudos de mídia, cultura e democracia (UFRJ)* 25–26: 283–90.

———. 2009. *Crime, proceder, convívio-seguro—Um experimento antropológico a partir de relações entre ladrões.* São Paulo: Dissertação de Mestrado em Antropologia, FFLCH—University of São Paulo.

———. 2010. "'Liderança,' 'proceder' e 'igualdade': Uma etnografia das relações políticas no Primeiro Comando da Capital. *Etnográfica* 14 (2): 311–35.

Marques, Ana Claudia. 2002. *Intrigas e questões: Vingança de família e tramas sociais no sertão de Pernambuco.* Rio de Janeiro: Relume Dumará.

Marques, Ana Claudia, and J. L. M. Villela. 2005. "O que se diz, o que se escreve." *Revista de Antropologia* 48, no. 1: 37–74.

Mingardi, Guaracy. 2007. "O trabalho da Inteligência no controle do Crime Organizado." *Revista de Estudos Avançados* 21, no. 1: 51–69.

Misse, Michel. 2007. "Mercados ilegais, redes de proteção e organização local do crime no Rio de Janeiro." *Revista de Estudos Avançados* 21, no. 1: 139–57.

Moehn, Frederick. 2012. *Contemporary Carioca: Technologies of Mixing in a Brazilian Music Scene.* Durham: Duke University Press.

Monod, Jacques. 1976. *Acaso e necessidade: Ensaio sobre a filosofia natural da biologia moderna*, translated by Bruno Palma and Pedro P. de S. Madureira. 3rd ed. Petrópolis: Vozes.

Nicholas, Ralph W. 1977. "Factions: A Comparative Analysis." In *Friends, Followers, and Factions: A Reader in Political Clientelism*, edited by S. W. Schmidt, L. Guasti, Carl H. Landé, and J. C. Scott, 55–73. Berkeley: University of California Press.

Nietzsche, Friedrich Wilhelm. 1979 [1873]. "On Truth and Lies in a Nonmoral Sense," *Philosophy and Truth: Selections from Nietzsche's Notebooks of the early 1870s.* Edited and Translated by Daniel Brazeale, 79–100. Atlantic Highlands, NJ: Humanities Press.

Palmeira, M. G. S., and B. Herédia. 1995. "Os comícios e a política de facções." *Anuário Antropológico* 94: 31–94.

Palmeira, Moacir. 1996. "Política, facções e voto." In *Antropologia, voto e representação política*, edited by Márcio Goldman and Moacir Palmeira, 41–56. Rio de Janeiro: Contra Capa.

Peel, J. D. Y. 1996. "1989 Debate. The Concept of Society Is Theoretically Obsolete. The Presentations: Against the Motion (1)." In *Key Debates in Anthropology*, edited by Tim Ingold, 67–71. New York: Routledge..

Ramalho, José Ricardo. 1979. *Mundo do crime: A ordem pelo avesso.* Rio de Janeiro: Edições Graal.

Sacramento, Paulo. 2003. *O prisioneiro da grade de ferro: Autorretratos.* Produced by Olhos de cão produções cinematográficas, São Paulo. 123 min, color, mini-DV, 35 mm, 1:1.85, Dolby digital (digital archive).

Santos, Getúlio Bezerra. 2007. "A hora e a vez de derrotar o Crime Organizado." *Revista Estudos Avançados* 21, no. 61: 99–105.

Schwarz, Roberto. 1992. *Misplaced Ideas: Essays on Brazilian Culture*, translated by John Gledson. New York: Verso.

Sobrinho, Wanderley Preite. 2013. "Três meses após promessa, famílias de PMs assassinados estão sem indenização." *Último Segundo*, January 28, http://ultimosegundo.ig.com.br/brasil/sp/2013-01-28/tres-meses-apos-promessa-familias-de-pms-assassinados-estao-sem-indenizacao.html, last accessed January 23, 2016.

Souza, Fátima. 2007. *PCC, a facção*. Rio de Janeiro: Record.

Strathern, Marilyn. 1996. "1989 Debate. The Concept of Society Is Theoretically Obsolete. The Presentations: For the Motion (1)." In *Key Debates in Anthropology*, edited by Tim Ingold, 60–66. New York: Routledge.

Swartz, Marc J., Victor Turner, and Arthur Tuden, eds. 1966. *Political Anthropology*. Chicago: Aldine.

Tarde, Gabriel. 2007 [1895]. "Monadologia e sociologia." In *Monadologia e sociologia e outros ensaios*, edited by Eduardo Viana Vargas, 51–131. São Paulo: Cosacnaify.

Telles, Vera da Silva, and Daniel Veloso Hirata. 2007. "Cidade e práticas urbanas: Nas fronteiras incertas entre o ilegal, o informal e o ilícito." *Revista Estudos Avançados* 21, no. 61: 173–91.

Toren, Christina. 1996. "The Concept of Society Is Theoretically Obsolete. The Presentations: For the motion (2)." In *Key Debates in Anthropology*, edited by Tim Ingold, 72–76. London: Routledge.

———. 2000. "Making the Chief: An Examination of why Fijian Chiefs Have to Be Elected." In *Elites: Choice, Leadership and Succession*, edited by J. Pina-Cabral and A. P. Lima, 113–29. Oxford: Berg.

Vargas, Eduardo Viana. 2000. *Antes Tarde do que nunca—Gabriel Tarde e a emergência das ciências sociais*. Rio de Janeiro: Contra Capa.

———. 2006. "Uso de drogas: A alter-ação como evento." *Revista de Antropologia USP* 49, no. 2: 581–623.

———, ed. 2007. *Monadologia e sociologia e outros ensaios*. São Paulo: Cosac Naify.

Velho, Otávio. 2007. *Mais realistas do que o rei: Ocidentalismo, religião e modernidades alternativas*. Rio de Janeiro: Topbooks.

Villela, Jorge Luiz Mattar. 2004. *O povo em armas: Violência e política no sertão de Pernambuco*. Rio de Janeiro: Relume Dumará.

———. 2010. "Apresentação." In Karina Biondi, *Junto e Misturado: Uma etnografia do PCC*. São Paulo: Editora Terceiro Nome.

Viotti da Costa, Emília. 2000. *The Brazilian Empire: Myths and Histories*. Chapel Hill: University of North Carolina Press.

Viveiros de Castro, Eduardo. 2002. "O Nativo Relativo." *Mana* 8, no. 1: 113–48.

———. 2007. "Filiação intensiva e aliança demoníaca." *Novos Estudos CEBRAP* no. 77: 91–126.

Wacquant, Loïc. 2001. *As prisões da miséria*. Rio de Janeiro: Jorge Zahar.

———. 2006. *Body and Soul: Notebooks of an Apprentice Boxer.* New York: Oxford University Press.

Wagner, Roy. 1981. *The Invention of Culture.* Chicago: University of Chicago Press.

Young, James Armour. January 28, 2016. "The Murder Rate Is Down in Rio—But Its Cops Continue to Kill." Vice News.

Zeni, Bruno. 2002. *Sobrevivente André du Rap (do Massacre do Carandiru).* São Paulo: Labortexto Editorial.

Index

Note: Page numbers in *italic* type indicate illustrations.

Wave of violence (2012), 145–54, 159–60, 162–63

Western thought: transcendental thinking and, 24, 26–27; two pillars of, xxii

White flag, 171n15; definition of, 77

Wives: boundary with inmate of, 125; dedication to husbands of, 10; group demand for better prison conditions by, 35; intimate search of, 7, 12–13, 14, 17, 63; PCC respect for, 20–21; PCC's importance vs., 175n12; prisoner treatment of, 21; punishment of *talarico* and 15, 166n5; visiting day and, 1–2, 4–8, 10–15, 20, 174n6

"Wrong" ideas, 168

"Zé Povinho" status (PCC non-involved person), 19